Translating Theory into Practice

A Student Guide to Counseling Practicum and Internship

Justin E. Levitov
Loyola University New Orleans
Kevin A. Fall
Texas State University

WAVELAND PRESS, INC.
Long Grove, Illinois

For information about this book, contact:
Waveland Press, Inc.
4180 IL Route 83, Suite 101
Long Grove, IL 60047-9580
(847) 634-0081
info@waveland.com
www.waveland.com

10-digit ISBN 1-57766-560-0
13-digit ISBN 978-1-57766-560-1

Printed in the United States of America

7 6 5 4 3 2 1

For Talya, Jana, Dylan, Blake, and Riley

CONTENTS

PREFACE

At one time or another, each of us has been asked questions about how we accomplished something that someone else was about to attempt. The mundane requests are not too difficult. But if we are passionate about what the questioner is trying to learn, we not only answer their questions but flood them with information because our enthusiasm for the topic drives us to be as "helpful" and complete as possible. The result is often an endless list of suggestions, comments, cautions, and encouragements. "Oh, by the way, be sure and take . . . "; "Once you get there you have to try . . . "; "Make sure that you talk to . . . "; "Did I mention that . . . "; or "You have got to get back to me once you finish so we can compare notes . . . "

Since we are counselor educators and practicing mental health counselors with a passion for counseling and teaching, we quickly discovered that we needed limits on the information we would ultimately include in this text. We know that much of what you will learn from practicum and internship will come through the unique experiences these courses offer. Your readings should not interfere with or replace those rich clinical opportunities. We continuously struggled with identifying the point where the information sharing needed to end and your personal experiences needed to begin. That said, we apologize in advance for those places where we might interfere with your experiential learning by being too detailed or too prescriptive. Our overarching goal is to offer a text that will help prepare you for the challenge of clinical training and improve your ability to learn from the personal and professional training experiences you will soon encounter.

Acknowledgments

We are grateful to a number of people who have helped in the creation of this text. We appreciate Waveland Press for its patience and support. Laurie Prossnitz is an extraordinary project editor. Thanks for so thoughtfully guiding this project through to completion and for calling after Hurricane Katrina to see if we were all right. Lori Meek Schuldt's meticulous editing improved the organization, clarity, and continuity of the text. Thanks for your painstaking attention to detail and for returning the drafts so quickly. We also gratefully acknowledge Leslie Midtbo's time, energy, and expertise. As a graduate assistant she spent many hours editing and reviewing copy as reliably as any well-seasoned professional. Our thanks also to Sarah Shelton for providing research support, tables, and copy editing.

We know that having the time to write a book is a gift given by a family to a writer. We are grateful to our families for their support, understanding, and encouragement. Finally, we acknowledge that without clients we cannot be counselors and without students we cannot be professors. That said, we offer our appreciation to countless clients and students who have enlightened us, taught us, and earned our respect. It will not be possible for you to identify exactly where these students and clients directly contributed to this text, but it is important for you to know that their influence, wisdom, and insights exist throughout.

Chapter 1

The Challenge of Translating Theory into Practice

During his first semester of college, Chris decided that as soon as he finished his bachelor's degree, he would directly enter a graduate counseling program. He had always wanted to be a counselor, and already was looking forward to greeting, evaluating, and treating his first "real client." So strong was his interest that at some level he felt that the counseling profession selected him, not the other way around. After all, his friends had always sought him out when they were troubled or concerned about their problems with school, parents, or other friends. He was a great listener, and his concern for them was real. In addition, the personal trait that others found most remarkable was his uncanny insight. He could define a problem, explain why it was happening, and identify realistic solutions better than anyone else could. He finished his undergraduate program in record time and was immediately accepted into the school's graduate counseling program.

While Chris enjoyed the counseling theory and practice courses as well as the counseling electives, he found them useful only to a point. Early in his graduate training, Chris had concluded that practicum and internship would be mostly a matter of continuing to do what he had always done so well with his friends. He would just listen carefully, determine what the client needed to do, and then advise him or her to do it.

As the time for practicum approached, Chris, unlike his peers, seemed unconcerned about the choice of a field site. He was confident that wherever he went, he would do just fine. He continued as he had through most of his training, spending more of his time helping other students with their myriad concerns rather than focusing on his own. Since he and his classmates were in the process of selecting a field site, he would carefully question others about where they wanted to work, what types of clients they would most prefer, and what they planned to do when they graduated. Once again, his insights proved invaluable to his cohorts as they refined their practicum choices and began to face this important element of their training.

As the practicum began, weekly group supervision meetings were filled with the questions with which all counseling novices struggle. Chris reflected on each one and rarely missed an opportunity to share his insights with other members of the group. Yet although he was sure that his advice was accurate and useful, he grew increasingly frustrated as one student after another seemed to become more and more uninterested in what he had to say. By the third week of practicum classes, Chris had become noticeably unhappy; at times he secretly dreaded having to attend the weekly group meetings. What's more, he sensed a struggle building with his site supervisor. Chris felt insulted when his site supervisor asked him why he rarely brought up questions about his own clients during group supervision meetings, preferring to discuss problems that other students were having at their field sites rather than addressing his own concerns. Chris misread the supervisor's intent when he incorrectly concluded that the supervisor was intimidated by him, a student with many natural skills needing very little direction.

It was not until the sixth week that Chris began to wonder about his progress in a more thoughtful and reflective way. He had completed intake evaluations on four clients. Two had not shown up for the next scheduled counseling session, and one had asked for a transfer to another counselor. Chris was becoming worried, confused, and at times angry about these developments. He knew that his advice was good and that the clients should be listening, but they were not. He found them frustrating. He wondered why these people weren't more enthusiastic about returning to meet with him and more willing to do what he recommended. His certainty about the clients' needs and the clarity of his expectations of them made the fact that they would not engage with him in the process of counseling all the more baffling. He knew things were not going well, but he was at a loss to explain why.

Chris's supervisor sensed his level of frustration and urged Chris to come in for an individual meeting. The supervisor recognized Chris's impressive strengths and abilities, but he also knew that the way Chris was conceptualizing the process was interfering with his ability to properly manage the important relationships that form the basis of clinical training. Though brief and to the point, the individual supervision inspired Chris to focus away from his advice giving in favor of developing his relationships with clients, supervisors, peers, and himself. Redirecting his efforts produced the hoped-for results, and within a couple of weeks Chris was experiencing a renewed sense of purpose, greater comfort with the process, and an obvious decrease in frustration levels. He actively participated in supervision by raising questions about his assigned cases, encouraging comments from others, and becoming more open to suggestions.

INTRODUCTION

Chris's first attempt at translating theory into practice contains many useful lessons for you as you move from the academic to the clinical focus of your training. While we realize that Chris's transition would be most valuable as a platform for discussion with your classmates and instructors, we can tell you that in general terms, Chris's experiences can be used to illustrate how one intern faced the challenge of simultaneously managing knowledge of theoretical information and key elements of his own personality as he tried to constructively relate to clinical supervisors, peers, faculty, clients, and himself. According to Kiser (2000), "Perhaps the greatest challenge for students in a human service field experience is not one of 'possessing knowledge' but one of 'making use of' that knowledge in practical ways" (p. xvi). While this can be a complicated and demanding process, the translation of counseling theory into effective clinical practice is also intensely rewarding. You can expect this process to produce a wealth of new insights about yourself and a greater appreciation for the forces that will help you develop into a competent, trained professional. As you enter this phase of your training, you should derive some comfort from the knowledge that you are about to negotiate the same path that every mental health professional before you followed as he or she underwent the critical professional transformations that practica and internships produce.

Because the counseling process relies so heavily upon the counselor-client relationship, each counselor must develop a clinical style that not only honors the counselor's individual character but also meets the multiple requirements of a healthy and effective clinical relationship. This reality, coupled with whatever wisdom we have gleaned from our practicum and internship teaching experiences, causes us to conclude that while you must make this transition from theory to practice, you must do so in your own way. Helping you make this important transformation while honoring the unique elements of your personality is the general focus of this text.

Do not be surprised if you have mixed feelings about this portion of your training—most counseling students do. If you are both eager to begin seeing clients and worried about how you will balance all of the elements that combine to form a successful clinical experience, you are not alone. Taking an academic course for credit and completing practicum or internship place very different demands upon you. It is one thing to study theory and quite another to apply theory in combination with key elements of your own personality so that you can craft an approach that allows you to ethically and effectively help others. The complexity of the task becomes clearer when you recognize that (a) each counselor is a unique individual, (b) each client is a unique individual, and (c) there are a number of different theories from which to choose. Any practical study of how these three highly variable components interact would be challenging. Fortunately, insights about yourself combined with your personal relationship to counseling theory, other professionals, supervisors, agencies, and ultimately clients follow predictable patterns. These patterns define and explain the forces that govern relationships, and these forces can be refined to improve your efforts to be helpful to others. This manual explores these relationships and offers suggestions on how you can translate theory into effective clinical practice. It is important to be thoughtful about these ideas because habits and patterns formed at this early stage are likely to endure throughout the course of your professional life.

Relationships

You will encounter various types of relationships during your clinical training. Each one is critical to your professional development; in the aggregate they will combine to help form you into a skilled clinician. While the counselor-client relationship may be the most obvious, a number of other relationships are equally critical. By carefully addressing each of these other relationships, you will discover valuable sources of information, support, guidance, and understanding. Ultimately, what you learn as you negotiate these relationships will greatly benefit your counselor-client relationships.

The following relationships and the term used to describe each, offered in no specific order, compose the types of interaction you can expect during your clinical work:

Student–Professor	Faculty Supervision
Student–Site Supervisor	Site Supervision
Student–Student	Peer Consultation/Peer Relationships
Student–Agency Staff	Work Relationships (other professionals and support staff)
Student–Client	Counseling Relationship

The first three relationships will be discussed in chapter 5. Chapter 4 includes information about working as an intern in an agency, hospital, or school. General information about the student-client relationship can be found in all of the chapters.

Just as a majority of mental health professionals subscribe to the notion that within the counselor-client dyad "it is the relationship that heals," counselor educators would likely agree that the five basic professional relationships listed on the previous page form students into trained counselors. These relationships, along with the lines of communication, are illustrated in Figure 1.1.

Figure 1.1 Clinical Relationships

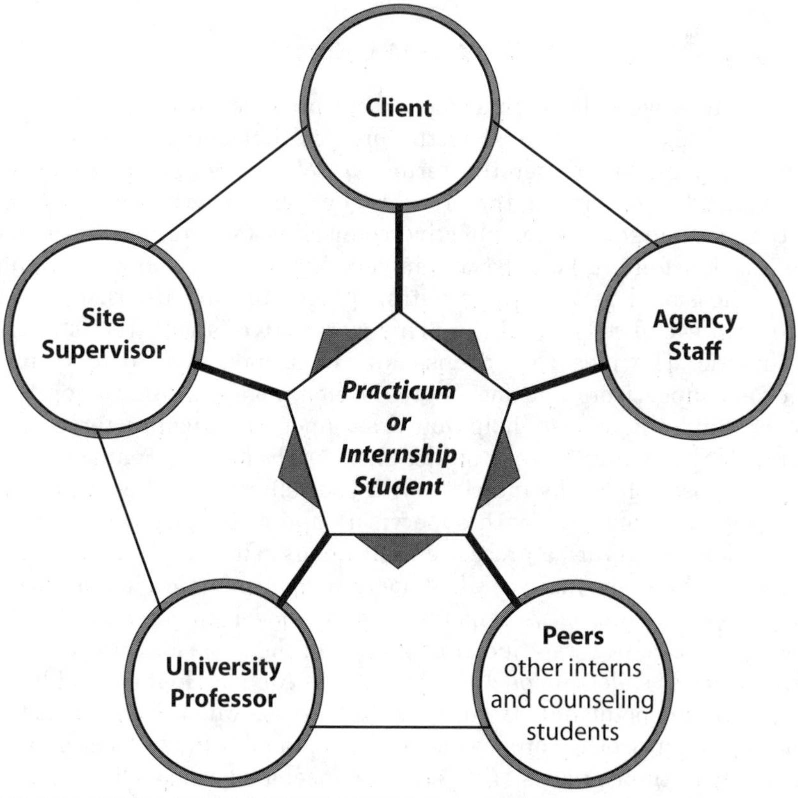

The network of interaction depicted in the figure reveals a range of opportunities for you to learn about self, others, and the mental health profession. Some of these encounters can produce personal reactions that are worrisome or disquieting while others may be positive and easy to embrace. Because of the potential for such a wide range of personal reactions, it is essential that professional relationships and mentorships be constructed upon a solid foundation formed from honesty, trust, respect, understanding, knowledge, and a shared commitment to personal and professional development. Reliance on such a foundation ensures that clinical training experiences can be used consistently to improve yourself, regardless of how personally difficult they may be. Learning new things about yourself, managing anxiety and uncertainty with greater skill, and developing better methods to communicate and work with people are as valuable to you as a counseling practicum or internship student as they are to the clients with whom you work. Improving your ability to interact in all five relationship areas ultimately ensures greater levels of success in the counselor-client relationship.

Counselor Formation

Because we believe that the effects produced by these five core relationships are so central to the process that transforms students into clinicians, we prefer the term *counselor formation* to counselor training when describing the process. The term *formation* implies that necessary ingredients for effective counseling (as well as those that may obstruct efforts) coexist within you. As a trainee, you will encounter professional relationships within practicum and internship that will help evoke these qualities. This perspective is both realistic and optimistic. The idea that counselors are formed instead of trained beckons supervisors and faculty to develop modes of interaction that honor your uniqueness, help you draw upon those characteristics of yourself that enhance your skills, and simultaneously manage those aspects of self that may interfere with your efforts to be helpful to others. Such relationships with supervisors and colleagues can motivate and guide you toward a process of continuous self-improvement, a goal that is shared by many skilled mental health professionals. What makes you unique is as important to the development and maintenance of the critical relationships that form the basis for counseling as any theory or collection of clinical skills. As Auxier, Hughes, and Kline (2003, p. 25) point out, "Counselors' identities differ from identities formed in many other professions because, in addition to forming attitudes about their professional selves, counselors develop a 'therapeutic self that consists of a unique personal blend of the developed professional and personal selves [Skovholt & Ronnestad, 1992, p. 507]'."

Counseling: Art and Science

Counseling is both an art and a science. As a science it relies heavily upon a growing body of research and theory to guide decision making and to encourage the proper use of counseling strategies. Advances in psychopharmacology, discoveries of more effective treatment protocols for specific types of psychological problems, and refined diagnostic criteria emphasize the importance of recognizing the more-scientific elements found in effective counseling. At the same time, "the practice of professional counseling is certainly not an objective science" (Osborn, 2004, p. 325) and because of its subjectivity, the counseling process calls for more-ambiguous yet equally useful skills of interpretation, expression, and relationship building, all of which are important to counseling outcomes. Research findings are useful, but findings alone rarely influence individuals enough to make the difficult changes that are necessary to improve the quality of their lives. Thus, if we accept that counseling is both an art and a science, then it follows that counselor formation, a process of evoking effective ways of balancing what you know with unique, useful, and often creative ways of delivering this information to clients, would be the learning model of choice.

By way of example, consider the problem of making an appropriate diagnosis, conveying that information to the client, and then providing counseling services. A purely scientific approach could produce a plausible diagnosis. The client could be notified of the diagnosis in a variety of ways, and a recommendation for treatment could be included in the diagnostic report. All of us know someone who had such information delivered in this way by some well-meaning professional of one sort or another. Interestingly enough, this model works, especially when the science is refined enough to produce consistently accurate diagnoses and consistently effective interventions. The professional in this scenario defines what is wrong and does something to correct it. Whether mental health will evolve to this level of science or even should evolve to this level of science forms the basis for a very interesting debate about personal rights and responsibilities. Suffice to say the discipline, for better or worse, remains as much an art as a science. In counseling, what we *do to* clients is important, but *who* we are and *how* we are in our relationship to them ultimately determines the success of our efforts.

Counseling Theory

Counseling theory offers a guide or framework from which counselors work to help others. Theories present serviceable explanations of human behavior and models for intervention. Working without benefit of a theory or theories presents a range of hazards. Counselors rely upon theory to guide them as they determine the nature of psychological problems, assess the level of seriousness, identify potential hazards, predict which efforts will be more successful and which will worsen symptoms, assess progress, identify treatment alternatives, and determine when counseling efforts have achieved maximum benefit.

As a practicum or internship student who has taken at least one or two courses in counseling theory, you can easily recognize the importance of theory. The problem that most students at this level of training experience has more to do with selecting a theory that makes sense to them and then learning the theory well enough to rely upon it in counseling sessions. Surveys and anecdotal evidence consistently illustrate the difficulties that students encounter as they (a) select a theory and (b) attempt to translate it into effective clinical initiatives.

While research studies identifying which theories are better suited to particular problem types are becoming more widely available, at this stage of your training it would be better to select a theory because it matches your personality and worldview. A number of useful texts exist to ease the process of selecting a theory (see, e.g., Fall, Holden, & Marquis, 2004). Consult one or more texts in advance of enrolling in the practicum or internship. You can and should expect site supervisors and teachers to question you about your theoretical orientation. While you may find this line of questioning unsettling, it is important. Your ability to espouse a theory, defend it, and effectively implement it will be a general expectation of anyone responsible for your supervision. Being thoroughly familiar with at least one theory is an essential requirement for this phase of counselor preparation. The following questions may be useful to ponder as you select a particular theory:

1. Are people influenced most by their emotions, thoughts, environment, or spiritual experiences?
2. What role does genetics play in behavior?
3. What role does pharmacotherapy play in behavior?
4. What role does family influence play in behavior?
5. Why do people persist in behaving in ways that continue to produce problems and distress?
6. What motivates or causes people to change their behavior?
7. What constitutes success in counseling?
8. Why does counseling work?
9. What is the role of the counselor?
10. What is the role of the client?

Answers to the preceding questions coupled with basic information about various theories and discussion with others will go a long way toward helping you find a theory that matches your personal assumptions about the nature of behavior and human experience.

Finally, we advise against adopting eclectic theories at this stage in your education. While eclectic models can be very useful, we believe that they are best left to highly experienced counselors who are in a position to choose elements of varied theories based upon their experience employing different theories over an extended period of time. For novices, eclectic approaches are problematic because choices about what to take from different theories may be more a function of chance than carefully thought-out decisions regarding what works best where. Enough theories exist for you to find at least one that makes sense to you without having to pursue an eclectic approach or, even worse, developing your own approach. The latter option has fallen from favor, but in the 1960s and 70s it was common for counseling faculty to require students to develop their own approaches to counseling. We were never sure why this alternative became so popular, but it is clear that the same forces that advanced counseling as a profession simultaneously suppressed practices like developing and relying upon your own theory of counseling.

Personal Risk

During the Loyola University New Orleans counseling program application interview, we tell new applicants that the study of counseling and the actual process of counseling clients can produce intrapsychic risks to students. By making this point, we inform new applicants that they will be personally affected by their exposure to the counseling curriculum and to their clients and that some of these effects can be disarming. We tell applicants that being affected in this way can help with their development so long as the effects are completely explored and properly integrated. One example we use to make this point came about during a training session at a regional conference. A familiar participant became noticeably upset as the presenter described a cognitive-behavioral treatment strategy for depression. This participant disputed the efficacy of the approach in such an emotional way that the audience became uneasy. Unbeknownst to many others in the audience, two of the participant's family members suffered with serious forms of depression, and neither one had benefited appreciably from the approach under discussion. Weeks later, in a discussion about the conference and the cognitive-behavioral session, the same participant volunteered that he thought he had been unfair in his reaction to the session and recalled that this form of treatment had not helped two members of his family. His ability to link his reactions to parts of his personal experience restored the balance between personal life and professional life that effective counselors need to maintain.

From the outset we encourage students to obtain counseling from our professionally staffed counseling and career services center whenever they encounter such reactions to course material or their clients. We offer the same cautions and recommendations to you because (a) your psychological health is important, (b) your personal issues can adversely affect your efforts to learn the material and help your clients, and (c) experiencing the counseling process as a client improves your understanding of it. Although not all counselor preparation programs require students to participate in personal counseling sessions, the need for students to obtain such support during the course of their training is quite common. Being open to the possibility of receiving counseling services is an excellent idea regardless of whether you are a beginner or an experienced counselor.

Professional Community

Counseling can be personally challenging because it is a solitary and often uncertain endeavor. Hours of individual therapy interspersed with brief periods of administrative activities like note taking and report writing can leave counselors with a seriously limited interpersonal sphere of interaction. As we have stressed, to be effective and healthy, counselors need a range of relationships. Counselors who believe that they are able to obtain all that they need interpersonally from the clients with whom they work seriously risk producing unproductive and unethical relationships with the very people they are trying to help.

In addition to isolation, counselors face a certain amount of ambiguity and uncertainty. According to Osborn (2004), "To a great extent, the focus or nature of counseling is subjective and often ambiguous. 'Absolutes' are elusive, 'exact personality profiles' cannot be captured, 'correct diagnoses' are ephemeral" (p. 325). This vagueness has the effect of creating an uncomfortable vacuum for novices. Under this type of pressure, students may leap to roles or models that they have observed rather than managing the anxiety in such a way as to propel them toward developing their own approach. "Playing the role of counselor," acting like their clinical supervisor, and imitating someone they have seen are all problematic examples of how the absence of explicitness can lead students to ineffective solutions.

Given that effective counselors rely almost exclusively upon what they know and who they are, the only way that they can gain some comfort with the process and simultaneously assure themselves that they are performing effectively is through regular interaction with other respected mental health professionals. While experienced counselors obtain this support through forms of supervision and consultation, we believe that practicum and internship students need to feel that they are participating in something that is psychologically larger. Practicum and internship students at Loyola University New Orleans are encouraged to see themselves as participants in a community of mental health professionals that includes faculty, peers, site supervisors, and various consultants. They are also expected to assume a level of responsibility to one another as each member of the community seeks to improve personally and professionally. With appropriate levels of trust, students quickly come to rely upon the members of their professional community for support and direction as they make clinical decisions, examine ethical concerns, explore counseling relationships, and form their unique professional identities. While all counselors, regardless of their level of training, benefit from contact with other professionals, novices find this type of support and professional interaction especially important to their development.

Summary

As you begin this phase of your training, expect to experience a range of emotions. While counseling can be deeply rewarding, it can also challenge you in complicated and often personal ways. Since effective counselors must merge who they are with what they know, your professional identity and clinical style will differ from others. If you think of this unique outcome as an opportunity rather than a source of frustration, you will be in a better psychological position to reap the full range of benefits that practicum and internship afford. Almost all that is accomplished in counselor formation occurs through various relationships. By taking the necessary steps to make these relationships healthy and productive, you can expect to gain much from your experiences.

Chris, the counseling student described in the introduction to this chapter, eventually translated the frustration and confusion he experienced into useful insights about himself and his work with clients. He achieved this outcome by taking the risk of letting others help him and support him in accomplishing his professional goals. His fear of not being as good as he thought he was did not block him from taking the steps that he needed to begin the process of becoming as skilled as he could be. It is no less important for you to search for and participate fully in a professional community. Do so by recognizing that the professional community places dual demands upon you: you are expected to give back as much as you obtain. Finally, recall that you are traveling a path that all who provide mental health services have traveled, albeit in their own way, before you.

Reflection Questions

1. Why do you believe Chris, the student described in the introduction, encountered so much difficulty with his transition to clinical training?
2. What do you expect to gain from clinical training?
3. What personal characteristics do you possess that will enhance your efforts to help others? Which will interfere?
4. Under what conditions would you pursue personal counseling?
5. Of the five relationships you must manage in clinical training, which will be easiest for you? Which will be most difficult? Why?

PART 1

PLANNING FOR CLINICAL TRAINING

In the chapters that follow, you will be guided through a process that will help you successfully plan and complete your field placements. You will be encouraged to review ethical standards from the vantage point of a practicum or internship student, engage in a system of self-assessment, determine where best you should complete your practical training, and explore clinical supervision issues.

Careful planning and personal preparation for practica and internships dramatically improve outcomes. Historically, counselor training programs exhibited a wide distribution of positions regarding clinical training. Stances ranged from sending students "off on their own" to find and complete fieldwork to providing carefully planned and highly organized courses with articulated agreements between the university, the field site, and the field supervisors. Ethical guidelines for the training of counselors have gone a long way to insure that the appropriate amount of time and attention is paid to this critical aspect of training. While these improvements have helped, you can also contribute by becoming thoroughly familiar with ethical codes, developing a willingness to learn more about yourself, exploring methods of enhancing the effects of supervision, and being prepared to identify the types of clients and agencies you would find most valuable.

As noted earlier, unlike content courses, practicum and internship produce a constellation of personal and professional responsibilities for which students must carefully prepare. The following five suggestions taken from "What Every Graduate Student Needs to Know" (Connelly, 2005) offers not only a realistic perspective upon which to build your skills but some encouragement as well:

1. You don't know everything. Mutual respect is the only way we have survived this long, so if something strikes you as (odd, repetitive, nonsensical, counterproductive—pick one) recognize that there are REASONS we do things the way we do. Listen, observe, learn. You can try to change it later.
2. The good news is, no one expects you to know everything. But you are expected to read assigned materials before class, to participate in discussions, and to challenge—and maybe defend—your current belief system.
3. You're not perfect, either. While perfection certainly is a goal, it is never TRULY attainable. This truism gives us all purpose.
4. You're going to make mistakes. (See item #3.) BUT when you do, especially when there's a client involved, you'll need to own up to them immediately and consult with someone who knows a whole lot more than you do (see item #1) to assess the damage and take steps to repair it.
5. Ramen noodles have provided sustenance to every grad student since Jung studied under Freud. We all survived.

(Reprinted from Connelly, A. R., 2005. What every graduate student needs to know. *Counseling Today, 48*(3), 22. The American Counseling Association. Reprinted with permission. No further reproduction authorized without written permission from the American Counseling Association.)

Chapter 2

Ethics of Clinical Practice for Student Interns

Anthony enjoyed the ethics courses more than any of the other graduate counseling courses he had taken. The idea that the study of philosophy, values, and logic could produce practical recommendations such as standards of professional behavior intrigued him. Undergraduate experiences in his chosen minor led him to believe that the study of philosophy was more about debate and the exploration of abstract ideas than it was about developing concrete recommendations for patterns of appropriate professional conduct. His undergraduate minor in philosophy propelled an academic interest in counseling ethics, but his personal and professional desire to complete his clinical training in a way that honored the ethical codes of his chosen profession created a different type of pressure upon him. He understood that what was once an academic exercise was now something that must be upheld and guaranteed to each client with whom he worked. Anthony also knew that he could not achieve this goal alone. He knew that it was impossible to develop a code that could identify all possible situations along with the correct action to be taken in each. Whereas some students may have been put off by the idea that ethical decision making required input from and dialogue with others, Anthony looked forward to it. For him, the topic of counseling ethics was going to become a living and dynamic process.

Jennifer, one of Anthony's classmates, and Anthony were assigned to the same site. They liked and respected one another and were frankly happy to have been placed together at the same mental health center.

Although this center had been popular with students from Anthony's program, it had been several years since anyone had been assigned there for clinical training. Anthony was relieved that at least he knew one other person who would be working with him during the semester. After participating in a day-long orientation, Anthony and Jennifer were introduced to their supervisor, Dr. Chelsea Palant. Dr. Palant scheduled the students for their weekly hour-long individual supervision sessions and reminded them that she would be available for consultation whenever either of them felt the need. She stressed the point that they were now working under supervision and that they should never feel that they had to make important decisions about their clients without input and support from their supervisor. Anthony quickly realized that he had entered into a training relationship that honored the fact that ethical and clinical decisions needed to be explored and discussed. Jennifer read the situation differently. She seemed almost offended by Dr. Palant's offer. She insisted to Anthony that she was quite capable of making many, if not all, of the decisions on her own. When he asked what she would do if she was uncertain or if she encountered a situation that was more serious than she felt she could manage, she abruptly said, "I'll ask you for help." While he was flattered that she had such confidence in him, her reply also made him anxious.

Minutes after settling into his practicum, Anthony was face-to-face with an important and worrisome ethical dilemma. Should he (a) contact his site supervisor and inform her of the problem, (b) remain silent about the situation and hope that Jennifer never needed to talk to him, (c) meet with and describe the situation to his on-campus faculty adviser, (d) talk directly to the faculty practicum instructor, (e) discuss the situation with another student in his program, or (f) meet with Jennifer? The options overwhelmed Anthony; worry about getting Jennifer into trouble if he told others about her position made him as anxious as did the fear that she would come to him for help or ask no one for help when she really did need to talk to her supervisor. It was not just Jennifer that Anthony was worried about. Jennifer's decisions could be potentially hazardous to her clients.

While Anthony knew that the codes would not contain specific information about how to handle this identical situation, they would offer some guidance as to how he might proceed. He was certain that it would be improper for Jennifer to avoid sharing important information about her clients with Dr. Palant. What he did not know was how he should proceed—that is, until he read the following section from the code.

> Informal Resolution. When counselors have reasonable cause to believe that another counselor is violating an ethical standard, they attempt to first resolve the issue informally with the other counselor if feasible, providing that such action does not violate confidentiality rights that may be involved. (ACA Code of Ethics, 2005, H.2.b)

Although Anthony found it difficult, he was able to meet with and talk frankly to Jennifer. He shared his concerns about being asked to assume responsibilities that he was not trained or prepared for and his fears that clients' concerns would not be properly addressed if Jennifer's supervisor were not involved. Jennifer instantly understood what she had done and what she would do about it. She recognized that because of her fears associated with asking people for help, she had placed Anthony in an awkward situation and risked not being as effective with her clients as she could be. She apologized and assured him that she would share her reservations about talking to Dr. Palant the next time that all three of them met.

Although the circumstances produced much discomfort, the outcome was even better than Anthony expected. Restored faith in his classmate, confidence in the process, and comfort with his supervisor buoyed him as he awaited the inevitable next ethical dilemma. Knowing where to find answers to important clinical and ethical concerns, knowing whom to talk to, and knowing what steps to follow did not make the decisions any easier, but they did combine to form a process that increased his confidence in being able to face future ethical issues.

INTRODUCTION

Anthony encounters an ethical dilemma within days of beginning his field placement. His choice to consult the code, develop a plan of action, and then take the necessary steps to resolve the problem is emblematic of a pattern that is repeated countless times by all mental health professionals. While Part 1 of the text may appear an unlikely place in which to lead with a chapter on ethics, we do so because we want to make the point that ethical concerns should guide *all* decision making. The choice of where you complete your clinical training is as much an ethical issue as is any other aspect of your work as a counselor. To further emphasize the point, ethics are so fundamental to the profession that we must turn to a discussion of them at the earliest possible opportunity. In this text, it is chapter 2.

Many counseling curricula include at least one one-semester course in Mental Health or Counseling Ethics. You may have taken such a survey course where the codes, decision-making models, and numerous case examples were covered. These courses offer valuable insights and information along with useful examples drawn from the experience of others. Clinical training, on the other hand, offers opportunities to combine what you learned from studying ethics with what you will personally confront as you gain clinical experience. Studying ethics and acting ethically offer different but equally valuable challenges.

We would be surprised, and even a little worried, if practicum or internship students reported that they were not concerned about the challenge of managing ethical issues. After all, ethical codes deal more with concepts than with specific acts, so an amount of ambiguity is inherent. Uncertainty about such important issues frustrates novices as well as experienced counselors. Since codes are based upon a values consensus, ambiguity is unavoidable, for several reasons. First, while specific sanctions do exist (e.g., sexual relations with clients are strictly prohibited), most of the code contains language that must be interpreted. Second, human behaviors always fall along a continuum where lines of demarcation between what is ethical and what is not are often blurry. Where is it appropriate to draw the line regarding, for example, physical contact between a counselor and client? Is a handshake prohibited? How about a pat on the back? Is it appropriate to hug clients? Finally, behavior has to be interpreted within the context in which it exists. For example, sharing personal information with members of an adult client's family would be a clear violation of confidentiality. On the other hand, if the client had threatened self-injury or suicide, such a disclosure would be an ethical mandate. Ford (1995) discusses the complexity of making ethical decisions, offers a caution to those of us who help students become counselors, and draws a reasonable conclusion about how students should think about the process in stating that "instructors might be concerned about making ethical behavior appear so complex and difficult that students will instead take refuge in cynicism [Abeles, 1980]. Students must understand that behaving ethically is neither easy nor impossible; it is both difficult and possible" (p. 5).

Ironically, regarding ethics, your lack of clinical experience can actually be beneficial. As a novice, you may be more attuned to the internal physical and emotional changes that signal the presence of ethical concerns than your veteran counterparts are. Veteran counselors run the risk of becoming cavalier about ethical concerns. Counseling can become routine to the extent that the internal emotional responses that alert us as an ethical dilemma begins to unfold now lack the impact they once had. Because it is crucial for counselors to be able to identify these internal emotional responses, we think that it helps to have a personally meaningful way to refer to them. To this end, we sometimes apply an animal metaphor suggested by several students who said that when they encountered ethical concerns, it felt as if *ferrets* were darting about inside of them. The metaphor is sensible because nausea and fluttering are examples of the gastrointestinal sensations often associated with anxiety. Counselors would be likely to have similar reactions in situations where ethical concerns were present. It would be a good idea to identify a metaphor for these reactions that makes sense to you. It can help you properly identify when ethical concerns are looming. Regardless of the metaphor you select, it is important to keep in mind the idea that "if it does not feel right, it probably is not right." As a counselor you will need to "trust your gut" as matters of ethical concern unfold.

Putting the pieces together that we have touched upon thus far, to achieve the level of ethical practice required of practicum and internship students you will need to:

- be sensitive to your reactions and to those of your client,
- couple the goals of helping your client with protecting your client's rights and well-being,
- thoroughly familiarize yourself with the code of ethics,
- know and be able to use at least one ethical decision-making model, and
- be prepared to consult with others *regularly* and *openly.*

Codes of Ethics

Within the mental health profession, codes of ethics vary by profession (counseling, psychology, social work, psychiatry) and by the relationships that they govern (counselor-client, agency-client, supervisor-supervisee, etc.). While counselor-client codes receive the most attention, for a practicum or internship student it is equally important to explore the codes that govern the relationships between you and your supervisor, field site, and college or university.

Counselor-Client

As a practicum or internship student, you are expected to know the code that governs your clinical work and to behave ethically. Your decision to enter the clinical component of your training affirms that you understand and have accepted this responsibility. We offer a limited review of ethics, selecting those areas of the code that are particularly important to students completing practicum or internship under university and field-site supervision. It is also important to understand that no single part of the code should be more or less important than another to you.

Several codes of ethics exist for mental health professionals (e.g., see appendixes A–D). While you are expected to be thoroughly familiar with the codes that govern your specific mental health subdiscipline, studying other codes can be helpful. Once you know your group's code, you might want to make comparisons to others. You can do so by selecting such common issues as confidentiality, dual relationships, and informed consent and then comparing how other codes deal with these universal concerns.

Variations from one code to another probably result from the subjectivity inherent in the underlying principles upon which most, if not all, mental health codes of ethics are based: *respect for autonomy, nonmaleficence, beneficence, justice,* and *fidelity* (see Kitchener, 1984 for a more complete discussion of these principles). In addition, codes of ethics are subject to change since they are linked to continuously evolving social and professional norms. Codes of professional conduct develop from (a) the interrelationship of the values of the society and the values of the profession and (b) a consensus that emerges between the society and the empirical practices of the mental health professions. Community standards for treatment are therefore dynamic. For example, the standard of *informed consent,* a concept based on the principle of respect for autonomy, illustrates how codes change in response to evolving social and clinical concerns. Informed consent stipulates that the client is given sufficient information upon which to base a decision about his or her care. Such information might include a description of the counselor's training and experience, risks associated with different courses of treatment, and expected outcomes. While this seems sensible, it has not always been the standard for treatment. Between 50 and 100 years ago, health professionals regularly withheld information from those being treated under the assumption that potentially disturbing information would be detrimental to the effort to cure them. Under such a community standard, it might be considered unethical to tell a cancer patient, for example, that he or she had a fatal illness. What's more, treatment decisions were regularly made with little input from the person being treated. Over time, this "doctor knows best" approach has evolved into its polar opposite: informed consent. This example underscores just how greatly values evolve over time and how necessary it is for these changes to guide practice.

While an in-depth discussion of counseling ethics is beyond the scope of this book, we offer a review of several practicum and internship concerns: informed consent, confidentiality, professional boundaries, and clinical competence.

Informed consent. Respect for autonomy is the principle that mostly underlies the concept of informed consent. Clients have a right and a responsibility to make independent decisions about their care; their choices must therefore be based upon complete and open disclosure of the methods used and the possible outcomes (positive and negative) anticipated. Counselors are obliged and ethically bound to provide their potential charges with a wide range of information. The counselor disclosure statement (CDS) is becoming an increasingly common way to inform clients. CDSs specify, in writing, the nature of the relationship between the client and the counselor. They are contracts that: (a) inform clients about the counseling process, (b) identify the counselor's professional training, clinical experience, and licensure status, (c) establish clinical and ethical boundaries, (d) identify courses of action when particular conditions exist, and (e) clarify expectations. CDSs honor many ethical mandates, including, for example, informed consent, limits of confidentiality, and duty to warn. The CDS is given to clients at the beginning of the first meeting or in advance of that meeting. In this way, clients are free to review the parameters of the relationship in advance of its formation. Student CDSs are especially useful because they specify from the outset that the client will receive counseling services from a *practicum or internship student* who is working under the supervision of a licensed professional.

The Louisiana Counselor Licensure Law and the rules stemming from that law require that counselors complete a CDS that includes specific information about each of the following topics:

1. Counselor identifying information
2. Qualifications; i.e., current graduate student working under supervision, completing practicum/internship
3. Description of the counseling relationship
4. Areas of expertise
5. Fee scales
6. An explanation of the types of services offered and clients served
7. Code of conduct
8. Privileged communication
9. Emergency situations
10. Client responsibilities
11. Physical health considerations
12. Potential counseling risks
13. Confirming signatures of client and counselor (supervisor and counselor intern)

(http://www.lpcboard.org/rules_for_declaration.htm)

Before CDSs were mandated, few if any counselors wrote and distributed them. In fact, many experienced professionals balked at having to design these forms once licensing boards required them. Despite the objections, counselors quickly realized that completing a CDS turned out to be a valuable exercise. It provides an opportunity to (a) reflect upon your choice of a counseling theory, (b) clearly define skills, abilities, and limitations, (c) consider many practical aspects of the counseling process, including limits to confidentiality, billing, scheduling, and client and counselor expectations, and (d) apply the ethical codes that govern practice. Preparing a CDS is an excellent way for you to explore ethical concerns before meeting with clients, and it will help you formulate answers to many questions that commonly arise in the course of providing counseling services. We require our practicum and internship students to prepare a rough draft, have it reviewed by other students, and complete a final draft based upon those peer recommendations. The time that you invest in this assignment will pay many dividends. And the final product, a written CDS, will benefit your clients.

Confidentiality. The confidentiality of the counseling relationship forms one pillar of its effectiveness. With such a guarantee, clients become free to expose troubling concerns and experiences that would under other circumstances remain suppressed or avoided. While confidentiality is based on several principles, fidelity, or "faithfulness to promises made and to the truth" (Welfel, 1998, p. 37) is particularly important. Clients expect and counselors must deliver confidential treatment. The promise that counselors make in this regard demands scrupulous adherence to the standards that govern the protection of their clients' information and identities. While your family doctor may say hello at a social gathering, as a mental health professional, you are not free to publicly identify yourself to clients. A simple greeting would unwittingly identify the other as receiving mental health services. We have rarely been able to successfully predict which of our clients will speak to us in public and which will not. To emphasize the point, we offer the following situation, which happened to one of us. A counselor was invited to serve on a board for a local community service program. The president introduced him to each member with brief, informal, threesome meetings. As he moved about the room, the counselor was surprised to discover that one of his clients was a board member of the organization. Had the counselor known beforehand that the client was on the board, he would not have accepted the invitation. As the president at last introduced the counselor to *his own* client, the counselor looked for some signal from the client, who quickly responded by saying that he was happy to meet the new member and asked him what type of work he did. The counselor asked the same question in return. The two men shook hands, parted, and headed for their respective seats. The next day, during the regularly scheduled counseling session, the client thanked the counselor for maintaining the confidentiality of their relationship.

Absent guarantees of confidentiality, many clients would be reluctant to explore important experiences and reactions in their lives. According to Jourard and Landsman (1980), self-disclosures are critical to the client's growth and development. They maintained that sharing information in the presence of a trusted "other" had two beneficial effects. While the counselor's empathic understanding of the client's concerns seemed the most obvious, the fact that the clients heard themselves more completely when concerns were uttered in the presence of another turned out to be the more curative force. Counselors and clients eventually use such information to develop plans to ameliorate difficulties and to access emotions that would otherwise be avoided.

Confidentiality has limits, and the management of them becomes yet another challenge of the ethics governing this aspect of the counseling relationship. Most jurisdictions and ethical codes stipulate that observing confidences cannot endanger the life of the client or the client's relationships. Counselors have a duty to warn if a real danger exists regarding the client's own life or the possibility that the client would injure someone else. This duty to warn is to a large extent based upon the interrelated concepts of nonmaleficence (doing no harm) and beneficence (doing good). Because counselors are, and should be, mandatory reporters of abuse toward children, older people, and people with disabilities, clients need to be aware of this limit to confidentiality as they enter the counseling relationship. Deciding whether a reportable threat to another person exists requires careful assessment, consultation, and action. You are working under supervision, however, so these decisions will always be made in consultation with supervisors. No one looks forward to making such a report, but openness, support, and experience make the difficult accomplishable. The fact that this possibility was covered in the CDS and discussed early in the counseling process helps. Fidelity, faithfulness to promises made, ultimately carries the counselor through this difficult process because "clients tend to trust truthful and honest counselors, even if the truth is painful or difficult" (Cavanagh & Levitov, 2002, p. 62). And such life-and-death concerns demand that you faithfully take steps to directly protect your client's life or others in his or her life. Protocols for assessing suicide and homicide risk are available and should be obtained from site and university supervisors.

While the ethic of confidentiality governs the sharing of information from a professional standpoint, *privileged communication* is the legal standard. Courts can and sometimes do subpoena records and counselors. Though the client owns the "privilege," such requests must be immediately discussed with the client because it is ultimately the judge who will determine whether the information and/or your testimony is required. There is little that counselors can do to prevent divulging such information if they are ordered to do so, beyond asserting their client's right to privileged communication. Supervision, consultation, and a phone call to the American Counseling Association's legal hotline are all important steps when legal action produces confidentiality and privileged-communication concerns.

While we are covering this subject, we would like to stress the fact that the client actually "owns" the information and can therefore dictate where and how it will be shared. Though not a limit to confidentiality, a client's request for his or her counselor to disclose information to others is actually quite common. The client may ask you to speak, for example, to an employer, another health care worker, or school officials (in the case of minors). The client's decision for you to take this action must be codified by completing a *release,* a written and signed document that stipulates to whom you can speak and in some cases what you are allowed to discuss. Clients will often ask you to discuss the decision to release information and to explore possible problems that may arise.

Confidentiality is a ubiquitous concern. Our lives as counselors are filled with occasions where the confidentiality of our clients must be fiercely protected. We quickly learn catchphrases like "I cannot confirm or deny . . ." as we respond to inevitable telephone and personal requests for information from others. We develop styles of interacting with other professionals that protect client identities. We limit what we say and where we say it. And we develop methods to guard the records and information that we obtain from our clients. Unfortunately, breaches of confidentiality sometimes occur. The principle of fidelity guides us under these circumstances as well. Being truthful to our clients, even in situations where the promise of confidentiality was not kept, is particularly important.

Professional boundaries. *Dual relationship* is the term often applied to clinical situations in which counselors inappropriately choose to begin counseling relationships with clients with whom they have a conflict of interest or in which clinical boundaries slip and produce inappropriate counselor-client relationships. Both unethical situations harm clients. The principle of nonmaleficence is most applicable here because the term means to do no harm or to protect clients from harm.

Counselors do not offer services to friends or family members. They resist counseling people with whom they have other types of relationships. For example, sanctions against dual relationships protect students from obtaining counseling from their professors. Supervision is not counseling. Each has a different set of goals and different means. Blurring the boundary between teacher and counselor is especially worrisome for students in the clinical portion of their training. As a practicum and internship student, you should be alert to improper invitations to shift from supervision to counseling. At Loyola University New Orleans, we draw a clear line, ensuring that students receive counseling from our counseling center and supervision from faculty. We offer more information about the differences in chapter 5.

Establishing and maintaining appropriate boundaries are essential clinical tasks to learn. The idea of a "slippery slope" is often used to describe boundary infractions that appear insignificant but actually mark the beginning of a serious change in the therapeutic alliance.

Unfortunately, counselors who take part in the erosion of these boundaries usually presume that they are exhibiting noble intentions as they unwittingly participate in what will eventually lead to countertherapeutic, in some cases dangerous, outcomes. Evidence that boundaries were poorly established from the beginning of the therapeutic alliance almost always surfaces when histories of problem-laden therapies are studied.

Implementing a course of action that focuses on the establishment and maintenance of boundaries is complicated by the fact that clients, for the most part, know almost nothing about mental health ethics. This naïveté produces confusion when your clients apply what they know about relationships in general to the counseling relationship. As a counselor, you may surprise or even insult them with your responses. For example, a client who offers many deeply personal replies to your questions may become frustrated when you correctly "process" rather than answer his or her questions about your personal life. You are appropriately more interested in discussing your client's need to know about you than in actually answering the questions, but the shift from what is commonly expected still feels awkward to the client. Although you may respond to client questions with versions of the statement, "This therapy is about you and should not focus on my life," the client may remain confused because such questions about you as counselor seem completely benign and consistent with social convention. Professional counseling relationships proceed in this unbalanced way so that ultimately clients share more and more detailed information about their emotional, social, vocational, and spiritual lives yet learn next to nothing about their counselors beyond that which can be obtained from reading the disclosure statement. The imbalance is striking to clients because people have come to expect others to share and risk as much as they do. Indeed, such a one-sided relationship is uncommon.

In addition, human beings quite naturally respond to others with a deepening sense of emotional closeness as more-intimate parts of the self are shared. Unfortunately, clients can easily mistake this form of closeness for the type found in a close personal friendship or love relationship in which, unlike the counseling relationship, both people share equally. If counselors and clients misinterpret the "contrived" closeness that clients experience from sharing so much of themselves for something other than a therapeutic or clinical relationship, serious problems develop. You will need to approach this aspect of the therapeutic alliance with caution and clarity so as not to allow your client to confuse counseling with the types of social relationships that form between people who mutually choose to share and respond to one another out of love or friendship. The value of appropriate boundaries for all counseling relationships cannot be overstated.

Clients can become frustrated, even hurt, when counselors correctly enforce various clinical boundaries. Such situations are often difficult for counselors and clients. Gift giving is an excellent example of a potentially difficult-to-enforce ethical boundary. In general, people are not comfortable with refusing gifts (counselors), nor are they accustomed to having their gifts refused (clients). Thus, managing ethical sanctions against accepting gifts from clients may feel unnatural and needlessly difficult. Counselors fear their clients' reaction when they return a gift; clients feel predictably hurt when their gifts are refused. Despite the discomfort, the need to maintain this boundary persists. Accepting gifts invites the client to change the nature and structure of the counseling relationship from well-bounded and professional to informal, casual, and friendly. If the gift is a sign of appreciation, it would be clinically preferable if the client used such an occasion to more completely appreciate the self rather than another. In any event, managing the boundary of gift giving becomes much easier after one or two experiences. You will find that being empathic and being firm are not mutually exclusive events. In most cases clients, even those who might initially appear hurt by your refusal of a gift, at some point express their appreciation for how you were able to maintain critical boundaries that in hindsight make better sense to them.

Counselors set boundaries with their clients by communicating with them. Therefore, our nonverbal reactions are as important as what we say. Skilled counselors learn to be consistent in both realms of interaction. Mixed messages are especially destructive to boundaries. Depending to some extent upon the client, something as seemingly minor as a pat on a client's shoulder as he or she leaves a session could undo what was verbally emphasized as the importance of a well-bounded professional relationship. Clients also need to know why such boundaries are important to the counseling process. For example, no clinician would question why a counselor would refuse an offer to come to a client's house for dinner. Counselors understand that the dinner would mark a change in the relationship from a professional alliance to a casual friendship. They recognize the worrisome decrease in objectivity, the countertherapeutic changes in expectations of the client for his or her counselor, and the plethora of confidentiality issues that would surface. Experienced clinicians may even recognize that the client's invitation may be prompted by undisclosed anxieties that the client believes could be resolved by being friendly with his or her counselor. Clients, of course, have no recognition of these and other factors, so the counselor is ultimately responsible for not only maintaining the boundary but also for explaining the benefits accrued from doing so. When counselors tell clients that they are ethically prohibited from, for example, accepting an invitation to dinner, they have only partially responded. It is important for the client to know why in some detail.

Consider the case of a client who unproductively began and ended counseling relationships with a number of counselors and was eventually referred to yet another counselor. During the intake interviews, the client discussed a long list of failed personal relationships in which she ended up feeling used and disrespected. While she did not identify the feelings, her loneliness and sadness were palpable. Note here that her personal history and her counseling history cued the counselor to relationship problems that signaled the potential for boundary problems in the newly forming counseling relationship. When the client asked the counselor for a hug and kiss good-bye at the end of the session, it came as no surprise. The counselor correctly declined and told the client that this issue would be the first order of business when they met for the next regularly scheduled meeting.

The client returned predictably hurt and angry. The counselor accepted that this was how she felt and responded by telling her that counseling must be a professional, well-bounded relationship and that the hug and kiss would have seriously interfered with that important goal. The counselor expressed having far too much respect for her and her struggles to allow the erosion of boundaries that were critical to her efforts to heal. The counselor explained that the hug and kiss might have reduced some level of her loneliness, but this counseling effort would be focused on more important and far-reaching goals, such as developing requisite skills for the formation of close personal relationships in her private life. The counselor knew that the client had a long history of repeating unproductive relationships, and allowing her to inadvertently do the same thing to the counseling relationship would have been counterproductive, disrespectful, and unethical. Once the counselor explained this last set of insights to her, she seemed to understand and appreciate the course that the counselor took with her. While her loneliness persisted, the groundwork had been laid so that she would be able use the counseling relationship to help herself on her journey to find intimacy in her personal life. This client, like most, encountered distortions and difficulties in her relationships with many people in her life. That she would inadvertently make similar problematic choices in a counseling relationship should not be a surprise; it is a major reason why counselors must scrupulously manage boundaries.

You can develop and maintain appropriate boundaries if you are willing to carefully honor them from the very outset of the counseling relationship and if you recognize the value of screening for potential dual relationships. Proper boundaries and clearly defined goals build trust and openness, critical elements of any effective clinical relationship.

Clinical competence. Because practicum and internship students are novices, concerns about their level of clinical competence are logical and common. After having trained many students, we recognize that your lack of experience fills you with (a) questions about what to do, when to do it, and how it should be done and (b) predictable worry about the fact that your clients are being treated by you, a counselor in training. Your supervisors respond to your inexperience with their own set of concerns coupled with an ethical and professional mandate to create a safe environment for you to grow into a mental health professional. The following section, Student-Institution, presents the ethical and practical guidelines that govern working under supervision. Your relationships to your university, field site, and supervisors have been carefully defined so that you can gain the requisite work experiences with actual clients and so that clients will be helped in the process. All professions recognize the risks and benefits that exist when theoretically trained but inexperienced clinicians enter this phase of their professional education. The medical school cliché "See one, do one, teach one" sarcastically pokes fun at the concerns professors and students must navigate as they help trainees gain requisite clinical experiences. Every trained mental health professional began by working with a first client in a practicum setting that was designed to accommodate the client's needs and the counselor's lack of experience.

Clinical competence is closely related to the principles of both beneficence, "the obligation to do good and to be of help" (Cavanagh & Levitov, 2002, p. 60) and nonmaleficence, to do no harm. These two principles are complementary; they say the same thing but do so from two opposing positions. Together they mandate that counselors take steps to insure that what they do is helpful and not harmful. It is easy to see how students, their supervisors, and their clients would be drawn to issues of clinical competence and the principles that underlie it.

We offer yet a second ironic example of how your lack of clinical experience is both an ethical concern and a clinical advantage. You already recognize that your lack of experience creates some discomfort as you ponder how you will answer client questions about such delicate matters as how much experience you have with their particular psychological problem or how many couples you have treated successfully. Some clients may also wonder how you could be helpful to them given that you are 20 years their junior. Such questions are common at the beginning of all counseling relationships; they are just more disturbing to novices. Your heightened sensitivity is useful because it motivates answers to questions that help you properly assess your level of competence and clarify the amount of supervision that you will need to carry out specific clinical assignments. The competency triad of (a) formal education, (b) supervised clinical/practical experience, and (c) continuing education offers an organized approach to determining competence in particular clinical situations. (We will return to the triad and offer greater detail in chapter 11.) As you encounter various types of clients, you can assess yourself on all three dimensions, make a determination, and establish a course of action that might include additional work in any or all of the three areas. It is important also to realize that your own psychological health can affect your ability to make accurate assessments. Consider the difference between feeling incompetent and being incompetent. Psychologically healthy counselors respond to concerns about competence by openly processing and discussing these concerns during supervision. This activity leads to growth and improvement. On the other hand, psychologically unhealthy counselors guard and withhold such information because they fear criticism. This trend leads to incompetence because honest assessment, feedback, and change are thwarted by the fears.

Being open to learning more about yourself and the way in which you work with clients does not end with internship. Trained counselors regularly obtain supervision when they opt to work with clients who have psychological problems that they have not previously encountered. They usually follow guidelines similar to those that you are exposed to in practicum and internship. For example, they would disclose the lack of training to the client (informed consent), identify that they would treat the client under the supervision of a clinician experienced in treating the client's difficulty (beneficence), and assure the client that the clinician would regularly monitor progress to determine whether a referral were necessary (nonmaleficence).

Ultimately, the issue of clinical competence helps us determine to whom we should provide service and who should be referred to other clinicians who possess treatment alternatives more appropriate to the particular client's needs. Unfortunately, competence is an important concern that can be easily and improperly influenced by clients themselves. During the evaluation process or when new information becomes available, a counselor may correctly determine that the client's needs call for a different type of mental health professional or someone with an expertise in a different area. Some clients balk at the recommendation and respond by insisting that the counselor continue to counsel them. Of course a common and problematic situation develops if the counselor acquiesces. Problems like this are not specific to counseling. Family medicine and internal medicine physicians are also subject to patients asking them to continue treatment even though the need for a referral to a specialist is indicated. Counselors must not only demonstrate competence in correctly identifying whom they can appropriately help but also demonstrate competence in effecting appropriate referrals.

Although site and university supervisors identify the types of clients that are appropriate for you and your level of expertise, you need to be aware of your concerns and be willing to share them with those who are responsible for your work. The ideal situation exists when you and your supervisor are in agreement about the types of clients that are appropriate for you. When supervisors feel that you are more skillful and competent than you think you are, they are obliged to help you recognize the gap and adapt to it. When you feel that you are more skilled and competent than your supervisors believe you are, another set of problems develops. In this situation, one of two concerns may exist: (a) your supervisors have misjudged your skill set, or (b) you have an exaggerated self-assessment. The former is remedied by allowing supervisors to gain more experience of your work, but the latter is a problem that can worsen rapidly and significantly. Self-assessment and assessments completed by others are covered in chapter 3. In any event, a harmony of opinion between you and your supervisor(s) concerning your level of competence is in all ways essential.

Student-Institution

To minimize risk to clients and to insure that counseling students obtain worthwhile clinical experiences, the education of counselors is guided by an elaborate set of ethics and policies. We have reviewed some of the ethical requirements that govern the counselor-client relationship, and we now turn to those that govern the relationship between the student and the college, university, or agency. As we review these codes and standards, you will see that the same five principles that guide the counselor-client relationship have a place in the student-institution relationship. Universities and their faculties as well as agencies and their site supervisors must also abide by codes of supervisory ethics and standards for supervision that form obligations to their counseling interns and to the clients who are served by them. An example of such standards and codes of conduct can be found in the published standards of the Council for the Accreditation of Counseling and Related Educational Programs (CACREP).

Accredited counseling programs abide by a range of standards that include, for example, class size for practicum classes (five students), internship classes (ten students), amount of supervision, type of supervision, and standards for performance. The "Clinical Instruction" section of the CACREP standards has been reprinted in appendix C so that you can more easily peruse this subset of the standards. The section opens with the following:

> Clinical instruction includes supervised practica and internships that have been completed within a student's program of study. Practicum and internship requirements are considered to be the most critical experience elements in the program. All faculty, including clinical instruction faculty and supervisors, are clearly committed to preparing professional counselors and promoting the development of the student's professional counselor identity.

The short goal statement offers a glimpse into a collection of standards that are both comprehensive and specific. For example, the number of hours completed at the field site, amount of time devoted to direct client contact, and individual/group supervision activities are all covered. Course syllabi are often designed around these criteria, so your review of them will offer an opportunity to identify the source of the requirements and a chance to determine the extent to which your course requirements are consistent with the CACREP standards. We would specifically recommend that you review sections H through M in appendix C. Becoming familiar with these CACREP standards can be very helpful when questions or concerns arise about course requirements, training experiences, and evaluation methods.

Student-Supervisor

Mental health codes of ethics usually include sections that address clinical supervision (e.g., appendixes A, B, C, and D). Of course, evidence of the five basic underlying principles can be easily identified in these codes. The Approved Clinical Supervisor (ACS) Code of Ethics offered by the Center for Credentialing and Education (2005) provides one set of particularly useful specifications. You can quickly relate one or more of the five principles to each numbered statement in the code. Item number 1 emphasizes respect for autonomy. Item 13 reflects the principle of justice, or "the expectation that counselors will act fairly and equitably" (Cavanagh & Levitov, 2002, p. 61). Counselors act justly when they understand and appropriately respond to cultural differences and the influence that such differences may have on the counseling relationship. See if you can identify which principles underlie the remaining elements of the code:

1. Ensure that supervisees inform clients of their professional status (e.g., intern) and of all conditions of supervision.
   Supervisors need to ensure that supervisees inform their clients of any status other than being fully qualified for independent practice or licensed. For example, supervisees need to inform their clients if they are a student, intern, trainee or, if licensed with restrictions, the nature of those restrictions (e.g., associate or conditional). In addition, clients must be informed of the requirements of supervision (e.g., the audio taping of all clinical sessions for purposes of supervision).
2. Ensure that clients have been informed of their rights to confidentiality and privileged communication when applicable. Clients also should be informed of the limits of confidentiality and privileged communication.
   The general limits of confidentiality are when harm to self or others is threatened; when the abuse of children, elders or disabled persons is suspected, and in cases when the court com-

pels the mental health professional to testify and break confidentiality. These are generally accepted limits to confidentiality and privileged communication, but they may be modified by state or federal statute.

3. Inform supervisees about the process of supervision, including supervision goals, case management procedures, and the supervisor's preferred supervision model(s).
4. Keep and secure supervision records and consider all information gained in supervision as confidential.
5. Avoid all dual relationships with supervisees that may interfere with the supervisor's professional judgment or exploit the supervisee.
   Any sexual, romantic, or intimate relationship is considered to be a violation. Sexual relationship means sexual conduct, sexual harassment, or sexual bias toward a supervisee by a supervisor.
6. Establish procedures with their supervisees for handling crisis situations.
7. Provide supervisees with adequate and timely feedback as part of an established evaluation plan.
8. Render assistance to any supervisee who is unable to provide competent counseling services to clients.
9. Intervene in any situation where the supervisee is impaired and the client is at risk.
10. Refrain from endorsing an impaired supervisee when such impairment deems it unlikely that the supervisee can provide adequate counseling services.
11. Supervisors offer only supervision for professional services for which they are trained or have supervised experience. Supervision should not include assistance in diagnosis, assessment, or treatment without prior training or supervision. Supervisors are responsible for correcting any misrepresentations of the qualifications of others.
12. Ensure that supervisees are aware of the current ethical standards related to their professional practice, as well as legal standards that regulate the practice of counseling.
13. Engage supervisees in an examination of cultural issues that might affect supervision and/or counseling.
14. Ensure that both supervisees and clients are aware of their rights and of due process procedures, and that you as supervisor are ultimately responsible for the client.
15. It is considered unethical for an ACS to supervise a relative or immediate family member.

(Revised 9/2005. Reprinted with the permission of the National Board for Certified Counselors, Inc. and Affiliates, 3 Terrace Way, Suite D, Greensboro, NC 27403-3660.)

The ACS code defines the nature of the relationship between counselors and their supervisors. It outlines what to expect from a supervisor, the supervisory relationship, and how to properly inform clients of your status as a person working under the supervision of a licensed professional. The parallels between aspects of the code governing counselor-client relationships and counselor-supervisor relationships are obvious. Dual relationships (item 15) are identified as problematic, and sanctions are imposed in both types of relationships. Issues of confidentiality, informed consent, and clinical competence are all included.

Making Ethical Decisions

While knowing and understanding the codes that govern practice and training are essential, they are not sufficient. You must be able to apply them effectively and willing to do so consistently. To achieve that end, researchers have developed protocols for ethical decision making. Each of the following models offers a slightly different, sequentially ordered protocol for effective, ethical decision making. Each begins by directing you to determine whether an ethical concern exists and ends with implementing an appropriate course of action.

Hybrid Model

This type of hybrid decision-making model is offered by Skovholt and Rivers (2004, p. 360) and based in part upon those of Corey, Corey, and Callanan (2003) and Kottler and Brown (2000).

1. Determine that an ethical and/or legal issue exists.
2. Frame the issue.
3. Review ethical guidelines, laws, policies of the work setting, and helping literature.
4. Consult with supervisors, colleagues, and/or other professionals.
5. Consider personal values.
6. Identify and consider various options for resolution.
7. Make a decision and act on it.
8. Accurately and fully document the issue, including all steps and actions taken.
9. Process the experience with supervisors and colleagues.

ACA Model

The ACA model is perhaps the most popular of all ethical decision making protocols. Forrester-Miller and Davis (1996) developed the following seven steps that comprise the ACA model:

1. Identify the problem and define it.
2. Apply the proper Code of Ethics.
3. Access the nature and depth of the problem.
4. Generate potential courses of action.
5. After carefully considering potential consequences for each option, select a course of action.
6. Evaluate the selected course of action.
7. Implement the course of action.

Employing a Model

Employing one of the available ethical decision-making models is an activity that will be repeated throughout the course of your career as a clinician. Disciplined attention to each of the steps will make it easier to integrate this approach into your clinical work; practice will increase your ability to make good decisions. We do not believe that one of the two protocols presented is necessarily better than the other, so we would encourage you to practice using both until you determine a preference based on your experience with them. You might start by identifying similarities and differences and then, having done so, hypothesize about why such differences exist. Once you understand the two models, analyze a potential ethical dilemma using each. This is a particularly effective exercise if you use it as an opportunity to work with peers. A good starting point would be the example situation offered at the beginning of this chapter.

Summary

Codes of ethics governing the counselor-client relationship are essential for obvious reasons. While this area of ethics usually gets the lion's share of attention, we also wanted to make you aware of and discuss the codes that govern the other important relationships in your life as a practicum and internship student. In doing so, we were able to illustrate that the same five basic principles influence all three relationship areas: counselor-client, student-supervisor, and student-institution.

We sought to demonstrate that ethics form one cornerstone of the profession and the counseling process. While it may not be easy to consistently follow the requirements of the codes, it is accomplishable and vital. We stressed the importance of openness and the need for supervision at this stage of your professional development. We know that ethical concerns can be worrisome, but we hope that you will also develop a sense of comfort from the idea that codes seek to ensure the proper treatment of those you counsel and those who are responsible for you as you learn to be a counselor.

This chapter on ethics is included early in the text because we believe that ethics should guide not only the counseling process but the counselor training process as well. We stress this point when we suggest that the selection of a field site is as much an ethical decision as it is an academic one. For example, you can easily recognize why a field site where you will be supervised by an old friend is problematic. However, it may be more difficult to recognize that certain settings may not be appropriate for you given the scope of your training or the fact that your own psychological health may be risked by working with certain types of clients. You will need to know a good deal about yourself and about the type of work done at sites you might possibly select if you are going to make a sound, ethical choice.

REFLECTION QUESTIONS

1. What reactions (feelings and thoughts) surfaced as you read Anthony's story in the introduction to this chapter?
2. What internal sensations do you experience that signal the presence of a potential ethical concern?
3. While the philosophical principles that underlie ethics have persisted for decades, mental health ethics are dynamic (evolving) rather than static (fixed). Why is this so, and what challenges does it place upon you as a clinician?
4. Under what conditions do you think you might be susceptible to allowing professional boundaries to inappropriately slip or erode?
5. What characteristics would you look for in a supervisor you were about to select for a discussion about a serious ethical concern?
6. What is the difference between thinking ethically and acting ethically?
7. What effect has reading this chapter had on your understanding of the opening story?

Chapter 3

Self and Program Evaluation

Formative and Summative Assessment

Dylan's internship site provided services to individuals with substance abuse problems. Several months' worth of successful interventions had improved Dylan's confidence and increased his comfort level with clients. Unfortunately, his very first client, after several months of successful work on a long-standing substance abuse problem, telephoned Dylan to let him know that he had begun to experience an unexpected and worrisome return of the same symptoms that originally brought him into counseling. Though Dylan knew that such relapses are especially common in substance abuse treatment, he was still worried. He was also uncertain about how to approach his client in light of this new information. At the beginning of their next counseling session, only a day or two after the phone call, the client opened with, "I'm slipping, but this time I know what to do: I have to return to the same basics that we spoke of when I first came into counseling!" Surprised that the client had so quickly come to rely on the products of the counseling relationship, Dylan asked him what specifically he meant by the comment. He answered without hesitation; he had been mulling over options for a while. He offered the following steps:

1. *Attend at least three AA meetings per week.*
2. *Contact his sponsor daily.*
3. *Return to complete his unfinished "third step."*

4. *Reassess his progress in counseling.*
5. *Channel unproductive worry and anxiety into actions that would benefit his long-term goal of sobriety.*

This level of problem solving arose in stark contrast to the chaos and uncertainty with which he presented when first entering counseling. Dylan realized that his client's decision making was no longer clouded. Actions were no longer hampered by the gridlock that forms from anxiety, uncertainty, and an inability to identify useful alternatives. Dylan recognized that his client could now not only sense when things were beginning to move in an undesirable direction but also identify and implement steps to improve his situation. This client had developed an effective system that he could activate on his own. The client reported that confidence and hopefulness now replaced his crippling fears because he now had an effective way to recognize when something was wrong, and he even knew what to do about it. This client confirmed what Dylan had always suspected: people will block themselves from attending to their concerns if they are overwhelmed or if they feel that they have no way of improving them.

INTRODUCTION

The example offers you a valuable distilled message: *Just as we cannot fix what we cannot see, we will not see what we cannot repair.* This message is equally important to you as a counseling student. You will be, if you are not already, making a number of key decisions about your professional future. To make good choices you will need to acquire accurate information, accept criticism, and act on what you learn. These skills are vital as you make decisions ranging from where you choose to complete your practicum or internship to determining your effectiveness as a counselor and isolating specific areas where improvement is needed. Throughout your professional life you will be expected to regularly assess the quality of your work and develop effective ways of ensuring that you are delivering services that meet acceptable standards of treatment. Knowing and using evaluation and assessment skills can prepare you for the professional journey of improving yourself and your ability to be helpful to the clients you serve.

Having spent so much time in schools and colleges, you understand how motivated people can be to obtain good evaluations (e.g., grades), how difficult it is to be open to criticism, and how valuable the positive and negative observations offered from others can be to your growth as a professional. As a counseling student, you probably also recognize the existence of internal forces that inhibit people from being able to attend to and process information that they may perceive as threatening to their self-concept or self-worth. These so-called defense mechanisms affect all human beings to some extent. At one extreme, heavily defended people cannot process anything that is contrary to their self-perception. Their chances of benefiting from criticism are seriously impaired. This depth of self-protection would make it difficult, if not impossible, to successfully complete clinical training. Clinical training demands a much greater level of vulnerability than does participation in content courses. It is no surprise that *evaluation* and *assessment* are terms that many people greet with feelings of uneasiness and defensiveness.

In an attempt to ease these predictable defensive reactions and improve the chances that students will be able to hear and act upon appropriate concerns, we often focus more on what can be done to improve instead of fixating on the deficiency. We encountered this valuable approach while one of us was serving on a team that was preparing materials for a university-wide accreditation process. We on the team knew going into the assessment that there were deficiencies. We also knew that being defensive about them was not going to improve our situation and that a rigid stance would only worsen the situation. Early in the meeting, one member of the team openly shared the dimensions of the problem with the assessment group. The group leader thought for a moment and then said, "We are not as concerned with the deficiency as we are with what you are doing to remedy it." We had been working on the resolution for some time, so the discussion immediately moved to the correctives and what we expected to happen once all the changes were implemented. Though this example refers to an organizational problem, you can be equally effective by employing the same problem-solving approach to help yourself and your clients. It honors the existence of areas where improvement is needed but does not stall at the point where the potential to tumble into unproductive defensiveness is highest. We have encountered this reality in both clinical settings and organizations and conclude that to be able to improve, we must visit our deficiencies, but we must be careful not to unproductively dwell there.

Our practical approach links assessment, information verification, identification of alternatives, establishment of priorities, and measurement of the overall effectiveness of problem-solving efforts into an organized system. The model draws upon several recognized paradigms: *institutional effectiveness* (IE) and *outcomes assessment* (OA; Nichols, 1991) to establish and evaluate personal and organizational goals through *total quality management* (TQM; Deming, 1986; *note*: though TQM was not named by Deming, the model is attributed to him) to create an organizational climate that fosters *continuous improvement.* Deming defined 14 steps that organizations must follow to achieve their goals. Four of these steps are particularly applicable to successful counselor formation. Offered in paraphrased form, they are:

1. Create constancy of purpose toward improvement.
2. Improve constantly and forever.
3. Drive out fear.
4. Institute education and self-improvement.

The combination of paradigms offers a model that is entirely consistent with the training of counseling students and the work of counselors in general.

While business management literature may seem an unlikely place from which to acquire theoretical models for helping counseling students maximize gains from experiential clinical training, TQM principles are actually quite applicable to mental health service agencies as well as individual mental health professionals like you. OA coupled with select elements of TQM produces reliable methods to assess institutional and individual strengths and weaknesses, identify alternatives, create environments that are conducive to productive change, and ultimately assess outcomes. TQM recognizes the importance of the individual to the system and recognizes that any change must be supported by the entire organization if it is going to improve.

Institutional Effectiveness and Outcomes Assessment

Since the late 1980s, academic settings of all kinds have come to rely upon IE and OA methods to assess and improve quality (Nichols, 1991). This change in methodology was considered a landmark event because assessment efforts moved from questions about what and how much academic institutions provided to students to questions of whether the desired results (outcomes) were actually being achieved. To accomplish this paradigm shift, institutions were first required to develop comprehensive *mission statements*. These mission statements were then translated into a number of highly specific goals. Finally, each goal was further defined by the creation of one or more measurable outcome objectives. The process of developing mission statements, goals, and outcome objectives is repeated in each academic and administrative unit of the institution, all of which must be aligned with the university-wide mission statement. The approach emphasizes the need for a high level of specificity and "measurable" outcome objectives.

IE and OA, though usually applied to academic settings, can easily be adapted to assess centers that offer mental health services and mental health training as well as to individual mental health service providers. As a student engaged in clinical training, you will find that the process of identifying your overall mission, specifying related goals, and creating measurable outcome objectives can help focus and direct your efforts to improve your clinical skills.

A realistic mission statement for an internship student, completing a community counseling program, might read as follows:

> Through participation in a range of supervised clinical experiences, I seek a level of proficiency that ensures that all clients in my care receive ethical and effective treatment. I recognize the need for supervision and look forward to full and open participation in a consultative process that will, in varying forms, span my career as a counselor. I expect to synthesize all elements of clinical training so that I can form a professional identity and adopt a professional demeanor that is consistent with existing standards for community counselors.

As we mentioned earlier, the mission statement becomes the genesis for a number of goals. To illustrate, we have slightly modified the CACREP Knowledge and Skill Requirements for Community Counselors into clinical training goals that correspond to the previously noted mission statement. In addition we have included one or more sample outcome objectives for each of the goals. We understand that you and your professors might develop goals and objectives that are different from those listed here. Such differences are completely understandable because community counseling is a broad field where no single or universal set of priorities exists. Our only purpose here is to offer an example of goals and outcome objectives on which to base a discussion of how models of assessment can be usefully applied.

Goals and Sample Outcome Objectives

1. Become familiar with typical characteristics of individuals and communities served by a variety of institutions and agencies that offer community counseling services;
   - 1.1 Describe the characteristics of the individuals served at your proposed or current field site.
   - 1.2 Identify one or more agencies that provide services to a similar population.
2. Know and be able to apply models, methods, and principles of program development and service delivery for a clientele based on assumptions of human and organizational development, including prevention, implementation of support groups, peer facilitation training, parent education, career/occupational information and counseling, and encouragement of self-help;
   - 2.1 Correctly identify a client's level of human and organizational development.
   - 2.2 Properly apply delivery systems that are deemed appropriate to the client's needs.
   - 2.3 Correctly assess the effectiveness of the system and make recommendations accordingly.

3. Implement effective strategies for promoting client understanding of and access to community resources;
   - 3.1 Identify at least three community resources that would be helpful to a particular client.
   - 3.2 Offer the options to the client using a clinical approach that ensures the greatest likelihood that the client will acquire the community resource.
4. Know and be able to apply principles and models of biopsychosocial assessment, case conceptualization, theories of human development, and concepts of normalcy and psychopathology leading to diagnoses and appropriate counseling plans;
   - 4.1 Correctly conceptualize the client by identifying his or her stage(s) of development, level of psychopathology, social concerns, vocational issues, and areas of identified strengths.
   - 4.2 Develop and implement a treatment plan that improves the client's biopsychosocial condition.
5. Know and be able to apply the principles of diagnosis and the use of current diagnostic tools, including the current edition of the *Diagnostic and Statistical Manual*;
   - 5.1 Offer a correct multiaxis diagnosis for the client.
   - 5.2 Demonstrate the combined use of interview, psychological test, and consultation information in making the diagnosis.
   - 5.3 Offer at least one additional diagnostic explanation for the client's condition.
6. Develop effective strategies for client advocacy in public policy and other matters of equity and accessibility;
   - 6.1 Identify at least three areas where improvements in equity and accessibility could be made within the agency or school.
   - 6.2 With permission and supervision, implement one of the noted improvements.
   - 6.3 Correctly assess the effect of the change.
7. Apply appropriate individual, couple, family, group, and systems modalities for initiating, maintaining, and terminating counseling, including the use of crisis intervention and brief, intermediate, and long-term approaches.
   - 7.1 Correctly identify an appropriate treatment for the client.
   - 7.2 Provide an acceptable rationale for the treatment choice.
   - 7.3 Identify expected therapeutic milestones.
   - 7.4 Demonstrate the ability to shift approaches when conditions warrant a change (e.g., moving to a crisis intervention approach from an intermediate therapy approach following the death of the client's spouse).
   - 7.5 Correctly assess the effectiveness of the intervention or mode of treatment selected.

7.6 Correctly identify alternative approaches that may be needed if a predictable change occurs in the client's life (e.g., the diagnosis of a serious health problem following symptoms that were not initially considered life threatening at the time the therapy began).

7.7 Correctly assess the efficacy of the change.

(Goals adapted from 2001 CACREP Standards for Community Counseling Programs, Section C: Knowledge and Skill Requirements)

An in-depth discussion of the preceding goals and objectives would be our first choice for a beneficial exercise. Of course, we will have to leave that activity to you and to those with whom you are training. On the other hand, we can use the matrix to make some observations that will help clarify the assessment issues that form the focus of this chapter. The first and perhaps most important conclusion that emerges from a review of the sample outcome objectives is the fact that for the most part, subjective criteria form the basis for determining whether a particular objective is met. Although more-objective criteria might be desirable, according to Bernard and Goodyear (1992), "Our profession is plagued with a certain degree of ambiguity that limits us as evaluators. . . . We are still unsure about what in therapy is therapeutic" (p. 106). Thus, clearly defined conclusions about what is right and what is wrong, what works and what does not, become difficult to glean. Counselors are faced with alternatives that must be weighed, actively discussed, and continuously assessed. Whereas experienced counselors may find this reality inspiring, you may find it troubling. Such subjectivity can produce levels of uncertainty about how best to help your clients and worries about what you specifically may need to do to successfully complete your clinical training.

The review of the objectives offers one other conclusion. To be effective, you will need to manage an impressive scope of responsibility, be able to apply the information you have learned, and acquire many new skills. Stated from an educational perspective, you will achieve a level of mastery that spans all of the categories that form Bloom's Taxonomy: knowledge, comprehension, application, analysis, synthesis, and evaluation (see Bloom 1984; Bloom, Englehart, Furst, Hill, & Krathwohl 1956). Abilities in each category of the taxonomy are vital to the task of helping supervisors teach students to translate theory into effective clinical practice (for a more detailed discussion, see Granello, 2000). Table 3.1 offers examples of the skills associated with each of the categories of the taxonomy. It illustrates the range of cognitive abilities required for clinical practice.

If the evaluation of clinical training poses unique challenges, what methods should be employed to properly manage what Bernard and Goodyear (1992, p. 106) refer to as "the burden of evaluation?" The most basic answer to this question is to (a) rely upon a model that uses formative rather than summative evaluation and (b) create working and learning environments that manage fear, encourage self-assessment, and foster continuous improvement as an overarching goal.

Educators make choices about which type of evaluation to employ by determining which one is more suitable to the material being taught and by defining the overarching goal of the assessment.

Table 3.1 Counseling Skills across Bloom's Taxonomy

Bloom's Categories	Skills	Examples
Knowledge	What When Name List Define	Recall of information related to client or case. Knowledge of core classroom-based information.
Understanding	Summarize Describe Why Paraphrase Interpret	Summarize facts related to the case. Predict consequences of interventions. Show comprehension of importance of data collection.
Application	Apply Demonstrate Construct Interpret Practice	Use research to make clinical decisions and decide on interventions. Apply theories to current cases. Problem solve difficult client issues.
Analysis	Analyze Classify Compare Contrast Experiment	Identify patterns of behavior in clients. Identify parts of client history that are relevant to presenting problem. Compare and contrast similar interventions with different clients.
Synthesis	Create Combine Integrate Design Generalize Hypothesize Construct Summarize	Combine information from different academic courses to apply to real-world problems. Conceptualize case, bringing together all relevant information. Design an intervention that uses all of the client's resources.
Evaluate	Appraise Assess Defend Evaluate Recommend Critique	Articulate a rationale for interventions. Assess the value or significance of a particular theory or intervention. Make choices based on reasoned arguments.

Adapted from Granello, D. H. (2000). Encouraging the cognitive development of supervisees: Using Bloom's taxonomy in supervision. *Counselor Education and Supervision, 40*, 31–46. The American Counseling Association. Reprinted with permission. No further reproduction authorized without written permission from the American Counseling Association.

According to Royse, Thyer, Padgett, and Logan (2006, p. 116), "Formative evaluations are employed to adjust and enhance interventions." On the other hand, summative evaluation is "evaluation designed to present conclusions about the merit or worth of an object and recommendations about whether it should be retained, altered, or eliminated" (Joint Commission on Standards for Educational Evaluation, 1981, p. 156). One common example of a summative evaluation is the final grade in a course. Summative evaluations, though clearly unavoidable, are much less useful to you at this stage of your training if you define usefulness as the extent to which assessment information can be used to identify deficiencies and illustrate specific ways in which you can improve.

Within the context of student clinical training, formative evaluation offers many important advantages. With a focus on adjusting and enhancing interventions, you can easily see the value of a process that establishes a continuous loop in which evaluation information guides decision making, development of serviceable alternatives, implementation of treatments, and assessment of effectiveness. Relying upon formative evaluation techniques will not, by itself, ensure successful acquisition of clinical skills. Subjective assessments, the complexity of the material which must be mastered, and the challenge of properly caring for a client as you learn cause emotional reactions that can blunt your efforts to develop into a skilled counselor.

Total Quality Management

When individuals are afraid, they are unable to experience other feelings, motivation diminishes, creativity decreases, and problem-solving skills are impaired. The effect of fear is universal–it is individually and collectively stifling. The management of fear is obviously an important and common counseling initiative, so why seek suggestions from a seemingly unrelated management initiative like TQM? The answer is that TQM deals with the issue of fear in a practical way; it recognizes how reliance upon shared goals and objectives can reduce the fears that hamper success, and it endorses the concept of continuous improvement. According to Suarez (1993), "The elimination of fear is necessary to create an environment of trust and cooperation, essential ingredients to initiating and sustaining a total quality effort, pursuing continuous improvement, encouraging innovation" (p. 1). Dr. W. Edwards Deming (1986) not only identified the management of fear as a fundamental requirement but also placed the responsibility for locating and correcting sources of fear squarely on the shoulders of managers and supervisors.

Since communication is such a central part of clinical training, Suarez's (1993) conclusion about the trust that can replace fear in the workplace is particularly applicable: "In general, the higher the trust, the more open the communication, and the more stable and predictable the cooperation. On the other hand, low trust leads to uncertainty and defensive behaviors" (p. 63). Because uncertainty and the likelihood for defensiveness are already high given the training task and the setting where interns and practicum students work, methods for managing both are vital. In summary, TQM principles aid clinical training efforts because they:

- direct professors and site supervisors to recognize the importance of a shared vision for training that includes mission, goals, and objectives,
- direct those who are responsible for training to bear the responsibility for managing fear within the work setting and the classroom, and
- foster a climate of continuous improvement.

Once a mission, goals, and objectives are agreed upon and supervisors have assumed their responsibilities (e.g., reducing fear and guidance), practicum and internship students face the task of continuous improvement. This task relies heavily upon knowing and properly employing assessment and evaluation tools. How you obtain information, how you verify its integrity, how you apply it, and how well you understand potential blocks to obtaining such information become central to learning.

Sources of Evaluation Information

As a counseling intern working with clients, you rely upon many sources of evaluation information. The intake interview is arguably the most basic, important, and widely used tool at your disposal. When clients share their inner experience, we become privy to the unique patterns that form and maintain the person we are trying to assist. The client's history, assumptions about the world, feelings, concerns, and perceived strengths and weaknesses are all essential requirements for any enterprise focused on helping someone make important life changes. You would be lost and unable to help without this critical information the client provides. At the same time, you also have the advantage of obtaining information from additional sources. Psychological, vocational, and academic testing can often identify important aspects of the client's life that are not as easily or directly obtained from interviews. Finally, information gained from others' experience of the client can also be incorporated as you complete the picture that forms from the constellation of evaluative information about the client.

As a practicum or internship student enrolled in a graduate program, you will have access to many similar sources of evaluation information in seeking feedback about your own skills and abilities. Assessment information obtained from various types of tests, supervisors and professors, peers, clients, and yourself can be used in combination to help you develop strategies to accomplish your goals, assess your progress, improve your clinical skills, and make wise career decisions.

Tests and Assessments

Just as various test instruments exist to aid clients, similar tools are available to help practicum and internship students. As OA worked its way through schools and colleges, a wide range of outcome instruments developed. One example of a collection of such tools can be found on the World Wide Web under the heading of "The Counseling Center Village" and located at http://ccvillage.buffalo.edu. Examples of client satisfaction surveys and summative assessment instruments that guide supervisors' assessments of students as well as students' assessments of their supervisors can be found on this Web site. The site sponsor invites counseling centers from all over to submit examples of assessment tools, and downloading forms is easy.

The clinical use of testing emphasizes the mechanics of test construction, norming information, and the conditions under which tests should be administered. As a graduate student who has taken at least one measurement and assessment course, you realize the importance of establishing reliability and validity for any measurement or assessment effort. Both concepts are easily defined. *Reliability* refers to the extent to which a test measures consistently. *Validity* refers to the extent to which a test measures what it purports to measure. According to Henerson, Morris, and Fitz-Gibbon (1987), "Validity and reliability help to determine the amount of faith people should place in an evaluation instrument" (p. 133). The process of establishing reliability and validity for paper-and-pencil instruments is fairly straightforward. We need not proceed any deeper into specific forms of reliability and validity, but it would be valuable to discuss some of the special challenges associated with assessing clinical or counseling outcomes.

Problems emerge when we shift our interests to traits that are more subjective, elusive, and difficult to define but no less important to assess. The truth is that we are regularly faced with the prospect of trying to measure such subjective or elusive constructs as feelings, intentions, or qualities of interaction. Measuring attitudes (our own as well as those of our clients), for example, is a highly subjective and complicated process. As Henerson, Morris, and Fitz-Gibbon state,

> The task of measuring attitudes is not a simple one. What's more, attempting to demonstrate attitude change, as some evaluations require, is probably the most difficult of all evaluation tasks. Why is this so?

> To begin with, the concept of attitude, like many abstract concepts, is a creation—a construct. As such it is a tool that serves the human need to see order and consistency in what people say, think and do, so that given certain behaviors, predictions can be made about future behaviors. An attitude is not something we can examine and measure in the same way we can examine the cells of a person's skin or measure the rate of her heartbeat. We can only infer that a person has attitudes by her words and actions. (1987, p. 11–12)

Fortunately, techniques do exist for measuring such constructs. In fact, qualitative methods were actually developed in part to solve this problem. *Process evaluation* is one such example of a qualitative tool that emphasizes "looking at how a product or outcome is produced rather than looking at the product itself; that is, it is an analysis of the processes whereby a program produces the results it does" (Patton, 1987, p. 23). Obviously such a method is particularly well suited to assessing process-rich enterprises like counselor training and counseling.

One additional qualitative approach is worth including. Patton (1987) recognized that "not only will outcomes vary along specific common dimensions, but outcomes will be qualitatively different and will involve qualitatively different dimensions for different clients" (p. 24). The idea that individualized outcomes can and should be measured parallels basic counseling expectations. Data collection techniques for either of the two approaches would include the use of interviews, direct observations, and the analysis of written documents (e.g., case notes) or psychological reports. Qualitative methods can be applied so that the unit of analysis becomes an individual and in our case that individual could be a client or practicum or internship student. That qualitative methods offer an alternative in situations where quantitative methods cannot be applied is but one piece of the evaluation puzzle. In a larger sense, reliance upon qualitative methods encourages a desirable paradigm shift in which the importance of process is elevated and the use of formative evaluation emphasized. Both of these by-products are equally important and vital to the clinical training assessment model offered in this chapter.

Supervisor or Professor Assessments

While supervision is covered in detail in chapter 5, several comments about supervisor assessments are worth including here. Many universities use a summative assessment instrument of one type or another on which to base judgments about final grades. It is crucial to obtain a copy of that instrument as soon as possible. Most supervisors and instructors recognize this fact and include a copy of it in the course syllabus or in the agency orientation materials. If it is not there, ask for it because you will need to take into account the agency and school performance criteria as you begin the process of developing your own goals and outcome objectives.

You should also be mindful of the fact that those who supervise your work are faced with two tasks that often create a dilemma for them. As people interested and involved in your development as a counselor, they assume a clearly formative role in your efforts to become a skilled clinician, but on the other hand, they are expected to provide a summative evaluation in the form of a final grade or perhaps a determination of whether you are ready to move to the next level of your training. You have a vested interest in both of these tasks and should do all that you can to insure that the formative assessments are directly linked to the summative evaluations. Developing and sharing goals and outcome objectives with supervisors, asking for help from them, and being clear about the fact that you cannot work in a setting that cultivates fear are all important tasks. While an imbalance of power between supervisors and students exists, the need to be clear about your needs and willing to share your concerns should not be diminished. While Deming maintains that managers must be responsible for managing fear in the workplace, your need to identify conditions that are interfering with your ability to achieve agreed-upon outcomes is equally important.

Peer Assessments

Counseling accreditation standards mandate group supervision, and so you will meet weekly with other students in your practicum or internship. Peers often offer suggestions, ask questions, and in some cases offer assessment information during the classes led by the professor or supervisor. Such peer comments can be useful as you refine your skills and develop treatment alternatives for your clients.

Of course, threats to objectivity exist. Fellow students may be uncomfortable offering critical comments for many reasons. They may worry that such comments might negatively influence the way in which others, including the supervisor, perceive them in the supervision group. They may fear that what they say could cause you or other members of the group to treat them more harshly. And friendships with other students (peers) may interfere with their ability to be completely honest about perceived difficulties. It would be unwise to rely upon peer evaluations alone as a basis for determining the extent to which you are achieving your clinical goals and growing as a professional. While obvious limitations exist, peer comments do occupy a place within the rubric of evaluation sources. If you recognize that peer comments are often censored and that peers may be more likely to take sides with you when differences of opinion exist between you and a common supervisor, you will be in a better position to accurately assess the level of influence to assign to peer assessments.

Client Assessment

Though clients are not commonly seen as sources of practicum or internship student assessment information, in terms of OA principles, they are probably the ideal resource. Unfortunately, not all agencies and schools collect this type of information. During a postdoctoral internship in a local university hospital setting, we were surprised to learn that all clients were asked to complete a simple questionnaire either following formal termination or after they stopped returning for counseling sessions on their own. Completed surveys, whenever they were received, became a focus of weekly individual supervision sessions. This process identified both areas where improvement was needed and clinical strengths. As the intern's collection of evaluations grew, the supervisor and the intern together were able to identify patterns that described how the intern was perceived by clients, and they were able to assess the efficacy of interventions from the client's perspective. While we cannot overestimate the value of such client assessments to one's development as a counselor, we must admit that we initially found the idea of client evaluations intimidating and worrisome.

Useful survey instruments exist, and they should be included in the list of assessment sources for all practicum and internship students. The University of North Texas counselor evaluation form is just one example of a useful tool for obtaining client assessments of practicum and internship students (see Form 3.1). While this form includes a number of Likert-styled items and sections for open responses, you might wish to develop a form of your own, once again relying upon objectives that you have specifically developed.

Some counselors have perfected an exit interview format that they use during the last session with a client to obtain assessment information. Asking clients what they found helpful, what they thought interfered with progress, and what they wished had been different during their counseling experience can provide useful insights. Objectivity and frankness are again issues of concern. It may be difficult for some clients to be as direct in person as they might be on an anonymously completed evaluation form. While the questions are important and probably should be asked, we are only suggesting that you would need to be cautious about conclusions given the potential threats that exist to reliability, validity, and objectivity. On the other hand, in cases where a client would be willing to or actually asks to share evaluative information about the counselor with the counselor's supervisor, some of the noted threats could be reduced. While this does occasionally occur, it is uncommon. We are sure that there are additional but as yet undeveloped routes to obtain client views of the counselors who work with them. You may be able to develop creative and ethical ways to acquire this valuable information.

Form 3.1 Counseling Experience Evaluation

COUNSELOR EDUCATION
UNIVERSITY OF NORTH TEXAS
COUNSELING AND HUMAN DEVELOPMENT CENTER
Counseling Experience Evaluation

Thank you for coming to the Counseling and Human Development Center. Through your use of this setting, your counselor has gained important professional experience. Now that you have completed your last session with your counselor, we are interested in your evaluation of this experience. Please do not put your name on this sheet. Feedback sheets will be collected by the instructor throughout the semester and shown to the counselor at the end of the term.

Your counselor's first name ____________________ Number of sessions attended_____

You came to this Center by way of: Self-referral ___________
Counseling class ___________
Other ___________ (Please explain briefly)

Please respond to each statement:

My counselor...	TO A LOW DEGREE 1	2	3	4	5	TO A HIGH DEGREE 6
seemed calm/relaxed	_____	_____	_____	_____	_____	_____
seemed confident	_____	_____	_____	_____	_____	_____
helped me feel comfortable	_____	_____	_____	_____	_____	_____
clearly explained expectations	_____	_____	_____	_____	_____	_____
seemed organized	_____	_____	_____	_____	_____	_____
conveyed acceptance of me	_____	_____	_____	_____	_____	_____
took an interest in me	_____	_____	_____	_____	_____	_____
seemed real—not playing a role	_____	_____	_____	_____	_____	_____
was warm/caring	_____	_____	_____	_____	_____	_____
seemed to understand me	_____	_____	_____	_____	_____	_____
was honest and direct	_____	_____	_____	_____	_____	_____
was supportive	_____	_____	_____	_____	_____	_____
helped me think about myself	_____	_____	_____	_____	_____	_____
helped me express my feelings	_____	_____	_____	_____	_____	_____
helped me make progress with the concerns for which I came to counseling	_____	_____	_____	_____	_____	_____

(continued)

What one thing did you like most about your counselor?

What one thing did you like least about your counselor?

If you were considering ongoing counseling, would you seek out this counselor? In answering this question, please do ***not*** consider such factors as location, cost, etc.; please consider ***only*** the quality of the experience you had with this counselor.

a. definitely.
b. probably.
c. uncertain.
d. probably not.
e. definitely not.

If you would like to explain your answer further, please feel free to do so below.

Please return this completed form to the practicum instructor. Thank you very much!

Used with permission of the Counseling Program, University of North Texas.

Self-Assessment

At the end of each clinical course at Loyola University New Orleans, supervisors usually ask students what they believe they have accomplished and what they hope to improve upon in the clinical course they are next scheduled to take. The students' answers are always interesting, useful, and indicative of the fact that they have thought about the questions. Unfortunately, we rarely have time to learn what specific information led them to their conclusions; what information, if any, they felt they needed but were unable to obtain; and how they actually assessed the accuracy of their conclusions. While you may experience the same time limitations in your own clinical courses, we hope this section may encourage and guide you to reflect more deeply on the sources of information and the efficacy of your own evaluative conclusions.

Human beings, like most living organisms, tend toward homeostasis, or balanced states. In nature, such a balanced state is usually considered healthy or adaptive. However, such is not necessarily the case in human beings. Unfortunately, regardless of how healthy or unhealthy a particular social or psychological homeostasis may be, individuals will tend to behave in ways that maintain that balance. This concept offers one serviceable explanation of why behaviors persist even when the people expressing the desire for change report great pain and distress from remaining in that balanced but unhealthy state. Fear of change and fear of the unknown are common explanations for the maintenance of behavior patterns that produce such self-destructive behavior. It is this tendency to homeostasis that must be considered when thinking about the process of self-assessment.

It is difficult for individuals to attend to information that has the potential to seriously interfere with the way they see themselves. Unfortunately, many students enter clinical training clinging to the hope that who they are, how they are, and what they are will be affirmed as ideally suited to the role of counselor. Much like the clients they serve, the drive to cling to a homeostasis forces them to look away from themselves and toward others with expectations that they will be affirmed and change will become the responsibility of those around them. To be sure, this predisposition interferes with the goal of continuous improvement and the pillars that form the concept of counselor formation.

Evolutionary information is the term that we apply to previously unknown facts that have the potential to change the way in which you perceive yourself, the world around you, and your thoughts and actions. The counseling process seeks to offer such information to clients, and in turn, we believe that clinical training should do the same. How, then, do you as a student manage the drive to homeostasis and eventually overcome blocks to obtaining the evolutionary information that produces self-improvement? Fear management is probably the most basic concern in the process. As discussed, faculty and supervisors will need to take the initiative here in ensuring a psychologically safe environment. But if fears persist even though the environment appears safe, outside therapy often helps. Attitude adjustments are also helpful. For example, it would be wise to think of all evaluative information as formative rather than summative. In this way you may be in a better position to avoid highly defensive reactions to what you may misperceive as indictments rather than suggestions for improvement. Also, many people will not consider something that interferes with their self-assessment if they feel that they will be hopelessly mired once the information is delivered and internalized. For this reason, formative assessment information should include recommendations for change and encouragement that the change is accomplishable. As we noted earlier, it does not help to unproductively dwell on a deficiency because doing so will eventually produce forms of defensiveness and rigidity that block internalization of the assessment information and stifle the pursuit of corrective action.

We are susceptible to perceptual bias in all of our endeavors, and we are especially biased when observing and evaluating ourselves. In other words, if objectivity is the major route to reduced perceptual bias, and being objective about oneself is difficult if not impossible, then self-assessment must be saturated with perceptual bias.

Difficulties with objectivity notwithstanding, there are a couple of methods that can be used to improve your ability to self-assess. Bernstein and Lacomte (1979, pp. 71–73) offer the following series of questions that would need to be answered prior to group or individual supervision sessions:

1. What was I hearing my client say and/or observing my client do?
2. What was I thinking about my observations?
3. What were my alternatives to say or do at this point?
4. How did I choose from among the alternatives?
5. How do I intend to proceed with my selected response(s)?
6. What did I actually say or do?
7. What effect(s) did my response have on my client?
8. How, then, would I evaluate the effectiveness of my response?
9. What would I do differently now?

Answering the questions in advance of obtaining peer and supervisor remarks will provide you with an opportunity to compare your responses to those of others. Where you encounter sizable differences between your answers and the comments of others, you should recognize the difference and explore the processes you employed to obtain your conclusions. For example, you might hear your client asking what you understood to be a benign question, "What is the fastest way to get in touch with you if an emergency occurs?" Others listening to the tape conclude that the client is actually in crisis and desperately seeking immediate help. It would not suffice to simply note the difference, blindly follow whatever your supervisor might recommend, and move on. You will need to carefully explore exactly how you may have missed the client's deeper meaning and develop methods for improving your skills in this area. Situations where your perceptions differ markedly from others are usually unpleasant but extremely valuable. Exploring those internal forces that tend to distort your observations can improve your ability to more accurately access varied forms of client communication.

The second approach replaces Bernstein and Lacomte's questions with a collection of goals and outcome objectives that you personally develop in consultation with peers and supervisors. You then assess the extent to which you are able to achieve the desired outcomes as you review samples of your clinical work. This model allows you to identify areas that may need improvement and assess the impact of any changes you implement. The process can also be expanded to identify any needed modifications to your goals and outcome objectives.

For instance, one subset of the outcome objectives offered earlier in this chapter could be easily used to assess an intervention:

1. Correctly identify an appropriate treatment for the client.
2. Provide an acceptable rationale for the treatment choice.
3. Identify expected therapeutic milestones.
4. Demonstrate the ability to shift approaches when conditions warrant a change.
5. Correctly assess the effectiveness of the intervention or mode of treatment selected.
6. Correctly identify alternative approaches that may be needed if a predictable change occurs in the client's life.
7. Correctly assess the efficacy of the change.

Once you have evaluated yourself on each of these objectives, you will need to consult with others to confirm your conclusions. Let us assume that when answering the first objective you discover that the selected approach has not produced the desired results, and a revised diagnosis confirms that the approach and the rationale for using it proved to be incorrect. When you identify a more appropriate way of helping the client and then implement it, you are not only correcting problems identified in items 1 and 2 on the list but also meeting criteria in items 4, 5, 6, and 7. That these outcome objectives are so interdependent comes as no surprise; all are based upon one comprehensive mission statement.

We can also use this example to demonstrate one other advantage of this self-assessment model. Let us assume that after making the identified changes you become worried about how long it took you to determine that you needed to alter your approach. Your concerns, further confirmed by a discussion with your site supervisor, eventually prompt a decision to modify outcome objective number 5 so that it now reads: "*After every third session,* correctly assess the effectiveness of the intervention or mode of treatment selected." Establishing a specific frequency for making the effectiveness assessment improves the outcome objective by responding to the noted deficiency. Additional modifications may be needed, but this is an expected result because the approach emphasizes continuous improvement. Ultimately, if you take the time to develop, modify, and pursue the goals and objectives that you create yourself, you will be in a much better position to properly utilize self-assessment tools.

SUMMARY

The counselor training program at Loyola University New Orleans hires actors to serve as clients for students completing, among other courses, counseling practice. Students videotape all of their sessions and obtain the following assessment information:

1. The instructor's assessment of a written verbatim analysis completed on a segment of one of the four tapes.
2. Peer assessment information obtained during peer consultations with other students who are "treating" the same client-actor.
3. Evaluative information provided by the actors who served as their clients during the term.

This counseling simulation that spans most of the semester not only gives students a unique opportunity to obtain a wealth of formative evaluation information, but it also gives them a chance to verify and implement their findings. With material as subjective as that which is contained in a series of counseling sessions, the task of verifying and interpreting data becomes complicated. Students eventually come to rely upon *triangulation,* a qualitative tool that causes the evaluator to take greater stock in a finding if its existence is verified by several unrelated sources. For example, if a student believed that he or she misinterpreted the client's meaning in a specific situation, next discovered that other people seeing the same client agreed that it was a misinterpretation, then had the misinterpretation confirmed by the instructor reviewing the videotape, and finally discovered during the last night of counselor-client (actor) meetings that the client felt misunderstood, the subjective observation would now have the status of an accurate conclusion because the finding had been triangulated using several sources.

If carefully defined goals and outcome objectives exist, the counselor has a good chance of taking this finding and using it to improve his or her skills. And all of this will be possible so long as fear is managed well enough to allow the student to risk identifying the deficiency and then to apply the principles that produce continuous improvement. In this summary we offer one microexample of how data are collected, evaluated, and applied. Counselor formation is actually a complex process based mostly on a long, interrelated, and continuous string of events like the one described in this summary. As we noted earlier in the chapter, the goal of continuous improvement begins early in clinical training, but it spans the life of your work as a practicing clinician.

Reflection Questions

1. How would you modify the sample mission statement to more properly reflect your own training priorities?
2. What are some personal fears that could interfere with your ability to actively participate in assessment activities?
3. What steps would you expect an instructor or supervisor to take to create a learning environment where fear is properly managed? Describe the steps in detail.
4. How would you collect formative evaluation information, analyze the efficacy of the information, and then develop an intervention that would improve the deficiency identified in the evaluation? Provide a hypothetical example.
5. What personal attitudes do you possess that could interfere with self-assessment efforts?

Chapter 4

CHOOSING A CLIENT POPULATION, SITE, AND SITE SUPERVISOR

Samantha found herself in a quandary. She planned to counsel children, so a field site that treated toddlers through early adolescents seemed an ideal choice. Finding such an agency did not at first look like much of a problem. But as she met with the site supervisors, she realized that scheduling conflicts were about to force her into something that she might not really want to do. Samantha's part-time job conflicted with scheduled intern hours at every single child-based center in the city.

Fearing that she would not be able to change her work schedule, she considered other types of sites for possible internships. The more she looked into these other placements, the farther she moved from her original plan of working with children. She realized that this was becoming a more difficult goal than originally anticipated. Samantha had invested a great deal in her counseling program, so veering away from her goal of working with children—especially at this stage of her training—worried, stressed, and even scared her. How could she continue to earn the money she needed to cover school expenses and still be able to attend the internship sites that matched her interests and career goals?

Samantha realized that she would have to be resourceful to solve this dilemma. In the end she had to delay entering the internship for a semester so that she could first arrange a more compatible work schedule. But what she later gained at the appropriate center working with her targeted clientele made the delay worthwhile. With hindsight she recognized that waiting one semester would not ultimately make much difference in her counselor formation, but settling for a field site that did not match her interests would have. She made a difficult but ultimately fruitful choice.

INTRODUCTION

Versions of Samantha's concerns arise for all students as they plan the practical component of their training. In the counseling program at Loyola University New Orleans, students complete both the practicum and the internship at off-campus field sites. We recognize that a number of other programs train students on-site, so the information in this chapter will apply mostly to those of you who will have to make important choices regarding where you complete your clinical work. That said, we regularly meet with students to discuss their choice of practicum and internship field sites, and each one gets a variation of this recommendation: Clinical training is the point where you will translate theory into practice. Where you complete your practicum and internships will greatly influence your development as a clinician. Take steps to clarify what type of counseling setting best meets your particular interests and career plans. And while we know there are many practical considerations that must be weighed as you make the choice, we want to emphasize the fact that in a perfect world, matching your interests and abilities to the site that best fits should be the highest priority.

We do not doubt that students understand the importance of selecting a field site, but despite our urgings, some eventually select sites that are not as good a match as they could be. For example, interns might select a substance abuse center not because they want to work with such clients but because the center is open in the evening. While the substance abuse center's schedule might allow them to continue a day job that would have conflicted with a more clinically appropriate placement, they have unquestionably shortchanged themselves. Graduate students and their professors make substantial investments in the counselor formation process. It is therefore all the more disheartening to faculty and students when field-site choices turn out to be compromises. Our attempts to forestall the problem have been only somewhat effective. During the graduate program orientation, we tell students that they will need a great deal of flexibility with respect to their schedule by the time they progress to the clinical training component of their program. The caution works only to a point. Life still has the capacity to interrupt academic and career plans in unfortunate ways. While we recognize that some students will not be able to overcome the practical limitations on their selection of a field site or may fail to correctly identify their particular interests, we remain concerned that choices made under these conditions will weaken this critical aspect of their training.

As suggested in the introductory example, there is one argument that does tend to mitigate the pressures caused by the practical side of the field-site selection process. We tell students that many graduates who were similarly challenged by practical concerns and who opted to select in favor of their counseling career goals realized later that they made the right decision and that they lost nothing by doing so. Thus, as you proceed through this section of the text, we ask that you do whatever you can to open yourself to the possibility of making an academically sound choice regarding the place where you will translate counseling theory into effective clinical practice.

Site Selection Criteria

Stewart and Stewart (1996b) maintain that professional goals as well as personal and practical considerations influence doctoral-level counseling psychology graduate student internship choices. Such students are expected to complete a one-year commitment at an approved site, often in another state. Though you will almost certainly choose from among a number of local facilities for your practicum or internship, many of the criteria that Stewart and Stewart identified are equally applicable to your selection process. Table 4.1 contains a list of both professional variables and personal and practical variables that we have adapted in part from Stewart and Stewart (1996a, p. 523). The lists illustrate how many diverse elements you will need to consider and how many important questions you will have to ask yourself before you begin the selection process. At the same time, the list is a bit deceptive. For example, the simplicity of the lead item, "Match with professional interests," belies the need for exhaustive reflection aimed at specifically identifying your professional interests. The same is true for the item dealing with clientele. Do you prefer working with adults or children? Would you like to work with families? Is substance abuse an interest? Are there types of psychological problems that you prefer not to encounter? Do your career goals include working with offenders, and if so, are there specific types of crimes of interest to you? Rather than taking a shotgun approach to managing these important questions, we can create more-manageable categories to guide you. In fact, the professional variables can be easily grouped into three categories: (a) professional interests, (b) site supervision and training, and (c) overall quality of the site.

Table 4.1 Site Selection Criteria

Professional Variables	Personal and Practical Variables
Match with professional interests	Impact of field site work schedules on current employment and family responsibilities
Ability to work with desired clientele	Number of semesters required by field site
Opportunities to obtain long-term or short-term treatment experience	Simplicity and ease of site application requirements
Opportunities for test administration and interpretation	Subjective feelings in interacting with site faculty during interviews
Ability to obtain specialized training	Receptivity and friendliness of faculty and staff
Amount and quality of supervision	Amount of needed or desired contact with peers during internship
Availability of live supervision	Ease of using internship's physical facilities
Ability of site to supply sufficient direct and indirect hours for course requirements	Level of personal safety at the site
Availability and amount of didactic experiences	Student sick leave and holiday policy
Extent to which site specifies its goals or objectives	Amount of travel required
Relative emphasis of training versus service	
Reputation and prestige of site	
Job opportunities after internship	
Opinions and feedback from present and past interns	
Ongoing opportunities to conduct research	

The listing of professional variables was compiled primarily from Megargee (1992), Stedman et al. (1995), and Tedesco (1979). The listing of personal and practical variables was compiled from Rodolfa, Haynes, and Kaplan (1995) and Stewart and Stewart (1996a).

Professional Interests

Professional interests are formed over time. They represent the combination of many personal factors and professional experiences. For example, you may be interested in one type of psychological problem over another because (a) a family member may have suffered with such a problem, (b) an interest surfaced while studying course material, or (c) work and life experiences heightened your interests. Of course, interest in particular psychological problems forms out of your personal, social, vocational, and academic experiences. The same is also true regarding your selection and comfort with certain counseling theories over others. You probably have already recognized that each counseling theory emphasizes specific aspects of human behavior while downplaying others. Each theory also identifies specific treatment strategies. Your personal values play a significant role in whether you will adopt a theory or reject it. For example, behavioral theories and the interventions associated with them might be easily embraced by one person and aggressively rejected by another. The adopter might stress the value of a highly organized and structured approach to *modifying behavior* while someone opposed to such a theory might passionately object by stating that "people are not laboratory animals." You cannot and should not overhaul your value system in an attempt to fit yourself into a site or a theory that exists in opposition to your core beliefs. Fortunately, there are various theories and many sites from which to choose. With this in mind, begin the process of selecting your field site by simultaneously reflecting upon your personal interests and the following professional-interest questions (with some possible responses following in parentheses).

1. What client age groups match your professional interests? And which do you feel you should avoid?
   (preschoolers, school-age children, adolescents, adults and older people)
2. What types of psychological or social problems interest you? What types of problems are beyond your interest, skill, or comfort level?
   (mood disorders, substance abuse, academic problems, relationship issues, criminal justice, school-related counseling issues)
3. Which counseling theories interest you? Which would be a poor match?
   (cognitive, client-centered, psychodynamic, family systems, Adlerian, Gestalt)
4. Which counseling modalities would you prefer?
   (individual, group, couples, family)
5. What areas of specialized training do you want to pursue?
   (parenting skills training; diagnosis-specific interventions, e.g., attention deficit disorder strategies)
6. What types of setting match your interests?
   (hospitals, clinics, schools, nonprofit mental health agencies, state and federal programs, employee assistance or personnel departments)

Discussing your answers to these questions with colleagues can help as you clarify where, with whom, and in what way you wish to complete your clinical training. This process also prepares you for the field site staff interviews that necessarily precede any placement. You will be better able to answer questions that are posed to you and clearer about the questions you will wish to ask of site personnel.

Site Supervision and Training

Sites vary greatly regarding the type of supervision offered, the number of additional training options available, and the extent to which training efforts are considered a priority within the site's overall goals and objectives. While most facilities provide one hour of individual supervision each week, this is actually considered a minimum requirement. Facilities may augment this time with group supervision, case conferences, and specialized training. Regardless of how supervision is offered, your supervisor will arguably be one of the most critical factors in your field site experience. The supervisor oversees your work, assumes professional responsibility for you while you are assigned to the center, and usually provides evaluative information to you and to your university. We alert you to the importance of the supervisory relationship in this chapter and then offer an in-depth discussion of the supervision process in chapter 5. The topic of supervision generates another collection of important questions that require thoughtful responses as you prepare to select a field site.

1. What type of supervision is offered (e.g., individual, group, or both)?
2. If you are selected, who will be supervising you?
3. If you stay more than one semester, will your supervisor change?
4. What priority does training take at the particular site?
5. Whom would you contact in case of an emergency if your supervisor is unavailable?
6. What additional training activities are offered? Are they optional or required of all students?
7. In addition to scheduled supervision, will your supervisor actually observe *live counseling sessions?*
8. How might possible disagreements between you and your supervisor be handled?
9. Does the agency have written policies governing practicum and internship students?
10. How many students are assigned to any particular supervisor?
11. What counseling theories do particular supervisors employ in their work?
12. Does the site rely upon or mandate specific supervision approaches?

Overall Quality of the Site

Information about particular sites can be easily obtained from other students who have worked there, occasionally from clients or client family members who may have been treated there, and directly from staff members. Other students are probably the most available resource and in many ways the best source. They can tell you about their firsthand experiences and fill you in on practical matters as well as the intangibles that are more difficult to assess (e.g., the overall atmosphere of the site). While students are a valuable source, it would be a good idea to recognize that your experience will never be identical to theirs. Each student's personality and work habits evoke predictably different responses from staff. We often observe differences in the way individual students might be treated at a particular site. This means that if you were to obtain information from one student that might sway your decision about a particular site, it would be especially important to talk to several other people as well before making a final decision. Questions that bear consideration in this category include:

1. What is the overall reputation of the field site as both a treatment and a training facility? (Some sites may not excel in both categories.)
2. Are the physical accommodations adequate? How are offices assigned? Where would you complete paperwork and maintain file material?
3. What arrangements exist for referral of more-troubled clients for psychological and psychiatric consults?
4. Are there well-defined protocols for psychiatric emergencies?
5. How are students integrated into the site and its mission?
6. Does the site offer a regularly scheduled formal orientation, or do you obtain the necessary information from other workers in a more informal way?
7. Does the site ever hire interns after they graduate?
8. Does the site subscribe to any particular counseling theory or treatment modality?
9. Have interns encountered any difficulty completing the assigned direct and indirect counseling hours?
10. Does the site have a good working relationship with the university and its faculty?
11. Are there any administrative or programmatic changes in the offing that could affect the quality of the field experience?

Interviewing at Potential Field Sites

Answers to the preceding questions and meetings with the faculty member who manages field sites should produce a short list of potential placements. At this point, you will need to follow your specific university-arranged protocol for applying to practicum and internship field sites. This process usually involves arranging interviews at one or more sites. Once you make a final decision, you are commonly expected to confirm the placement with the site and with your professor. The essential part of this stage of the process is the on-site interview. All of the work you completed in identifying your interests and matching them to particular sites makes preparing for the interview much easier. The interview has two basic purposes: (a) for site staff to determine whether they want to include you as a practicum or internship student and (b) for you to determine whether the site meets your needs and expectations. You should already have a pretty good idea of what you believe you need and expect, but we have not talked much about what the site staff may be pursuing in a student.

What do supervisors look for when selecting practicum and internship students? A local assessment completed by one coauthor called for 20 site supervisors to rank a number of student characteristics. Table 4.2 contains the results of that survey in order of importance.

Table 4.2 Rank Order of Supervisor's 12 Selection Criteria

Rank	Skill or knowledge competency	Mean	Standard deviation	*N*
1	Counseling ethics	2.70	1.68	20
2	Counseling skills	3.20	2.60	20
3	Communication skills	3.80	2.01	20
4	Self-awareness	4.75	3.09	20
5	Counseling theory	5.50	2.60	20
6	Ability to work under supervision	6.15	3.08	20
7	Diagnostic skills	6.90	3.82	20
8	Group leadership skills	7.05	2.87	20
9	Case management skills	7.60	3.15	20
10	Knowledge of multicultural issues	7.85	2.85	20
11	Writing skills	8.65	2.53	20
12	Knowledge of referral agencies	10.60	2.60	20

It comes as no surprise that supervisors would place such a premium on ethics and counseling skills that they rank first and second, respectively. Supervisors will be responsible for all of your work, and regardless of whether they were responsible, they would want to ensure that your clients are ethically and effectively treated. Supervisors would also recognize that absent effective communication skills and self-awareness (ranked third and fourth, respectively), the counseling and supervisory relationships would be hopeless enterprises. This four-part cluster of top skills reflects the elements that have the highest priority for the supervisors surveyed in this study. Of course, a large and more diverse sample would go a long way toward helping generalize these findings, but we believe that they do tend to confirm anecdotal evidence regarding the priority that supervisors place on certain aspects of potential applicants' training and abilities. It is also interesting to note that these competencies and their relative ranks tend to match the core training areas identified by Bradley and Fiorini (1999) in their national study of programs accredited by the Council for the Accreditation of Counseling and Related Educational Programs (CACREP). You would be well advised to consider how your training and skills in each of these areas can be shared during the interview. Of course some of your competencies will be assessed simply as a function of participating in the interview. Communication skills and to some extent self-awareness will surface immediately and consistently. Your knowledge of counseling skills and, perhaps even more important, your regard for counseling ethics will need to surface in more-topic-specific discussions. You should be prepared to answer questions about counseling ethics, skills, and theory. While you may not have all the answers, you should be able to illustrate what you would do if you did have a question about any one of these key topics.

Supervisors hope that the field site experience will have an impact on you as you complete your work. They are not looking for fully formed counselors. Rather, they are hoping to find students who have basic skills, are open to learning, are willing to follow recommendations, are enthusiastic about supervision, and are interested in helping the types of clients who frequent the field site. If these basics are present, the field site staff will usually take comfort in helping you develop clinically and take pride in your work because it will often reflect their model of caring for clients. Of course, difficulties in one or more of the basic areas can produce undesirable outcomes. Imagine how difficult it would be for site personnel to work with a student who lacked basic skills, tended to ignore directives, withheld information during supervision, and generally disliked working with the clients served by the center. Obviously the site supervisor-student relationship would be severely compromised, and serious concerns about the well-being of both the student and the clients served by the student would surface. You can easily see how crucial it is for everyone involved that you make a sound decision about where you will complete your clinical training.

Summary

Counseling students who complete their practicum or internship at an off-campus site must weigh a number of important variables as they enter this phase of their training. Practical concerns can easily overtake professional goals and vocational interests when weighed against the need to earn a living. But careful planning and a willingness to be flexible as the clinical component nears can make sound clinical decisions accomplishable. An amount of self-reflection aimed at solidifying career goals and specific professional interests is the only valid way of properly narrowing down your choices for a suitable placement. Gathering basic information from a variety of sources about each of the sites under consideration not only makes for sounder decisions, it also helps you prepare for the inevitable preplacement interview. This interview helps the facility personnel determine whether you fit their program, and it gives you a chance to ask the questions that you need answered to determine whether the site is a good fit for you. Finally, knowing the characteristics that potential supervisors value when deciding on a counseling intern can also guide you as you prioritize your preclinical training efforts. The choice may be a difficult one, but planning, reflection, and information from experienced sources ensure the likelihood of success.

Reflection Questions

1. What practical concerns will you have to take into consideration when selecting a practicum or internship site?
2. What steps will you take to ensure that you choose an appropriate site, one that meets your professional and personal needs?
3. What do you expect will be the most difficult part of choosing a site?
4. Which skills do you possess that will appeal to a potential supervisor? Which skills need to be enhanced?
5. What will be the most important professional variables in your decision-making process? Which will be the most important personal and practical variables?

Chapter 5

Clinical Supervision
Rights and Responsibilities

It was not until Jana received word that the pretrial diversion program had accepted her for internship that she realized how much she wanted to work there. She hoped to eventually seek employment as a federal probation officer, and the pretrial diversion program was just the sort of training experience she needed. Jana knew a great deal about the program because two of her friends completed internships there. She especially liked that she would be working with first-time offenders. She knew that second chances were rare in life, so helping offenders take advantage of this opportunity could be rewarding and challenging. If these clients successfully completed the program, their arrest records would be expunged or erased.

During the program orientation, Jana learned about the criminal justice system, office policies and procedures, and the counseling strategies that the staff identified as useful when working with offenders. Although it was all fascinating, it was also intimidating. Jana did not know Della, her assigned supervisor, and none of the other students Jana knew had ever worked with her. The idea of reporting to someone about whom she had almost no information became a source of concern. This person would be supervising her work, directing many of her activities, and evaluating her performance. Jana had no idea what to expect, and she was worried. At the same time, she trusted and liked her university practicum instructor, so his comments about how good Della was as a supervisor provided some reassurance. There was a lot riding on this final component of Jana's training.

Introduction

Jana's concerns about her supervisor are understandable. As we noted in chapter 1, practicum and internship can be seen as a collection of important relationships. This chapter explores arguably the most critical pair–the supervisor-supervisee relationships with your site supervisor and your faculty supervisor (course instructor). We will define supervision as well as identify the ethical and clinical boundaries of this relationship. And because supervision is a collaborative process, we include steps that you can take to improve your clinical, personal, and professional results.

The field experience courses offered in the counseling program at Loyola University New Orleans are consistently taught by full-time faculty. We know that this is not always the case at other universities. We know that students, if they are to achieve their full potential, require a challenging setting in which fear and anxiety are properly managed. The clinical component is the point at which students must rely the most upon the relationships they have developed with their professors. A successful supervisor-supervisee relationship demands levels of openness and understanding that can develop only when teacher and student work cooperatively over an extended period. Thus, the time spent advising, teaching, and working with students makes us uniquely suited to helping them through the rigors of clinical training. For these reasons, we especially enjoy working with our students as they complete practicum and internships. And teaching these classes gives us a rare chance to assess the overall effectiveness of the curriculum.

Supervisory relationships and experiences form novices into counselors and ensure an appropriate level of care to the clients with whom students work. Whenever we reflect on our own professional development, we first recall the cadre of supervisors who guided and supported our efforts at becoming a counselor. Mostly we were supervised by one person at a time, but one of us during a postdoctoral internship reported to five supervisors. Yet even the potentially frustrating situation of sorting through contradictory recommendations proved remarkably helpful. In the end, the tactical complications produced by multiple supervisors proved a minor inconvenience when measured against what was learned from the professional community these experienced clinicians created. Indeed, skilled supervision is a precious and critical component of the counselor formation process.

Counselor Supervision

As you will learn, counseling supervision is a very special mentor-mentee relationship. Its existence illustrates the confidence that experienced clinicians have in novices' abilities to provide services to clients as they learn their profession and the commitment that experienced clinicians have to training. As professors we are constantly impressed by the extent to which agency and school personnel are willing to supervise our students and the amount of time they volunteer to help our students become seasoned professionals.

Defined

Bradley (1989), citing the 1969 Committee on Counselor Effectiveness of the Association for Counselor Education and Supervision, described counselor supervision as:

> 1. being performed by experienced successful counselors (supervisors) who have been prepared in methodology of supervision;
> 2. facilitating the counselor's personal and professional development, promoting counselor competencies and promoting counseling and guidance services and programs; and,
> 3. providing the purposeful function of overseeing the work of counselor trainees or practicing counselors (supervisees) through a set of supervisory activities which include consultation, counselor training and instruction, and evaluation. (p. 4)

The definition identifies who can supervise, the basic goals of supervision, and the routes that should be taken to bring supervisees to an appropriate level of clinical competence. It intimates that while each student's personal and professional development will be different, all must meet basic standards for treatment and that oversight of their work must be properly carried out.

Some years later Bernard and Goodyear (1998) offered the following description as they sought to define supervision:

> An intervention provided by a more senior member of a profession to a more junior member or members of that same profession. This relationship is evaluative, extends over time, and has the simultaneous purposes of enhancing the professional functioning of the more junior person(s), monitoring the quality of professional services offered to the client(s) she, he or they see(s), and serving as a gatekeeper of those who are to enter the profession. (p. 6)

This definition reflects the ethical and clinical concerns that evolved with respect to counseling in general and clinical training specifically. The relationship between an experienced practitioner and a novice seeking to enter the profession must always address the student's need for experiences whereby he or she can develop requisite clinical skills and competencies while protecting the safety and well-being of his or her clients. Supervisors are ethically and legally responsible for the care of the supervisee's clients, but their responsibilities also extend to their supervisees and to the counseling profession.

The definitions also reveal the existence of a potentially problematic dual relationship. On the one hand, supervisors seek to enhance their charges' professional and personal growth, yet on the other hand, they must evaluate them and make judgments about their suitability as professionals. This suitability to the profession also includes an assessment of how psychologically healthy or safe it is for certain supervisees to provide mental health services to their clients. Offering counseling services to clients brings with it risks to the counselor's mental health and psychological well-being. Supervisors must occasionally intervene in ways that protect the student from such psychological risks or injuries. One example involved a student who worked as an intern in a substance abuse treatment center. During the course of this internship, memories of being raised by a parent who struggled with substance abuse problems surfaced. The intern became depressed and angry. It became difficult for the intern to be objective with clients because of the countertransference. The supervisor identified the difficulty, referred the intern for counseling, and with the intern's permission met with the intern and the site supervisor to develop a plan. The intern responded rapidly to counseling and supervision efforts. Settling the countertransference issues not only resolved the intern-client conflict but created a deepened level of empathy and understanding and a stronger therapeutic alliance.

Supervision is a process with a broad scope of concerns, some of which conflict with others. These definitions also suggest how delicately balanced the process is. By recognizing the need to manage these complexities and identifying methods to do so, you will be in a better position to cooperate effectively. We begin by establishing the boundaries that differentiate supervisory, consulting, and counseling relationships.

Delineating Supervision, Consultation, and Counseling

Because the types of relationships formed and the goals of supervision, consultation, and counseling are different, confusing one for another or allowing one to evolve into another produces problems. You will need to understand the differences and to recognize the boundaries that differentiate each type. The distinction between supervision and consultation is easily made. In *supervision* the supervisor has ethical and legal responsibility for the client even though he or she is not directly treating the client. You work under supervision when you are a student, when you are completing required hours for licensure, and when you learn new techniques and procedures to which you have not been exposed. *Consultation* also relies upon interaction with an experienced clinician, but in contrast to supervision, the consultee retains sole responsibility for the client from ethical, legal, and clinical standpoints. Experienced counselors regularly use consultants to assess their clinical judgments and to ensure that clients are treated effectively and ethically. Consultants are expected to share the most up-to-date and sound information they possess and identify the limits of their knowledge. Mental health professionals are expected to regularly consult with other professionals throughout the course of their professional lives.

Although it is fairly simple to discriminate between supervision and counseling, erecting and maintaining the appropriate boundaries that prevent supervision from morphing into counseling can be problematic. In the course of supervision, many of the supervisee's personal issues may arise. This is actually a desirable trend because surfacing such issues motivates us to (a) learn more about ourselves, (b) resolve our psychological struggles, and in turn, (c) improve our ability to be helpful to others. But the supervisee's personal issues must be addressed in a counselor-client relationship, not in the supervisor-supervisee setting. Shifts to *counseling,* in which the supervisor becomes the counselor and the student becomes the client, are problematic and should always be avoided. Cautions against such a shift are couched in the restrictions that prohibit dual relationships. Being a teacher, a supervisor, and a counselor to the same person will produce conflicts. While a supervisee's desire to speak more deeply about a personal issue that is directly affecting his or her ability to work effectively with clients may be greeted with interest by the supervisor, it must be referred to another setting where the supervisee can meet privately with a counselor. Since all supervisors are also counselors, they must remain vigilant to such boundary problems. They can easily develop clinical interests in their supervisees that will interrupt supervision. Such limits should be discussed early in the supervisor-supervisee relationship so that when any amount of erosion occurs, both parties will be prepared to identify the change and take appropriate corrective action.

Goals of Supervision

Like most human endeavors, supervision works best with clearly defined goals whereby progress can be easily measured and correctives rapidly implemented. Bordin (1983, p. 38) offers the following set of simple, clear, and, taken together, comprehensive goals:

1. Mastery of specific skills
2. Enlarging understanding of clients
3. Enlarging awareness of process issues
4. Increasing awareness of self and impact on process
5. Overcoming personal and intellectual obstacles toward learning and mastery
6. Deepening understanding of concept and theory
7. Providing a stimulus to research
8. Maintaining the standards of service

The transition from student to clinician requires success in all eight areas. Counseling is a theoretically and ethically bound process that relies upon the proper use of a diverse collection of tools (skills, abilities, and attitudes) that reside within the counselor. Such broad-based goals are essential because client personalities and the struggles they confront differ markedly. The larger the skill set, the wider the range of clients you will be able help. Thus, you should expect supervision to improve your ability to make clinical sense of an ever widening collection of client issues and to tailor your interventions by correctly selecting from the many skills that are available to you. Supervision helps you correctly negotiate the gaps between what you know, what you need to know, and what you should actually do as you respond to the challenge of clinical work.

Stages of Supervision

Because supervision is a relational process, it follows predictable stages that mirror what one would expect in the counseling relationship. For example, Beitman's (1987) stages of psychotherapy (engagement, pattern search, change, and termination) can be adapted to the supervisor-supervisee relationship, though the topics and focus would of course differ from those found in a counseling relationship. To begin with, engagement is no less important in the supervisory relationship, but the purpose of that relationship is different. A relationship bound by trust, respect, and a shared sense of purpose makes it possible for supervisees to discuss sensitive information that must be revealed if they are to improve. Absent a strong relationship, supervisees will be reluctant to talk about the embarrassing or difficult situations that often arise during counseling sessions. Imagine how difficult it might be for you to share information about a counseling session that you know contained errors in judgment or clinical interventions without some sense that you would be accepted, respected, and guided toward an appropriate resolution. Research shows that fear and shame associated with actual as well as presumed errors and concerns about being evaluated negatively consistently block trainees from disclosing as much as they should (see, e.g., Barnes, 2004; Hiebert, Uhlemann, Marshall, & Lee, 1998; Skovholt & Ronnestad, 1995). Clients are not likely to speak about deeper or more embarrassing experiences if their level of engagement with their counselor is not sufficient with respect to trust, understanding, and confidence that the disclosure will be used productively. Supervisees will also avoid such discussion if they do not feel the relationship can properly manage the sensitive information and because they may fear that negative evaluations will jeopardize passing the course or, worse, being blocked from entering the counseling profession at all! It is not surprising that, according to Ronnestad and Skovholt (1993):

> In supervision, the anxious student may tend to discuss in supervision only clients who show good progress, choose themes in which he or she is functioning well, or choose a mode of presenting data that allows full control over what the supervisor learns. For example, video or audio-taping may be resisted. This is a delicate area that demands tactful handling by the supervisor. Fortunately, this changes with increased experience. (p. 398)

The importance of the supervisor-supervisee relationship is further emphasized when you consider how much important information can be screened from the supervisor when supervisee fears and anxiety are not properly managed.

Recognizing the developmental nature of the process, Hill, Charles, and Reed (1981) offered the following four-part model that identifies the developmental changes you can expect to experience as you become a skilled clinician.

1. Sympathy—counselor anxiety and confusion
2. "Counselor stance"
3. Transition
4. Integrated personal style

You can expect to cycle through these stages as you progress through the clinical portion of your training. The first stage is the most difficult. With an abundance of theoretical information and almost no experience in translating theory into practice, you may, not surprisingly, feel anxious and confused. The pressure of caring for someone with a psychological malady and the desire to be as helpful as possible as quickly as possible create their own maelstrom. Add to it the desire to be evaluated positively by the client, the site supervisor, and the faculty supervisor, and you easily recognize the source of your tension and just how critical it will be for you to properly manage the inevitable anxiety that this early stage produces.

The most common reaction to the stress of the first stage is to "act like a counselor" because at this point you do not know how to be one. Fortunately, the second stage offers opportunities to try various approaches that you have seen or heard about as you attempt to develop effective methods for helping your client and interacting with other mental health professionals. While there are obvious advantages to "trying on these hats," they are, in all cases, approaches that work for others but not necessarily for you. During the transition phase of the third stage, you are finally able to assess the efficacy of efforts in terms of how well they match your own personality, skill set, values, and goals. Some strategies will seem fine, others will be completely inconsistent with how you define yourself, and many will need to be modified before you will be able to incorporate them into your approach. As this stage proceeds, you will observe the emergence of an ethical and effective approach to clinical work that "fits" you and makes sense to you. Incorporate all of these elements and you will develop an integrated personal style and achieve the final stage of development. Experienced counselors will tell you that no one remains at this stage. Whenever you encounter new challenges, expect to revert to earlier stages as you work to integrate into your personal style whatever you may need to be helpful under these more demanding conditions.

Ultimately, you can use Beitman's stages to assess the nature or level of your relationship with your supervisor, and the stages of development to identify your level at any particular point in your clinical training. As we intimated earlier, it would be difficult if not impossible to achieve higher levels of professional development without a commensurate supervisor-supervisee relationship. For example, to traverse the transition stage of the developmental process, the supervisory relationship would need to have evolved to the change stage. At this level, the relationship would have developed enough trust and confidence to manage the anxieties that would interfere with exploring alternatives, assessing efficacy, and internalizing those that should be incorporated into an integrated personal approach. Problems often arise when supervisor and supervisee try to accomplish a developmental task without having achieved the necessary relationship level. When this does happen, a quick assessment can guide both participants to a serviceable solution. If, for example, the student is trying to accomplish a developmental task that requires perhaps more "engagement" or "pattern search," the supervisor and supervisee can redeploy their efforts at enhancing the supervisory relationship (engagement) or developing more alternatives (pattern search) and then return to the developmental task. While we know that this may sound simplistic, in practice it really does work. Students will even use these exact terms during supervision meetings. An intern once responded to a recommendation made by a classmate by saying, "I need more pattern search before I commit to following the recommendation." The class knew what the student meant and immediately cooperated by offering additional patterns (in this case, treatment suggestions) and waiting for the student to find one that formed a better match.

Evaluation

Chapter 3 illustrated the importance of evaluation in the process. That chapter emphasized the role that evaluation will play in your professional growth as you work under supervision, and it stressed the fact that emotional reactions to being evaluated must be effectively regulated in order to gain the maximum benefit from your practicum and internships. You may wish to review that chapter during your supervision.

SUPERVISION PROCESSES

As a practicum or internship student, you can expect to be supervised in both individual and group formats. The CACREP standards (see appendix C) require both individual and group supervision for practicum students and group supervision for internship students. At Loyola University New Orleans, we offer individual supervision on an as-requested basis in addition to the regularly scheduled groups for our internship students. Internship students often take us up on this open offer for individual supervision sessions.

Individual and group supervision sessions usually include case presentations, reviews of taped (audio and video) sessions, reviews of verbatims (when taping is not permitted), general or specific emergent site or agency concerns, ethical or clinical emergencies, and topics of special interest (e.g., new techniques, counseling theory, community mental health concerns). Student presentations on these topics usually generate rich discussions that help clarify and expand the student's concerns and questions. The clearly defined issues can now be linked to clinical treatment alternatives. Group supervision has the advantage of a larger pool of people from which to draw suggestions, but individual supervision can also produce a rich collection of useful interventions, especially if supervisor and supervisee share the responsibility.

Since alternatives are useful only if they are implemented, the next phase of the supervisory process explores why the student should make the change and how it should be carried out. If can be difficult to adjust your view of the client's issues and challenging to enact new clinical interventions. Simulations and role-playing exercises are used at this point because they offer a serviceable model of what exactly to do, and they can bring to the surface unanticipated client reactions that will need to be managed. For example, consider the case of a practicum student whose client does not allow him to speak. Each session is basically a monologue. Whenever the student does try to interrupt, the client quickly speaks louder and faster, blunting every effort to enter into a dialogue. During group supervision, the student is comforted by the unanimous support from classmates, all of whom confirm how difficult the client is to engage. The student also explains that it would feel very rude to interrupt the client with any more force than that which has not as yet worked. The student asks for answers to two specific questions. Why would people block a counselor from dialoguing with them? What should be done to interrupt this countertherapeutic situation? Group discussion not only helped the student understand that the client's undisclosed fears would be causing the engagement block but also produced several ways of confronting the client. A role play exercise was the only other step that the student needed before being able to incorporate the new insight into the client's struggle and implement the confrontation. The exercise was repeated several times so that the student could practice responding to several client responses to being confronted.

The choice of how to carry out role plays and simulations should include student input. You may end up playing the part of your client, portraying the counselor while another student plays the role of the client, or simply observing while two other students assume the roles of counselor and client. No matter the format, this exchange of information is quite useful—it forms the content of supervision. But human encounters always create process concerns in addition to the content. These process concerns are equally important in supervision. Two such processes, *parallel process* and *countertransference* are uniquely important in supervision. When properly managed, they enhance students' clinical skills.

Parallel Process

Parallel process occurs when a particular element of the counselor-client relationship replicates itself in the supervisor-supervisee relationship. This remarkable effect occurs frequently but can easily go undetected. Experienced supervisors train themselves to notice when parallel process events occur and to use the material the events create as they dialogue with their supervisees. Parallel process affords supervisors an in vivo teaching tool that if properly managed can have a profound positive influence on their supervisees. We recall an incident not too many years ago in which a supervisee, while reviewing a case during group supervision, became noticeably frustrated with and demanding of the supervisor. He turned to the class and said, "I am getting nowhere with the people I am trying to help, and supervision is a waste of time!" The other students' nods of understanding seemed to calm him some, but the frustration was still palpable. One student asked him if he still wanted to discuss the case he had been scheduled to present. He said he did, composed himself a bit more, and began the case presentation. He offered the usual basic information about the client and then stated that "the client was very angry at" him. The client told him that he was not helping at all and demanded that he immediately become much more proactive in solving his problems for him or he would ask for another counselor. The student closed by saying that he did not know what to do, but he had to do something or he was going to "lose" the client.

Parallel process had been discussed earlier in the term, but the intensity of this supervisee's experience made it almost impossible to identify. Such emotionally intense situations are common reasons why parallel process can be difficult for supervisees and supervisors to detect. In our real-life example, the supervisor also had difficulty identifying the parallel process because of his own emotional reaction to seemingly having failed his supervisee. The client's highly charged demand for answers and for someone to be responsible for him had fired through his counselor (the supervisee) and was making its way to the supervisor. Once the supervisor's own defensiveness subsided he was able to correctly label the parallel process and invite the supervisee to join him as they worked their way through the concerns together and eventually back to a useful way of properly managing the client's issues. The successful resolution of this episode produced many desirable results. The supervisee left the session with a better understanding of his client, some strategies for increasing client responsibility and accountability, greater confidence in his ability to be helpful, and more willingness to identify and work through the next inevitable parallel process issue. Because the other members of the class vicariously experienced the parallel process concerns, they became more skilled at identifying and resolving them.

According to Borders and Leddick (1987, p. 44), "The 'reflection process' [Searles, 1955] refers to the supervisee unconsciously behaving like the client in an effort to communicate subtle client dynamics to the supervisor." The previous illustration, though not too subtle, is a good example of a "reflection process." However, the reflection process is not the only parallel process effect. As Doehrman (1976) suggests, parallel process could also explain why some counselors assume the role of their supervisors when counseling their clients.

It is equally important for students to be alert to this effect because it can inadvertently interfere with your overall effectiveness with your client. A student who was confused about her client's psychological problems asked her supervisor for help in developing a good diagnosis and treatment plan for a particularly challenging client. Although the client was a new transfer to her, the client had been seen at the clinic for several years by various counselors, but experienced only minor improvement in her condition. A rich discussion ensued, replete with important hypothetical explanations about the client's problems, conclusive diagnostic findings, and several potentially successful treatment plans. Unfortunately, the discussion between the supervisor and the supervisee was replicated when the counselor met with the client. On tape the pair sounded like two experienced professionals talking about someone they were about to help. Years of therapy made the client psychologically savvy enough to switch the counseling session to a consultation. Unearthing this parallel process produced many interesting and ultimately useful insights. The student realized that the client had actually participated in similar countertherapeutic encounters with previous counselors. Once the student understood her contribution to the parallel process, she successfully helped the client recognize and own her part in the problematic encounter. This parallel process encounter eventually paved the way for the student to help a client who had floundered in several previous attempts by other counselors.

As we have illustrated, during individual supervision, the supervisor's response will determine to a great extent whether the parallel process issues will be handled in a helpful or problematic way. A supervisor who acts defensively will only increase the frustration levels and prolong the deleterious effects of the parallel process encounter. Working cooperatively, on the other hand, offers the supervisee a model for dealing more effectively with the client and a chance to learn more about himself or herself as a counselor. Thus the onus for a successful outcome rests on the supervisor and his or her skills in managing parallel process enriched encounters. We need also mention that group supervision offers the opportunity for other students to help detect and resolve parallel process concerns. Supervisors appreciate the value of multiple observers, so they encourage all members of the group to be sensitive to parallel process concerns whenever and with whomever they arise.

Countertransference

Transference patterns can be illuminated in many counseling relationships. The tendency for clients to project feelings from another relationship in their life onto the counselor is legendary. But countertransference, the process of the counselor projecting onto the client, is an equally important clinical concern—one that is often identified and tended to by supervisors. Countertransference is not, in and of itself, a problem, but how you react to these feelings can be.

Consider an overly dependent client who, in the course of a session, asks the counselor a number of questions that urge the counselor to take responsibility for choices that should fall to the client. Assume also that the counselor, when confronted with these questions, unwittingly *reacts* in a directive and paternalistic way. In this example, the counselor "acts out" the countertransference, and as a result, the client experiences yet another unhealthy relationship where someone (in this case the counselor) jumps in and takes responsibility, eventually making choices that the client should have made.

Unfortunately, in this example, countertransference directs the counselor's behavior. Had the counselor recognized the countertransferential feelings and talked them out instead of acted them out, the client would have benefited from the countertransference-propelled interaction. A more aware counselor would have told the client, "I know it would be wrong to do so, but for some reason I feel like I want to give you advice and make decisions for you." The client might have responded by saying, "You know, this happens to me a lot but no one has ever said that it was wrong to do so, like you just did." The client might even have asked the most therapeutic questions, "What do I do that invites people to criticize, direct, and take responsibility for me? Why do I do this? What can I do to change?" This example stresses the point that countertransference should not be avoided but rather should be carefully identified and diligently talked through with clients. Countertransference offers clients important clues to how they are perceived by others and where they may need to focus their energies. And, for the counselor, it can highlight personal concerns that may need to be addressed in the counselor's individual or group therapy.

Implementing Supervisory Suggestions

A portion of weekly supervision time should be allocated to discussions regarding the implementation of recommendations and suggestions. You should always be prepared to: (a) describe how you tailored your clinical efforts in light of what you learned during supervision, (b) discuss the steps you took to carry out recommendations, and (c) provide an assessment of how efficacious the changes actually were. You often have some latitude in how you carry out general suggestions, but you must also be prepared to act when a specific course of action is needed. There are situations in which you must carry out a specific set of instructions ordered by your site or faculty supervisor. For example, during a case presentation, your supervisor confirms that the information shared by your client meets the criteria for a compulsory report to child abuse authorities. You would be expected to discuss your concerns, if any, about this course of action and then immediately carry out the request as is consistent with the agency or site policies. While you may feel uncomfortable about having to make the report or you may judge the situation as less severe and not warranting such a report, you are still required to proceed. Students sometimes respond to such feelings or thoughts by delaying action or ignoring what they have been told to do. When a student senses that this may be happening, and we know that it can be hard to recognize, it is vitally important to discuss the reluctance immediately with either or both supervisors. We recall one case where a student had delayed acting for a full week. During the next group supervision, he revealed that he had not complied with the supervisor's request. He was directed to immediately leave class, report to the field site, obtain the client file, call in the report, and have the field supervisor call to confirm that all of the steps had been completed. Although supervision is normally a collaborative experience that produces alternative courses of action whereby students choose among the options, there are times when a prescribed set of steps must be followed.

Maximizing Supervision Effectiveness

Many students and a surprising number of supervisors take a somewhat passive stance with respect to supervision. Absent directions to do otherwise, students will often do little to prepare for individual and group supervision sessions. And supervisors may leave the responsibility of what will be discussed completely in the hands of the students, many of whom have not thought much about what they need from the process and how they plan to go about getting this help. Students may also lose sight of the fact that there are steps that they can personally take to reduce heightened levels of fear and anxiety that can adversely affect their participation. Given the potential for these problematic situations to occur, we offer several strategies that you can use to ensure that your supervisory experiences deliver all that you want and need from them. Beinart (2003) offers the following useful suggestions:

> Supervisees need to take responsibility for taking an active part in supervision. This involves playing a part in a collaborative relationship, showing interest and enthusiasm, identifying needs clearly, arriving at a supervision meeting properly prepared having thought through issues and priorities, being open and receptive to feedback and being prepared to give clear and honest feedback to the supervisor. It is not helpful when supervisees fail to raise issues that they are struggling with, get defensive when offered feedback or do not take the advice of their supervisor without good reason or discussion. (p. 50)

The author's recommendations can be converted into action once you understand the forces that affect supervision and identify the methods and strategies that must be implemented. These suggestions not only improve the amount and quality of information shared, but also positively affect the process and enhance the supervisor-supervisee relationship. We suggest a protocol for planning out your specific supervision experiences as well as methods for managing the anxiety that inhibits professional growth. These strategies will help you eventually develop requisite levels of self-efficacy.

Planning for Supervision

Perhaps the best way to prepare for supervision is to follow a protocol that directs you to answer a number of important clinical questions about the client and the course of treatment. Preparing these responses will ensure that you will be able to deliver the prerequisite information that your supervisors and classmates will need if they are going to be helpful to you. And as you prepare the case material, you will also be able to more accurately identify the questions to which you will be seeking answers during supervision. This level of preparation facilitates properly formed and focused clinical questions and the ability to share a sufficient amount of background information. You and your audience will be in a much better position to explore the concerns and make good recommendations.

Form 5.1 is an example of a case presentation form that may be used to organize pertinent case information. There are many types of case presentation forms and supporting documents. Form 5.1 should be treated as a draft document because you will need to modify it to meet your specific site and supervision needs. You should also feel free to add other sources of information (e.g., genograms, test results, therapy summaries) that you deem helpful, in formats that honor confidentiality concerns. The best way to prepare good materials is to carefully anticipate what you will be asked and what you will want to know. Most students become efficient after preparing only a few consultations.

Form 5.1 Sample Case Presentation Form

Name: ______________________ Date of presentation: ______________

Name or Client ID: ______________ Date of session: ________________

Type of presentation (Circle one):
Audiotape Videotape Written Verbatim Written Case Presentation

Presenting concern(s) bringing client to counseling (in client's words):

____

____

Your theoretical orientation: ____________________________________

Your perception of the client's concerns based upon your theoretical orientation:

____

____

Client's identified counseling goals:

1. ____
2. ____
3. ____
4. ____

Number of times client has been seen: ____________

Relevant clinical history and background (attach a genogram for family issues):

____

____

____

____

Diagnosis:

____

____

(continued)

Perceived strengths and resources:

____

____

____

Specific issues and questions to be discussed in supervision:

1. ____
2. ____
3. ____
4. ____

Recommendations suggested during supervision:

1. ____
2. ____
3. ____
4. ____

Changes implemented and assessment of effectiveness: Useful (y/n)

1. ____
2. ____
3. ____
4. ____

Follow-up questions:

1. ____
2. ____
3. ____
4. ____

We often recommend that students prepare a genogram of the client's family. Copies, with information properly coded to protect confidentiality, are shared with the supervisor and other members of the supervision group. With a little practice, students quickly learn to prepare detailed genograms that convey a remarkable amount of useful information in a condensed format. Participants appreciate having this data once they learn how to read the chart and develop serviceable interpretations of the client's difficulties as well as sources of support.

Managing Anxiety

Frankly, as supervisors, given the amount of responsibility placed upon students and the challenge of successfully completing clinical training, we would be concerned if a student did not report levels of concern, worry, or anxiety. In our opinion, too cavalier an attitude may be even more problematic than unhealthy levels of anxiety. Appropriate levels of anxiety or worry are desirable because they motivate you. Healthy anxiety makes you function more effectively and motivates you to pursue the information, skills, and techniques that you will need to improve. Appropriate levels of anxiety may also allow you to be more sensitive to changes in yourself and in your interpersonal relationships. Such heightened sensitivity ensures that you will attend more fully to the content and the processes found in each of the relationships that form novices into skilled professionals.

Unhealthy or extreme levels of anxiety interfere with your ability to counsel clients, they obstruct relationships with supervisors, they disturb interaction with peers, and they make it very difficult to understand yourself. When disturbances simultaneously occur in all of these relationships, progress is simply not possible. Supervisors suggest that their supervisees pursue personal or group counseling when they detect crippling levels of anxiety. Such counseling is often helpful because it reduces anxiety levels and has the added benefit of giving the student firsthand experience as a client.

Extreme levels of anxiety require swift outside intervention. A supervisor who tries to help a student in distress risks morphing supervision into counseling and violating important clinical boundaries. But what should be done when you sense a level of anxiety that is not so severe that it requires external intervention yet strong enough that it has begun to diminish your effectiveness? First, you should do everything in your power to prepare for each element of clinical work. Prepare yourself in advance for each counseling session as well as for each supervision meeting. Following the protocol offered in the previous section will reduce anxiety because preparation manages the fears produced by uncertainty and dealing with the unknown.

Second, you need to manage the anxiety that each of us faces as we deal with busy lives and the demands of working under supervision. Fortunately, Fitch and Marshall (2002) have identified a number of common themes and recommendations for cognitively restructuring thoughts (see Table 5.1). The result is a serviceable model that not only forewarns you but identifies improved ways of thinking about these concerns that reduce anxiety to more adaptive and appropriate levels. If you experience one or more of these sources (themes) and find the cognitive restructuring tools ineffective, you would be wise to discuss the matter with your supervisor and pursue outside counseling. Unresolved fears and anxieties can blunt the effectiveness of clinical training and even cause you to unwittingly diminish your training opportunities. Students with such fears will often avoid taking cases that could improve their skills or will even select sites that seem "safer" because they believe that they can avoid too much attention.

Table 5.1 Common Anxiety-Related Thoughts of Practicum Students

Major Theme	Positive Self-Talk/Cognitive Restructuring Thoughts
Will this affect my job	I need to prioritize my semester and plan ahead for my job and practicum. Although it will take time away from my job now, learning to counsel students can improve my work.
Listening to audio-taped sessions in class	I assume everyone in class is basically starting from the same point, so my tape will not stand out. My tapes do not need to be perfect. It takes time to get good at this, so be patient.
Counseling skills are inadequate	It is confusing to know what to do; however, if I stay focused and follow my training, I will be fine. Students are not as fragile as I think. As long as I am positive and focused, I will be fine. Change takes time and patience; also, they are responsible for their own change, not you.
Lack of conceptualization skills	I will not always know what to do. It is OK to ask for help with this case. It will take time to learn how to apply the theories.
Course demands and time commitments	I can handle the stress if I break the demands down into smaller pieces. You eat an elephant one bite at a time. Other students have survived before me so I know it can be done.
Personal stressors	Learning to be an effective counselor takes time away from family and friends so I will have to manage time carefully this semester. I need to stay focused on my training, although other things in my life are very demanding. Being less effective with my counseling will only make things worse.

From Fitch, T. J. and Marshall, J. L. (2002). Using cognitive interventions with counseling practicum students during group supervision. *Counselor Education and Supervision, 41*, 335–342. The American Counseling Association. Reprinted with permission. No further reproduction authorized without written permission from the American Counseling Association.

These outcomes are unfortunate and avoidable. As counselors, we are particularly interested in helping clients identify their fears, manage their anxiety, and pursue their goals. We should be willing to do exactly the same for ourselves. Supervisors can often detect when their supervisees are not working to their potential or selecting appropriate field placements. But you should also be willing to question your client choices and discuss with your supervisors field site alternatives that anxiety may have eliminated from your list of options.

Counselor Self-Efficacy

Counselor self-efficacy (CSE), as described by Barnes (2004), forms the final goal for students working under supervision. CSE is defined by Larson and Daniels (1998) as "one's belief or judgments about her or his capabilities to effectively counsel a client in the near future" (p. 180). A series of effective counseling experiences, support from supervisors, an enlarged pool of counseling skills, varied opportunities to make and evaluate clinical judgments, knowing and applying protocols (e.g., suicide assessment, child abuse assessment), and useful formative evaluations combine to increase levels of CSE.

CSE is important for two reasons. First, CSE helps students move from the sympathy and counselor stance stages to the transition and integrated personal style stages. Second, according to Barnes (2004) and Larson and Daniels (1998), interns and practicum students who have higher levels of CSE can integrate evaluative information more effectively. CSE plays a significant role in supervision and the extent to which you will be able to use the wealth of information that supervision produces. You can do a great deal to increase CSE by identifying what you specifically need to build your confidence in working with clients and describing how you will obtain it. Supervisors appreciate supervisees who have thought their way through these questions and who have some idea of what would be helpful for them.

Since developing CSE has risks attached to it, there are steps that supervisors can take to help students more safely expose themselves to the situations that develop CSE. According to Barnes (2004),

> Modeling an appreciation for constructive feedback, or observations of strengths and areas in need of continued growth, is important to facilitating trainee self-reflection. This can be accomplished by establishing a collaborative environment in which the supervisor or counselor educator seeks constructive feedback from the trainee about his or her experiences in supervision or training during each session. (p. 63)

This type of modeling guides students by introducing a common style of communicating as they share and integrate feedback. While being able to communicate productively with supervisors and other clinicians is essential during clinical training, your need for these skills will persist throughout your life as a mental health professional. Consultation and supervision require that you communicate with professionals and integrate what you learn in essentially the same way.

Jana and Della Revisited

Della had supervised many internships during her 15-year tenure in the program. She appreciated Jana's enthusiasm, knowing that it would carry her through challenges she would soon face. Della also knew that she would have to support, understand, and encourage Jana if their supervisor-supervisee relationship was going to form the foundation for the positive clinical outcomes that they both anticipated.

Della and Jana met about a week after orientation for the first of many weekly supervision sessions. Della explained how important it would be for Jana to feel comfortable discussing all aspects of her work in the program. She told Jana that creating a climate of openness would be a responsibility shared by both of them. Della told Jana that she would also have to rely upon her to provide feedback concerning how effective the supervision sessions were and identifying areas that might need improvement. Della closed by telling Jana that she hoped that they would be able to form something called "a professional community." Della defined the term to mean a collection of professionals, all of whom are focused on self-improvement and share the common goal of delivering quality and ethical care to clients. She emphasized the need for mutual respect and understanding coupled with a willingness to confront difficulties and resolve differences. This type of working relationship, formed from optimism and encouragement, would be a unique opportunity for Jana. Della's introduction reduced Jana's anxiety and buoyed her spirits. She felt confident that their working relationship would be able to resolve the inevitable difficulties, improve her skills as a counselor, and introduce her to a profession where consulting with other professionals will continue throughout her career.

SUMMARY

Supervision is a process that is based upon a clearly defined and well-bounded relationship between a supervisor and one or more supervisees. Because there are risks associated with novices providing treatment, supervisors assume an impressive range of responsibilities. They are responsible not only for their supervisees but also for their supervisee's clients. And supervisors are responsible to the counseling profession. They are expected to make decisions and to act in the interest of the client, the supervisee, and the profession. In the last case, supervisors may be seen as "gatekeepers," individuals who seek to ensure that only competent clinicians are allowed to enter the ranks of the profession.

Supervision is a relationship that follows predictable stages and needs to be properly cultivated. It is also a relationship that if not properly managed can erode into counseling. Students and supervisors risk serious problems if such a dual relationship surfaces. When effective, supervision helps manage fear and anxiety, and it offers new ways of understanding clients, treatment alternatives, a source of very useful evaluative information, and a setting in which to openly discuss a range of topics (e.g., ethics, counseling theory, research).

As a participant in the process, you can do a great deal to improve outcomes. You can carefully prepare for all of the events in which you participate during clinical training. A shared sense of responsibility helps, as does a willingness to be open, involved, and engaged. You can train yourself to be an active participant by managing fears and anxieties, learning about parallel process, studying the effects of countertransference, modifying the supervision form to meet your particular needs, and being an active participant. Supervision is a precious opportunity for growth, and there is much that you can do to enhance your involvement in it.

Reflection Questions

1. What steps would you take to make sure that a supervisory relationship did not become a counseling relationship?
2. What behaviors might you see in yourself if you were at the "counselor stance" level of development?
3. What would be appropriate fears or anxieties for students about to begin their clinical training?
4. How could you tell if levels of anxiety had increased to the point that they would affect your work? What would you do?
5. What will you do to ensure that you receive the maximum benefit from your practicum or internship?

PART 2

COUNSELING CLIENTS
BOUNDARIES, GOALS, EMERGENCIES, AND CAVEATS

The four chapters in this part provide an overview of the "nuts and bolts" of the counseling process. Most of what is covered here you have probably discussed in your courses and probably are thinking, "Why cover this again?" The purpose of walking through the stages of counseling, from beginning to end, is to remind you of the basics of the counseling process. From this foundation, your practicum and internship experience will begin to grow.

Chapter 6 deals with the formation of the therapeutic relationship. It is our premise that practicum is all about learning how to effectively connect with another human being who is seeking your help. The chapter covers the formation of the relationship and revisits an old friend, empathy. The information in this chapter is akin to the eye of the storm; no matter how chaotic the counseling session, you can always trust the skills of relationship development.

Chapter 7 explores the process of searching for patterns in your client's life as a means of gaining better insight into the client's world and learning about what the client wants to change. Using formal methods such as assessment and diagnostic tools, as well as informal strategies such as the unstructured interview, you can discover clues about the client's dysfunction and assets. The chapter also covers the importance of goal setting in the counseling process.

Chapter 8 deals with the complexities of change. Every counselor in the world likely wants nothing more than for the clients to *change*. The chapter examines change not as an isolated element of the counseling process but as highly dependent on the counselor's ability to form a therapeutic relationship and collaborate with the client in accurate goal setting. Although it is beyond the scope of this book to illuminate all the ideas about change, we have distilled the areas of change into three spheres: cognitive, emotional, and behavioral. We discuss counselor strategies for each sphere.

Chapter 9 highlights the important stage of termination. Sometimes, we are so eager to begin the counseling process and move toward the change stage that we forget to prepare our clients and ourselves for a positive parting. We believe that how you end a counseling relationship is just as important as how you begin it. The information in this chapter will guide your exploration and practice in terminating and alert you to ways that poor terminations can be avoided.

Chapter 6

Client Intake
First Steps in Forming the Alliance

One of the most fascinating aspects of the counseling profession lies within the energy of the first counseling session. As you wait for the client to show up, the countless possibilities for the emerging relationship may rush through your head. From the superficial curiosities ("I wonder what he will look like") to deeper reflections about self ("I wonder if she will think I'm a good counselor") to musings about the path counseling might take ("I wonder what the real issue will be"), all these thoughts occupy that space as you anticipate the first session. The inherent anxiety is actually beneficial because it helps you see each client as an individual, not just a "problem." When you allow yourself to anticipate, you open yourself up to an exciting part of counseling: the connection between two people who have never met and yet are about to embark together on a powerful journey of growth. This chapter explores the ways you can use the anxiety creatively to facilitate a solid foundation for counseling. As you will see, the first steps of counseling are filled with far more than superficial paperwork and history taking. Done right, the first few sessions set the tone for the remainder of the journey.

The Importance of First Contact

Counseling begins from the first contact between client and counselor. For most, the first meeting is on the phone as the client attempts to set up an appointment. From that moment, both client and counselor are engaged in a parallel process of assessment and engagement. Consider the following excerpts and think about what the counselor and client might conclude from the interaction.

Phone Dialogue 1

CLIENT: Um . . . yeah. I don't know why I'm calling. My wife thinks I need to come in.

COUNSELOR: Would you like to make an appointment?

CLIENT: I guess. I don't know. I really don't have time, but I can try.

Phone Dialogue 2

CLIENT (leaving message on machine): Hi. My name is Amy and I would like to make an appointment. I need one as soon as possible. I'm really anxious and can't seem to get my life together and it's getting worse. Please call me back.

COUNSELOR (calling back two days later): Hi. I got your message and my next open appointment is in two weeks. Would you like me to pencil you in?

In these two brief interactions, you can probably draw some conclusions about the individuals. Without ever meeting the client in the first dialogue, what are your impressions? Most observers would say that this client is hesitant to enter counseling, and the main areas of potential resistance include feeling pressured into counseling and his time schedule. Paying attention to these dynamics may help you form the alliance with him and increase the likelihood of a positive counseling outcome.

From the client's perspective, in the second dialogue, what are some of your impressions of the counselor? The client may assume that the counselor will not be attentive due to the long wait for a return phone call or may even feel like the counselor's skills are weak based on the lack of concern in the face of urgent client symptoms. The client may feel ignored or not taken seriously, which could affect the alliance and even lead to the client not following through on the appointment.

Attending to the client's dynamics during the first contact can provide key information about the client, and being aware of your interaction can be a powerful first step in the alliance process. Once the client gets to the appointment, the therapeutic process can really get rolling. We believe that the first stage of counseling is designed to:

1. *Gather information about the client.* This information will help the counselor develop a phenomenological view of the client's world.
2. *Orient the client to the process of counseling.* The orientation includes both explicit activities, such as informed consent, and implicit actions, such as the way the dialogue progresses in the session.

3. *Formulate tentative goals.* Collaborative goal setting allows client and counselor to agree on some possible outcomes of counseling. Counselors use assessment, both formal and informal, to help facilitate realistic goal setting.
4. *Test the alliance.* Not all counselors and clients are good matches. As the relationship develops, both parties need to decide if it has the potential for a good working relationship.

These steps in engagement of a client are congruent to the steps of a forming relationship between supervisee and supervisor. As you begin supervision, your supervisor will be exploring your style and skills in order to get a realistic picture of you. He or she will also orient you to the process of supervision, covering the topics discussed in chapters 3 and 5. You will also learn a lot about the skill and manner of your supervisor through the supervisory dialogues. Together you will discuss goals for your training and determine whether the relationship is solid enough to provide an opportunity to work towards those goals.

First Meeting and the Purpose of Paperwork

On the day of the first session with a new client, most counselors report a sense of anxiety and nervous tension about the meeting. This feeling is normal; a person is about to come see you with expectations that you will help, but you know nothing about the person. The very fact that you have the privilege of connecting with another human being in this way may be anxiety provoking. Plan to arrive early for the appointment. Clients may arrive late, but you must not because it conveys a lack of professionalism and a tone of disrespect for the client's issues. When the client arrives, greet him or her by introducing yourself and proceed to the next step in the process, which for most sites includes filling out paperwork.

Paperwork at some agencies can be overwhelming. We have worked in places where the forms clients have to fill out read like novellas. If the paperwork packet at your site is more than five pages long, you may explore the possibility of mailing it to your client prior to the first meeting or asking the client to come early to the first session to complete the necessary forms. All forms should serve a purpose in the treatment of the client. At a minimum the packet should include an informed consent document (professional disclosure statement), a consent to reveal confidential information form (to share pertinent information with other members of the client's treatment team; school counselors, psychiatrists, etc.), and a background information form.

While it may not be essential for clients to sign the release of confidential information form or fill out the background questionnaire immediately, it is important for the client to read, understand, and sign the informed consent document before discussing any issues. The professional disclosure statement, discussed in chapter 2, orients the client to the boundaries of counseling, explains the role of the client and counselor, outlines fees and appointment issues, and specifies the exceptions to confidentiality. By reading the form and asking questions about the content, the client is able to make an informed choice about whether to participate in treatment. Not only does the discussion provide the client with needed information about the counseling process, it also provides an excellent opportunity for the counselor to engage the client in a cooperative relationship before the presenting problem emerges. Thus, the document becomes more than a piece a paper; it may also be considered a vital element of the engagement process. For an even more detailed discussion of the purpose of the professional disclosure statement, see Cavanagh and Levitov (2002, pp. 62–79). A template is available online at www.lpcboard.org.

The other forms can also be used as methods of alliance building. Discussions about the consent to release confidential information can reveal other professionals who are working on the issue and the client's perception of their role in the process. Background information forms can provide jumping-off places for the dialogue. For example, most background forms cover broad topics such as presenting problem, medications, prior diagnoses, family constellation, and substance use, any of which can be places to begin the counseling (e.g., "I see that you mention you made the appointment to discuss your father's recent illness. Tell me a little more about that."). In addition to the general topics, it is also important to have a space on the background form for the client to note any feelings of suicide or homicide. These areas can be addressed at the very beginning of counseling to deal with or rule out a crisis situation.

The overarching goal of these first few minutes of the beginning session is to orient your client to the counseling process and begin the relationship formation. Using the paperwork as a means to initiate the dialogue serves the client and the alliance more effectively than does approaching the paperwork as a meaningless task: it is meaningless only if you fail to integrate the activity into the alliance process. Once the dialogue has begun, your understanding of the client can deepen.

Basic Elements of Alliance Formation

There is so much information about what to do with clients that it can feel overwhelming. In fact, trying to distill all the relevant information into one chapter was overwhelming to us! As we sat surrounded by the mountain of literature, we imagined that this is what it must feel like to practicum and internship students as they try to decide what to do to form a relationship with a client. We then thought about suggestions we give to our students: "Alliance forming is about the *relationship*. When you feel stuck, go back to the basics." So that's what we're going to do in this chapter: go back to the basics; that is, those popularized by Carl Rogers (1961), but widely accepted as alliance-building methods. We will use the elements of *empathy, unconditional positive regard,* and *congruence* to focus on the nature of alliance formation. Remember those?

Empathy

There is probably not another concept discussed in the counseling literature as universal as empathy. By now, you have probably discussed empathy in several of your courses, and if asked to describe it, you might say empathy is "being in touch with another person's feelings" or "walking in the client's shoes." Empathy has historically been viewed as an important part of the alliance building between counselor and client. Rogers and Stevens, who included empathy as one of the necessary and sufficient elements of change, clarify the concept in terms of the role of the counselor: "To sense the client's inner world of private personal meanings as if it were your own, but without losing the 'as if' quality, this is empathy, and this seems essential to a growth-promoting relationship" (1967, pp. 92–93).

In order to form empathy in the client-counselor relationship, we must be able to touch the inner world of the client (e.g., see with his or her eyes) without losing our own sense of self in the process (e.g., the "as if" quality). At its most superficial, empathy can be experienced as an emotional connection between counselor and client; an acknowledgment of the affective domain of the client. Through that validation, the client feels understood. For example, consider the following exchange and comments:

> CLIENT: I am so tired of having to do all the work in my relationship.
>
> COUNSELOR: You feel frustrated over not being appreciated.
> (Counselor chooses to reflect the feeling of frustration felt empathically in the client's statement.)
>
> CLIENT: Yes! It seems like nobody ever gives me respect.
> (Client responds positively, feeling understood and validated.)

If we stopped here, the example would capture the essence of typical discussions regarding empathy. However, empathy can be viewed as more complex than a mere conveyance of emotional reflection. Barrett-Lennard (1981) defines empathy as a cyclical interchange between counselor and client and outlines a five-stage model that helps illuminate the complexities and pathways of empathy as an alliance-building skill. The five steps of the cycle will be briefly explored to add depth to your awareness of the role of empathy.

Step 1. The counselor actively attends to the client as the client actively expresses an aspect of self. In this step, the counselor is responsible for preparing for the client's self-expression through evidence of an *empathic set,* which is accomplished through being aware and attentive. The client is responsible for providing information; the stimuli for empathy. Simply put, the counselor must pay attention to the client, and the client has to say something to which the counselor can pay attention. Even though this step seems easy to accomplish, poor listening skills, stressful or emotional life distractions, or other factors can impede the counselor from being fully present for the client and thus disrupt the empathic connection before it has a chance to benefit the client.

Step 2. The counselor recognizes and can relate internally to the emotional content within the client's statements. Using intuitive sensing, counselors must attune themselves to the inner world of the client. It is here, in step 2, that you must place one foot firmly in your own experience to draw upon that knowledge as well as to anchor yourself and, at the same time, move the other foot into the world of the client by being curious about the client's own perspective. At first glance, this step might also seem easy, but consider the following client statement: "I am so upset that my husband left me." To adequately respond in an empathic manner, you first in your own mind connect and identify all the relevant emotions: pain, loneliness, sadness, anger, and so on. You mentally draw from analogous experiences in your own life to verify the accuracy of these initial feelings (this is the foot in your world). You then add in the context of what you know about the client, the client's nonverbal cues while speaking, and any other information regarding the client that may be pertinent (this represents the stepping into the client's world). Without internal reference to your own knowledge, it is impossible to intuit feelings of others. Without access to the client's world, you are left with only your own feelings, and the probability of empathic failure increases. Plainly, without both feet, you are standing on shaky ground.

Step 3. The counselor conveys understanding of the client's emotional content. In this step, the counselor must frame a verbal response that demonstrates understanding of the client's world. The most common method is a reflection of feeling. Reflections of feeling can be phrased in a tentative ("You *seem* to feel disappointed") or certain ("You *are* disappointed") manner depending on the current state of the empathic connection. Tentative reflections carry less potency but may work well with beginning relationships or with clients who are suspicious, whereas reflections with a high degree of certainty convey more understanding and work well to deepen the empathic bond. It is also important to note that in addition to the counselor's words, the nonverbal communication is equally important in conveying empathy. Body posture, facial expression, and voice tone are all empathy-enhancing tools at this stage.

Step 4. The client attends to the counselor's response of understanding. This step is beyond the counselor's control. Obviously, most clients are in a state to hear what the counselor is saying, but some client factors may make the reception difficult, if not impossible. High levels of emotion might impede the listening skills of the client. For example, someone who is sobbing may miss what the counselor says. Severe psychopathology such as psychosis, panic attacks, or mania may make it difficult for the client to adequately receive the empathy of the counselor. Although the counselor cannot control these limitations, it is the counselor's responsibility to note these dynamics and work them into the treatment plan.

Step 5. The client provides feedback to the counselor regarding the accuracy of the counselor's statement and the resulting impact on the empathic connection between client and counselor. If accurate, the counselor's empathic reflection will allow the client to feel understood and validated, and thus the alliance will be enhanced. Often the feedback is offered with little more than a "Yes!" followed by deeper self-expression. It is the validation and understanding that facilitate the depth exploration. Even when the counselor's attempt is inaccurate, it still allows for a positive relationship impact, in that the reflection offers the client a chance to check the accuracy and correct the mistake. Feedback of this type often goes as follows:

> COUNSELOR: You seem angry about being betrayed.
>
> CLIENT: Not angry, I was livid! How could my lover do that to me?

This example illustrates how even perceived inaccuracies can be helpful to the alliance formation. The elegance in step 5 rests with the client's feedback, which allows for deeper understanding of the client's phenomenological worldview. The critical part of empathy is that the counselor is making a sincere attempt to understand the subjective view of the client, and the cycle demonstrates the unfolding of the process. As the counselor and client move together through the cycle, the alliance is formed.

Unconditional Positive Regard

If empathy is the path to connecting with the client's world, unconditional positive regard is the way of accepting the client's right to see the world in his or her uniquely personal manner without judgment from the counselor. Rogers (1961) noted that unconditional positive regard is "a warm, positive and acceptant attitude toward what is in the client. It means an outgoing positive feeling without reservations, without evaluations" (p. 62).

In the beginning stage of counseling, clients are sensitive about disclosing embarrassing or shameful aspects of their life for fear that the counselor will reject or look down on them like so many people have done in the "real world." Conveying unconditional positive regard creates a safe environment for the client to discuss and explore painful parts of life, and it defines a unique aspect of the counseling relationship.

Much like empathy, unconditional positive regard is more complicated than most people suspect. It may seem intuitive that a counselor needs to accept the client and honor the client's right to a personal worldview, but clinical reality presents challenges to a counselor's ability to feel unconditional positive regard, most often when the client's worldview is significantly divergent from the counselor's own values. Issues such as parenting, domestic violence, religion, sexuality, and personal ethics all create potential rifts in the alliance due to problems with the counselor's ability to convey unconditional positive regard. Consider the following dialogue:

CLIENT: I am so depressed. I can't believe all that has happened to me this year: the divorce, the lost job, my illness . . .

COUNSELOR: It sounds like you have been through a lot over the past year. Tell me more about what that's been like for you.

CLIENT: It just wears me down. It's hard to go on day by day with all this on my back.

COUNSELOR: I can see that your experiences have really taken their toll on you emotionally and physically.

CLIENT: Thanks. It's nice to have a place to come and talk. Most people tell me to pull myself up and get on with my life. That just adds to the stress.

COUNSELOR: Like you could just snap out of it, right?

CLIENT: Right! I don't know, you know, sometimes I get so angry too.

COUNSELOR: Tell me about the anger.

CLIENT: Well, I used to be spiritual, you know, go to church and all that. But how could God turn his back on me? How could he let all this stuff happen to me?

COUNSELOR: Well, maybe it's all happening for a reason.

CLIENT: What?

COUNSELOR: Well, I guess I am asking if now is the time to move away from something that has historically been a support for you.

CLIENT: I guess I never viewed it as a support. If it was supporting me, why did I fall so hard?

The dialogue demonstrates how easily unconditional positive regard can begin to fade. In the first four interchanges, the counselor does a nice job of creating a safe environment for the client's expression. Notice how the counselor stays with the feelings, allows for deeper exploration, and connects with the client's perspective. Once religion enters the discussion, however, the counselor seems a bit shaken. The first response ("Well, maybe it's happening for a reason") seems to take the client by surprise. It's almost as if the counselor lost focus, as though the counselor was in tune with the client and then became momentarily distracted, and the distraction pulled the counselor back into the counselor's own world. The second comment is an attempt to reenter the client's world, but it is still rooted in the counselor's own belief system. It is as if the counselor's own possible belief that religion *should* be a support is interfering with the unconditional positive regard for the client's belief that religion has ceased to be a support.

Congruence

When a counselor is able to be genuine with the client, the client feels like he or she is relating to a real person. Rogers (1961) described congruence as a condition in which "the feelings the therapist is experiencing are available to him, available to his awareness, and he is able to live these feelings, be them, and able to communicate them if appropriate" (p. 61).

Many counselors impede congruence by erecting a rigid professional facade, placing extreme emotional distance between client and counselor. Hidden behind the impenetrable wall, the counselor may appear aloof and impersonal to the client. Counselors who adopt this approach have probably translated the "therapist as a blank screen" theme too literally. When counselors do not come across as real people to their clients, it makes it more difficult to relate and thus inhibits the relationship.

On the other hand, being too open and glib can be experienced by the client as abrasive or even cruel. Every counselor has thoughts and feelings during the course of the session that, if stated concretely, could be damaging to the client. For example, if the counselor is feeling bored in the session due to incessant client storytelling, then blurting out, "You are boring me to tears with your inane stories!" may be congruent, but it is not conducive to alliance building. The art of congruence lies with being able to convey the emotion in a way that is helpful to the client.

Now that you are aware of some ways congruence can go wrong, let us explore some examples dealing with common, yet complicated, counseling situations related to congruence. The first example takes us back to the counselor feeling bored.

CLIENT: I don't know but when I was 15 I remember my mom took me to this weird store and we shopped for hours for little rabbit statues that were supposed to be made out of clay, but it seemed we never really found a rabbit made of clay but we did find some really neat clay statues of porcupines, or I guess, they really weren't statues, but more like figures because figures are smaller than statues and when I think of statues, I tend to think of museums and not so much about things that go in houses. Anyway . . .

COUNSELOR 1 (too distant): Uh-huh . . .

COUNSELOR 2: (abrasive): Stop! I can't take this anymore. You are rambling, and it's putting me to sleep.

COUNSELOR 3: (appropriately congruent): Let me jump in here a minute. I am sure there is something you really want me to know, but I am getting lost in all the words and details.

In the three examples, notice the difference in tone and probable client reactions. The too-distant example will likely produce more storytelling on the part of the client, and the boredom will morph into anger or resentment in the counselor. The abrasive response has a high probability of producing an embarrassed or defensive client response. The appropriately congruent response highlights the counselor emotion, and the counselor notes the reason (words and details) but takes responsibility for the feeling. This allows the client to feel less defensive and facilitates insight by offering multiple pathways of exploration, both within the counselor-client relationship and in relationships the client has outside of counseling.

Our second example deals with counselor fear.

MALE CLIENT: I think all women are full of crap. They just try to manipulate and screw men over. It makes me so angry I just want to strangle them sometimes. Don't get me wrong, I love the ladies, but down deep inside, I know I can't trust them. I never have met one I could trust or that didn't stab me in the back. Every time I think of it, I just want to take it out on the first woman I see.

FEMALE COUNSELOR 1 (too distant): I can tell you are really frustrated by the women who hurt you.

FEMALE COUNSELOR 2 (abrasive): Well, I'm a woman! I feel threatened by you and want you out of my office!

FEMALE COUNSELOR 3 (appropriately congruent): I have to say that I feel fearful and intimidated, being a woman and listening to your obvious anger, but I am also sensing a lot of hurt in your voice. I wonder if you could talk specifically about feelings of trust in our relationship.

In this example, the counselor's feelings of fear and intimidation are normal responses to the client's expression of disdain for women. The client is probably keenly aware that his behavior produces fear—

some might say that is even his intent—so pretending to not have feelings could possibly lead the client directly to not trust the counselor. Being abrasive may honor the feelings, but they are communicated in a way that increases the chance of a hostile or defensive client reaction. The appropriately congruent response directly conveys the feelings of the counselor in a nonthreatening manner and openly offers the client an opportunity to explore the feelings within the context of the relationship. While this approach does not guarantee the client will respond in a self-reflective manner, it does increase the probability that the dialogue that follows will be alliance enhancing rather than destructive.

Questions

Most of us are taught that the easiest way to get information is to ask a question. However, counselors are aware that they want the engagement process to feel less like an interrogation and more like a dialogue. Knowing the difference between two types of questions can aid in the development of the alliance.

Closed-ended questions can be answered minimally, usually with such one-word answers as yes and no. Examples of closed-ended questions include:

Are you having trouble at school?
Do you ever feel like you don't belong?
Can you imagine yourself getting better?

Clients responding to these closed-ended questions with one-word answers will provide little real information for the counselor. Even worse, the lack of information often prompts the counselor to ask even more questions, often leading the interview to feel more like an interrogation than an engagement process. Put yourself in the client's seat and consider the following dialogue:

COUNSELOR: Your mother asked you to come here today because of some issues you were having with your soccer coach. Is that accurate?

CLIENT: Yeah, I guess.

COUNSELOR: Do you think you have issues with your soccer coach?

CLIENT: No.

COUNSELOR: Are you having problems with your mom?

CLIENT: No.

COUNSELOR: Can you describe your relationship with anyone you might not get along with?

CLIENT: Not really.

COUNSELOR: Do you sometimes feel that no one really understands you?

CLIENT: Yes.

OK, that's enough. We hope by now you get the idea how uncomfortable a long series of closed-ended questions can be for both client and counselor. Even if you are not feeling particularly uncomfortable, you probably see the limitations of the information gathered by closed-ended questions.

Conversely, open-ended questions encourage the client to answer with elaborated answers, allowing for greater detail and sharing. One type of open-ended question really isn't a question at all but more of a prompt for further exploration. This type begins with, "Tell me more about . . ." Consider the same counselor invitation that was used on the closed-ended question example:

> COUNSELOR: Your mother asked you to come here today because of some issues you were having with your soccer coach. What do you think about your relationship with your coach?
>
> CLIENT: Um, I don't know. I don't think I really have a problem with him.
>
> COUNSELOR: So you think everything is going pretty well. If there was something you could change about the relationship, what would it be?
>
> CLIENT: Well, he's pretty hard on me. When he yells at me, I just don't want to listen to him at all. I just tune him out and that really pisses him off.
>
> COUNSELOR: Tell me more about how you tune him out.
>
> CLIENT: I just hear him getting on me and it's like he isn't recognizing how hard I am working. He just wants to focus on the negative. It hurts, but I would never let him know that.
>
> COUNSELOR: What would happen if you did let him know?
>
> CLIENT: Oh man, I bet he would really get on me then, for being a wimp.

Did you notice how different the tone and amount of information gathered is when using open-ended questions? It feels much less like an interrogation session and allows both client and counselor many opportunities for discovery.

Obviously, as you form the relationship with your client, you are going to utilize all of these elements and more. The main point of this chapter is that although the beginning stages of counseling are anxiety provoking, forming an alliance is best constructed by remembering the *basics*. When you encounter new people, their life is known to them but is completely unknown to you. It's like sitting in front of one of those 3-D art posters. The entire picture is there, but you can't see it yet. To see it, the first step is not complicated: relax and don't try too hard to see it. Applying this approach to counseling is like letting the picture of the client's life unfold through the process of connecting.

A Word about Premature Terminations

Often in the early phases of counseling, clients decide to not return. These "premature terminations" are usually not preceded by discussion or processing of the reasons for leaving. Instead, clients just stop coming. The consequence for ending counseling early leaves the client without help and support for the issues at hand. Researchers believe there are some ways to minimize premature termination. Some of the strategies include precounseling education, effective client screening, short-term treatment contracts, and appointment reminders (H. Bernard, 1989; Murphy & Cannon, 1986; Reis & Brown, 1999; Walitzer, Derman, & Connors, 1999). In addition, researchers note the importance of the counselor-client relationship and the ability of the counselor to access affective content of the client as viable methods for preventing client dropout (Ogrodniczuk, Joyce, & Piper, 2005; Tyron & Kane, 1993).

In addition to the maladaptive effects premature termination may have on the client, the event may also impact the counselor in a negative manner. The abrupt ending of the counseling relationship can leave the counselor feeling incompetent, rejected, and hurt. As one intern reflected,

> I had only met with Josie twice, and I thought things were going well. Then she just stopped coming. She didn't call me to cancel. She just no-showed and did not return my calls. I have no idea why she stopped, and I keep thinking I did something wrong. It feels so unfinished. I can't believe I got dumped!

Premature termination is confusing and hits at the core of insecurity about your professional self. It is important to note that clients leave counseling early for a variety of reasons, and not all of them are counselor related. According to Garfield (1994), up to 57% of clients end treatment prematurely, with most completing no more than four sessions. Due to the uncertainty of the termination, it is a good idea to think about the many possible reasons and reflect on ways you can influence future clients to decrease the likelihood of clients leaving without processing.

Supervision provides an excellent venue for discussing the complex feelings associated with premature termination. Within group supervision, you will undoubtedly hear from other interns who have experienced the same issue and be comforted by the fact that you are not alone. Individual supervision can be used to explore deeper personal reflections about your professional identity and discuss plans for modifying the ways you form alliances with clients. Through supervision, you can realize the goal of learning to change what you can and becoming comfortable with what you cannot.

Summary

This chapter highlights the important elements of the beginning stages of alliance formation. From the initial contact with the client, the counselor has an opportunity to build rapport. Even tasks that might seem tedious, such as attending to paperwork, provide important information to both client and counselor about the process of counseling.

Three core concepts were used to define the basics of alliance formation: empathy, unconditional positive regard, and congruence. Although these are familiar concepts by now, they represent foundational pieces that will set the stage for success in the counseling relationship. As rapport deepens between counselor and client, the client feels more comfortable sharing important aspects of self that will increase the potential for exploration and growth. The cohesion between client and counselor decreases the probability of premature termination and facilitates movement to the next stage of continued assessment, pattern search, and goal setting.

Reflection Questions

1. What concerns do you imagine will surface as you prepare for the meeting with your first client?
2. How can you respond empathically to a client whom you have just met and hardly know?
3. How will you provide "unconditional positive regard" to your clients as you listen to their difficulties or embarrassing moments?
4. What do you think it means for a counselor to rely heavily on closed-ended questions?
5. As counselors become more skilled, they tend to be able to engage with a wider range of clients. Why do you think this change occurs?

Chapter 7

Assessment, Pattern Search, and Goal Setting

In chapter 6, we discussed ways to form a therapeutic alliance with the client. Utilizing empathy and a spirit of curiosity, counselors can enter the lives of individuals to facilitate change. Once you have the connection, a deeper level of exploration begins. As the landscape of the client's life unfolds, the counselor can recognize patterns that are unique to the client. In these patterns, the counselor can identify strengths and areas for growth. This chapter highlights some of the basic concepts associated with this part of the counseling process.

Assessment and Diagnosis

There are many schools of thought and external pressures (e.g., from insurance companies) that encourage counselors to begin the counseling process with a formal assessment and diagnosis that guides treatment planning. Learning to use the *Diagnostic and Statistical Manual of Mental Disorders-IVTR* was probably a part of your formal graduate training. While we believe that assessment and diagnosis are important, we also believe that the information can be incorporated into the counseling process so that it adds to the rapport building rather than detracts from it. In our own clinical practices, we have remarked on how the amount of paperwork has decreased the longer we have been in practice. We have found that it is sometimes just as efficient to get the information by dialoguing with the client.

A useful way for seeing how the elements of relationship building, assessment, diagnosis, and treatment connect is featured in Figure 7.1. This figure illustrates an interrelated, cyclical process whereby

Figure 7.1 Connections among Relationship Building, Assessment, and Treatment

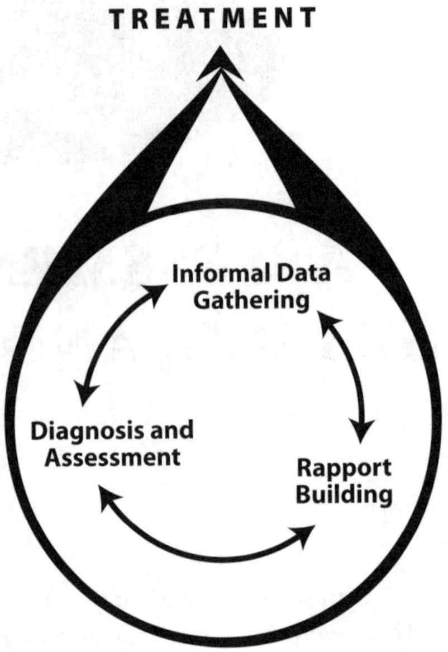

each component of the cycle builds onto and into itself to further the goal of treatment.

Assessment Tools

Formal assessment tools can serve as a valuable resource in complicated cases. Deciding when to use formal assessment tools requires deliberate decision making on the part of the counselor. Seligman (1994, pp. 69–72) recommends that counselors consider these important points when deciding whether to use psychological testing:

- Consider what information and knowledge you are looking to find in the assessment.
- Consider whether your current informational sources (client, intake form, family members, external records) can provide the information you seek. If not, can the assessment provide the missing information?
- Consider the client's perspective regarding being "tested." If the client's reaction is apprehensive, working through those feelings and assessing the impact on the therapeutic relationship is important.
- Choose the tool that gives you the best chance of acquiring the information you need. Choose tools that provide reliable, valid, and meaningful data.
- Develop a method of incorporating the results into the counseling process. Think about how you are going to process the infor-

mation with the client and be ready to discuss how it will benefit the client's treatment.

Once you weigh the benefits and disadvantages of testing, you probably have an idea of what testing should be done. The following are some of the common categories of assessments available. The list is brief, but you have already taken a course in assessment, so this should serve as a reminder and quick resource.

Personality tests. Personality instruments are designed to assess personal, emotional, social, and behavioral patterns of the individual. These tools are most often self-report based, that is, taken by the client from the client's perspective. They can range from comprehensive instruments such as the Minnesota Multiphasic Personality Interview-II (MMPI-II) and the Myers-Briggs Type Indicator (MBTI) to more specifically focused instruments such as the Beck Depression Inventory (BDI) that addresses levels of mood disturbance. Also in this category are the projective personality tests such as the Thematic Apperception Test (TAT) and the Rorschach Ink Blot Test. These tests are most often given as part of a psychological testing battery administered by a psychologist. They are useful in providing information and clarification of personality patterns, especially with regard to diagnosable conditions.

Interest inventories. These assessments measure a client's likes and dislikes, primarily in work and academic pursuits. The Self-Directed Search (SDS), the Strong Campbell Interest Inventory, and the Kuder General Interest Survey, Form E are all examples of such inventories. These tests are widely used by counselors as methods for helping clients gain insight into their relative satisfaction or dissatisfaction with a chosen vocational or academic path.

Career development inventories. These assessments examine the client's progress along the accepted stages of career development, including associated attitudinal and cognitive factors. Whereas the interest inventories assess the content of career choice, career development inventories evaluate the process and the client's current place in that process. Examples of career development inventories include the Adult Career Concerns Inventory (ACCI), Career Decision Scale (CDS), Career Development Inventory (CDI), and Career Maturity Inventory (CMI). These tests are common in vocational counseling offices, especially on college campuses, and many can be accessed for online administration.

Measures of ability. These tests encompass all assessments of aptitude, achievement, and intelligence. Aptitude tests try to predict a person's future performance; for example, the American College Test

(ACT) and the Scholastic Aptitude Test (SAT) are used to predict success in college academics, and the Graduate Record Exam (GRE) is used to predict academic success in graduate school. Achievement tests are designed to measure learning at selected academic intervals. Examples include any state educational test or the nationally used California Achievement Test. The intelligence tests, such as the Stanford-Binet, the Wechsler Adult Intelligence Scale (WAIS), the Wechsler Intelligence Scale for Children-Revised (WISC-R), and the Wechsler Preschool and Primary Scale of Intelligence (WPPSI), are used to quantify the elusive "intelligence quotient" (IQ). All of these tests are extensively used in educational and vocational settings, and to some degree, the intelligence tests are commonly included in psychological testing batteries.

Diagnosis

Diagnosis is a criteria-structured system that corrals commonly co-occurring symptom clusters into labels that describe types of psychopathology. Based on the medical model, the most commonly used systems of diagnosis are the *Diagnostic and Statistical Manual of Mental Disorders-IVTR* (*DSM*) and the *International Classification of Diseases, Clinical Modification,* 9th edition. Someone once said, "Diagnosis is the art of information gathering." That statement resonates throughout clinical work and teaching. To be a good diagnostician, one must know how to obtain information. If the counselor does not get accurate information, the diagnosis and the treatment will be degraded. Quality information is generated when the counselor connects with the client and enters the client's world (empathy). This is how empathy and diagnosis are intertwined.

According to Seligman (1998, pp. 92–95), the purpose of the *DSM* for counseling professionals is to:

- provide a universal language of mental illness to improve communication among mental health professionals
- improve research reliability by providing criteria for identifying the disorders
- seek approval from insurance companies that require a diagnosis for reimbursement
- predict the progress of the disorder and create treatment plans accordingly that match the diagnosis

As a basic overview, the *DSM* system of diagnosis allows the counselor to make use of the clinical interview, compiling and organizing the symptoms into categories. The system funnels the information into the finished product: a multiaxial diagnosis of the client. The axes are as follows:

Axis I: Clinical Disorders
Axis II: Personality Disorders, Mental Retardation
Axis III: General Medical Conditions
Axis IV: Psychosocial and Environmental Problems
Axis V: Global Assessment of Function (GAF)

Used correctly, the system is designed to provide a compact method for describing the dysfunction of the client in a comprehensive way. For more detailed explanations of the diagnostic process, please consult the *Diagnostic and Statistical Manual of Mental Disorders-IVTR* (American Psychiatric Association, 2000) and Morrison (1995).

Informal Methods of Information Gathering

Formal assessment tools and diagnostic labels help validate key areas of problems in the client's life, but they often fail to describe the specific impact the symptoms have on the individual sitting across from you. You could round up 50 people with the diagnosis of major depressive disorder or a BDI score of 8 and they would all be different in their presentation. Why? Because although assessments and diagnostic tools help identify the problem, they fail to capture the idiosyncratic nature of the problem. Figuring out how the diagnosis fits into the fabric of the client's life is an extension of the engagement stage. The better the connection you have with your client, the more information you will be able to access and fit into the bigger picture.

Although there are many informal ways to get the information you need, allowing the client to talk about what life is like can begin the pattern search process. Each theoretical school has its own "important life areas" list that helps structure the interview and give the counselor the best vantage point of the client's world, but Summers (2003) provides a comprehensive transtheoretical list of areas that might be useful to keep in mind as we explore pattern searching:

- *Medical history:* general health issues and problems
- *Psychiatric history:* previous diagnoses and treatment experiences
- *Social competencies:* how they connect and disconnect with people
- *Behavioral patterns:* problematic patterns that "get me in trouble"
- *Family system:* family of origin exploration as well as current intimate relationships (if the client has children, parenting issues)
- *School or work history:* educational background, work background, and relationships with colleagues and those in authority
- *Friends:* social relationships, both quantity and quality
- *Leisure activities:* hobbies, free time
- *Spirituality:* belief in a higher power

Making Sense of It All: The Process of Pattern Search

As the relationship deepens, more and more information about the client's world becomes available to the counselor. The flood of information must be processed and distilled in a manner that is useful to both client and counselor. Each theory has its own method for conceptualizing this wealth of information, but all emphasize the importance of seeing the patterns in the client's life. According to Beitman (1987), "The goal of the pattern search is to define patterns of thought, feeling, and/or behavior that are within the client's ability to influence and that, if changed, would lead toward a desirable outcome" (p. 82). In this section, we discuss the many ways a counselor can look for patterns and as a result help the client move toward change.

Developmental and External Sources

The list provided by Summers (2003) outlines several of the developmental and external resources for information that can provide the counselor with excellent pattern search material. During the intake sessions, the counselor can guide the client to discuss any or all of these issues as a way to get a clear perspective of the client's world. The more areas the counselor explores, the more clearly the patterns emerge. Consider the following case excerpt exploring a few of the areas. See if you can hypothesize about this client's patterns.

Case Excerpt 1 (Family of Origin)

COUNSELOR: You have made several remarks about your relationship with your parents. Have you always been caught in the middle of their arguments?

CLIENT: Oh yes. I mean, I'm 46 now and I'm still getting sucked in. Ever since I was a child, I recall it happening. My father worked long hours, and my mom took care of me and my sister. I could tell she would get tired of hanging out with us and resented my father working all the time. He would come home and they would start screaming at each other. Neither one really respected the other. Sooner or later, my dad would get tired of yelling at my mom and would turn on me and my sister. Then later my mom would come to me and try to console me.

COUNSELOR: And now you are the one who is expected to console her?

CLIENT: Yeah, she calls all the time, complaining about my father and how hard it is living with him. She just wants me to listen because she thinks I can relate. To tell you the truth, it's very draining.

Case Excerpt 2 (Friendships)

COUNSELOR: Tell me a little about your support network of friends.

CLIENT: I have a pretty good group of about five girlfriends. They are great.

COUNSELOR: What do you bring to the friendship group that makes you a contributing member?

CLIENT: I'm a nice person.

COUNSELOR: How would you define "nice"?

CLIENT: Well, I am like the "go to" person of the group. If someone needs something, I'm there for them. People know that I am available to talk to them if they have a problem. Whenever there is a disagreement among the group, I am the one people look to as a mediator. Just last week, Charlotte and Tara got in this huge fight, and I must have spent all night and most of the next day talking with each of them on the phone until I brokered a truce. I was worn out. That happens a lot.

Case Excerpt 3 (Parenting)

COUNSELOR: As a mother of two small children, you must have a lot on your plate. Tell me about your relationship with your kids.

CLIENT: Yes, Abbey is 6 and Allistair is 4. They are quite the handful! I really enjoy them though.

COUNSELOR: What do you enjoy?

CLIENT: Just being with them. I can tell they love me very much. I left my pretty demanding job after Abbey was born. I just couldn't work and be a mom. It was too much. I really like being there for them. I get to make them breakfast, really all the meals. I get to see all their "first" things, like walking and talking and stuff like that. I think I am much more connected to them than my husband. I like that connection.

COUNSELOR: They need you.

CLIENT: Oh yes! I mean, they are little kids, so I think that is pretty normal.

COUNSELOR: That's the fun side of being a mom. Is there any part that you would like to change?

CLIENT: I would like a little more help, I think.

COUNSELOR: You mean from your husband, Lucas?

CLIENT: Right. I just feel overwhelmed sometimes by having to do everything. I know I don't do it all, but sometimes it feels like that.

Based on the case material, can you detect some common patterns in the client's life? Probably most apparent is the fact that she enjoys being connected to other people. Isolation does not seem to be a common behavioral pattern for her. Along with her desire and ability to connect is a pattern of how she connects with others. In each of the areas, she reports being in the role of "helper." In her family of origin, she helped and is still helping her mom with the tension experienced with husband/father. In her friendships, she mediates disputes and provides other services. With her kids, she is the primary caretaker. Another evident pattern associated with her role can be seen in the emotions that are experienced as a result of that role. For the client, she experiences joy and a sense of belonging that is associated with being needed. Unfortunately, that feeling is often followed by a sense of being drained, exhausted, and overwhelmed. We hope this exercise has demonstrated how the use of external information can illuminate patterns. Although such information may seem like more than enough to establish some workable patterns, paying attention to experiences in the here and now can also provide clues to the client's world.

Here-and-Now Sources

The therapeutic relationship is a gold mine of pattern search opportunities provided that you have established a meaningful rapport with the client. As you learn about the client's external world, the primary thought on the counselor's mind should be, "How are these relationship dynamics occurring in our relationship?" For example:

> CLIENT: My husband and I don't get along very well. We really haven't for several years. I tend to go along with what he wants to do and never get my own way.
>
> COUNSELOR: It seems you give in but resent not being listened to. (Empathic reflection. Counselor notes relationship pattern and wonders how it will manifest in the counseling relationship.)
>
> CLIENT: Yes, that's it. I guess I suffer in silence. You are right, I want to be listened to, but I just suck it up and then hate him for pushing me around.
>
> COUNSELOR: I'm thinking about what that would look like in here. I haven't noticed that lately, but I wonder how I would know if you thought I was pushing you around? What would suffering in silence look like?
> (The counselor, having noticed the pattern, brings it into the here and now of the counseling relationship.)

In this example, the counselor is making use of a relationship pattern that has not yet appeared in counseling. Addressing it now allows the counselor and client to share responsibility for addressing it should it arise in the context of future sessions. Consider another example:

> CLIENT: My parents have always been there for me. It seems like whenever I stumble, there they are, ready to pitch in and rescue me from harm. It's been like that all my life, and here I am, at 40, and they are still taking bullets for me.
>
> COUNSELOR: It seems like you are ambivalent about their role. On the one hand, you appreciate their support, but on the other, you wonder if it's too much.
> (An empathic statement designed to get the client to go deeper. Counselor is also noting the pattern emergence of dependency on others and is thinking about how that pattern has manifested within the counseling sessions.)

CLIENT: Yeah, it's weird. I don't want to let go, but they don't either.

COUNSELOR: Tell me more about the fear of letting go.
(Empathic statement naming an emotion, fear.)

CLIENT: Well, I want the support, so it's scary to think about doing life all on my own. When I get scared, I get anxious, and when I get anxious, my parents get anxious and jump in to rescue me.

COUNSELOR: It seems like you use the anxiety as a signal of distress, so others will know you need help.
(Identifying the pattern.)

CLIENT: Yes, I think that's right.

COUNSELOR: I've noticed that in our relationship as well. You get very nervous and talk about anxiety when we address some topics. I wonder if you are letting me know you need help with those issues.
(Addressing the pattern in the context of the counseling relationship.)

CLIENT: Yes, I guess I do that, now that you mention it.

In this example, the counselor identifies the external relational pattern and discovers an example of how it is operating in the counseling relationship. By identifying it and using the counseling relationship as "evidence," the client and counselor now have a here-and-now testing laboratory for working on that pattern.

There are also times when the counselor will have a reaction to the client but does not have any information that the pattern exists outside of counseling. In this aspect of the counseling relationship, the counselor uses the contemporaneous counseling experience as a basis for hypothesizing about a possible pattern.

CLIENT: I'm sorry I missed last session. I got real busy and just forgot to call.

COUNSELOR: Well, as we have discussed, this is your time. If you make an appointment, it is your responsibility for coming and working.

CLIENT: I know. I know. Wow, you don't have to make me feel so guilty about it. You know, if you would call and remind me, that would help. You know how I tend to forget things.

COUNSELOR: You would like me to be responsible for your coming to counseling?

CLIENT: Well, I guess calling to remind me is a little much, but would it be too hard for you to call if I'm late? You know, to give me a little warning that I might have missed it? If you had called, I could have made the session. I'm only five minutes away.

COUNSELOR: Hmmm . . . that still feels like you wanting me to take responsibility for your stuff. When you make those suggestions, I have an internal pull to say, "OK, I'll do that." I'll have to monitor times when I feel that pull. I wonder if you have that effect on other people.

In addition to the use of the counseling relationship as a method of marking patterns, counselors also note dynamics in the client that may point to common threads of import. Tracking emotions, which ones appear and when they disappear, as well as tracking the cognitive and behavioral antecedents and corollaries is an effective pattern search strategy. Consider the following emotional patterns exhibited by clients:

> A 15-year-old boy tears up whenever the topic of his recently deceased father comes up. His sadness is immediately followed by squirming in the chair, face rubbing, and a desire to change the subject. He most often changes the subject to how angry he is with his mom's nagging.
>
> A 40-year-old man reports feeling anxious when discussing issues of intimacy. The anxiety manifests as fidgeting and increasing his rate of speech. Explorations into the anxiety and possible things he could do differently are met with blaming ("She just wanted me for my money") or boasting ("I could have anyone I wanted; why would I want her?").
>
> A 6-year-old girl in play therapy responds with fear every time an adult male toy is present in the room. She avoids the toys and through symbolic play discusses how the "little bunny rabbit is scared of the big bull." Following the emotional and behavioral pattern allows the counselor to discover elements of physical abuse in the child's home.

There are many methods for identifying the patterns in the life of the client. Once some common themes emerge, the client and counselor can begin to formulate goals for counseling. These goals will serve as the guidelines for assessing growth or stagnation in the counseling process.

Goal Setting

It is difficult to set realistic goals before you have a deep understanding of the client. That is the reason we put goal setting toward the end of this chapter. In essence, goal setting begins from the moment you first interact with the client, for relationship building is a goal, but it is rarely explicitly discussed in the counseling session. Other counseling activities such as assessment, diagnosis, and pattern search are all counseling goals, but they are not the reason the client is coming to counseling. These *counselor goals* must be met in order for the counselor to be in a position to fulfill the *client goals.* Having worked on the foundation of fulfilling the unspoken counselor goals, we can now turn our attention to the client goals as the threshold that will allow us to move toward change.

Whose Goal Is This Anyway? The Process of Goal Alignment

As patterns emerge, issues of import will seemingly become apparent to client and counselor. It is common at this stage to encounter several types of goals. They often break down into the following categories:

- *Client goals:* what the client wants to change
- *Counselor goals:* what the counselor believes should be changed
- *External participant goals:* what family members or other interested parties think the client should change

In the best possible scenario, all of the categories focus on the same goal. Unfortunately, that rarely happens. In most cases, slight variations exist in the exact nature of the desired change. The process of goal alignment allows for the counselor to dialogue with the client and find a goal that is reasonable and attainable from all perspectives. Consider the following case.

A 15-year-old boy enters counseling at the request of his parents. The parents are disturbed at the son's lack of responsibility for his schoolwork (grades have dropped), his family life (he refuses to do chores or participate in family time), and his behavior with friends (he has been in trouble for fighting). The son complains that his parents are smothering him and he just wants to be "completely free." He maintains that everything would be just fine if they just left him alone and let him do whatever he wanted. During rapport building and pattern search, the counselor learns that the parents typically "crack down" on all their children when they reach middle adolescence. The counselor also learns that prior to this year, the son's behavior had been, by all accounts, "responsible" (good grades, family participation, solid friendships).

Based on this case material, the following goals emerged:

- *Client (son) goal:* "Complete freedom. I want them to leave me alone."
- *External participant (parents) goal:* "Responsibility."
- *Counselor goal:* "Wow, this is difficult."

The counselor experiences difficulty because the goals seem so disparate and the counselor cannot really buy into the client's goal. For goal alignment to work, the counselor must have a good rapport with the client, characterized by an empathic connection with the client. The counselor must be willing and able to "see" beneath the client's goal, which can be accomplished only through empathic understanding. In addition to expressing empathy, the counselor must also discern the patterns at work in the client's life. Using these two elements, the counselor can facilitate goal alignment. Here is what it would look like in our example scenario.

The counselor looks beyond the son's desire for "absolute isolation" and combines it with an understanding of the client's interaction with the family before the disruption. The counselor hypothesizes that the client wants "independence" but not total independence. He wants some freedom and respect for his work and accomplishments. The parents also want him to take responsibility, but they are so smothering that the client feels like there is no hope of being treated as responsible. The counselor tests the idea:

> COUNSELOR: If you could create a schoolwork strategy that would get you the grades you wanted, what would it look like?
>
> CLIENT: I would do it all by myself. I wouldn't have my parents hawking over me all night.
>
> COUNSELOR: That sounds irritating. What do you do when they hawk over you?
>
> CLIENT: I give up.
>
> COUNSELOR: That probably drives them crazy! What happens to your schoolwork?
>
> CLIENT: It doesn't get done. I know I am hurting myself, but why should I do it if they are pestering me? If I do good, all they will say is, "See, without us, you would fail."
>
> COUNSELOR: So you are trying to show them that they are not helping you?
>
> CLIENT: Yeah, but that's not working very well either. They blame me either way.

The hypothesis has been tested, and a goal emerges that both parties can agree to:

- *Shared goal:* Increased responsibility *and* independence. The parents and client will formulate a plan on each of the concerns that allows the client to be primarily responsible for success. Definitions of each term, *responsibility* and *independence*, will be created so evaluation of progress can occur. As the client experiences success, the client will enjoy continued independence. If the client chooses irresponsible behavior, consequences (loss of independence) will result.

Although the entire counseling process would be much more detailed, the purpose here is to demonstrate how one can take goals that seem incongruent and use the power of empathy and pattern search to uncover a workable goal. Building on the foundation of the therapeutic relationship allows for the counselor to engage the client in goal formation and alignment. The deeper the connection, the better the patterns are illuminated. The more illuminated the patterns, the more meaningful and accurate the goal. The greater the meaning and accuracy of the goal, the better the opportunity for change to occur.

There are occasions when goal alignment is not possible. They often occur when clients are interested in pursuing a goal that does not fit with the skill or values set of the counselor. When the issue is a counselor skills deficit (e.g., the client wants to learn assertiveness skills and the counselor does not feel competent in that area), then a referral to an expert in that skill area is indicated. A conflict of values is a more serious problem. Hutchins and Vaught (1997, p. 150) list several client-based goals that cannot be "embraced" by counselors:

- The goal to harm self or others.
- The goal of developing or participating in behaviors incongruent with the counselors' belief system (learning ways to join a gang or hate group; wanting to learn how to better control and manipulate members of the opposite sex).
- The goal of learning unsafe or illegal practices (how to deal drugs, steal from your work without getting caught, or lose an unhealthy amount of weight).

The inability to accept individuals into counseling for reasons such as these rests on the fact that all of the examples represent a discordance between the client's values and those of counselors and the profession of counseling. Counselors who encounter clients expressing such goals can dialogue about the appropriateness of the stated goal. If the client is persistent, when necessary, counselors must then take steps to protect the client or others as dictated by ethical code and legal precedent. The clash in values creates an unviable foundation for empathy, and without the rapport, treatment will suffer. In the end, if the dissonance continues, the counselor recognizes that a referral to a different counselor is the most professional course of action.

Elements of a "Good" Counseling Goal

Now that you know the types of goals and how to align the goal when the types are incongruent, it is time to learn about formulating goals that have the best chance of producing change. Clients come into counseling with an idea of what they want to change but often have only vague notions of how to get there. Building a solid foundational therapeutic relationship, followed by a thorough search for patterns in the client's life, positions the counselor-client team to both identify goals and set a course to achieve them. However, setting an appropriate goal is sometimes more difficult than it seems. Cavanagh and Levitov (2002) outline the key elements of effective counseling goals.

- *Goals must be specific and measurable.* If you ask a client, "What would you like to have happen as a result of your work in counseling?" you will likely get the answer, "I want to be happy." Happy is nice, but it is not a good counseling goal at face value. Why? Well, the answer is because happy is vague and has many different definitions depending on whom you ask. To make "happy" a good counseling goal, we have to specify what happy looks like to the client. For example, the client may say, "Happy for me means fighting less with my husband over money." This is a specific definition of *happy,* and it can also be measured. The client can keep a log of conflicts with her husband over money and assess, day by day, whether or not she is achieving her goal.

- *Goals must be realistic.* Good counseling goals have a reasonable probability of attainment when the client's strengths and limitations are factored into the equation. Consider two men who enter counseling with the stated goal, "I want to increase my comfort in my intimate relationships so I can get married with less anxiety." Sounds good, right? The first man has been dating the same woman for three years and has been engaged for three months. The second man has a history of failed relationships and has not been in a serious relationship for two years and has no prospects. We hope you can see that the goal is more realistic for the first man as compared to the second client. An additional comment about realistic goals addresses the expectation for change. Realistic goals understand that change is a process, not an absolute. So, framing change in terms of "less anxiety" is more realistic than setting the goal as experiencing "no anxiety."
- *Goals are often hierarchal.* It is rare for a client to enter counseling with one goal. Usually, counseling goals are multifaceted and complex. When this occurs, it is important to work with the client to prioritize the goals. In many cases working on one goal leads to the emergence of another goal, or making progress on a goal makes it easier to then address another issue. For example, a high school junior may enter counseling to work on getting a full-time job for the summer. As you learn more about the client, you discover that the parents are opposed to him working because his grades have been slipping. Working on the goal of improving his academic performance and his relationship with his parents may take precedence over working on job exploration.
- *Goals must be evaluated frequently.* If you and your client have done all the difficult work in formulating a good counseling goal based on the elements discussed above, make sure you follow through and assess progress. One of the benefits of goal alignment is that the counseling has direction, which limits the feeling of wandering aimlessly through the sessions. Both client and counselor should participate equally in the evaluation process. When progress is not being made, it can be addressed openly, and if necessary, the goal should be realigned.

Summary

This chapter continues the process that began with rapport building. As the counselor connects with the client, more information becomes available and patterns emerge. There are many strategies for obtaining good information about the client. Assessment tools, diagnostic systems, and informal intake interviews all provide the counselor with data for pattern searching. The information streams depend largely on the empathic relationship between client and counselor; the more the client trusts the counselor, the more information is disclosed.

Counselors use these external sources of information to see themes in the client's life. The counselor can also use and compare the external information with the in-session behavioral and emotional patterns of the client. Using the counseling relationship provides an in vivo experience of the patterns and acclimates the client to the use of immediacy in the change process. Once some preliminary themes are identified, goal setting becomes a collaborative process that sets the stage for the work ahead.

Reflection Questions

1. Consider your own personal philosophy on the use of assessment. Under what conditions would you feel comfortable referring someone for psychological or vocational testing?
2. What are some patterns in your own life? How aware are you of your own patterns? What are some patterns that you have tried to change in your life? What was easy and difficult about changing?
3. What obstacles might interfere with good goal setting in counseling? How would you work with the client to overcome the resistance?

Chapter 8

HELPING CLIENTS CHANGE

By this time in your training, you have learned some skills and techniques for helping your clients move toward change. Chapters 6 and 7 outlined the first necessary steps for the process of therapeutic change. Developing and maintaining solid rapport and participating in thorough assessment and goal setting are activities that create an atmosphere conducive to producing change. Yet change is a nebulous concept. People are not machines, for which we can easily diagnose the problem, apply a specific tool, and guarantee a positive result. Various schools of thought and numerous counseling theories supply us with philosophical and scientific explanations of how people develop, become maladjusted, and use counseling to change. The fact that there are so many different theories of how to help people change should tip you off that change is not a concrete dynamic. It is beyond the scope of this chapter to address the many facets and nuances of change, but we can outline specific spheres of change and common client resistance to the change process.

BASIC CONSIDERATIONS IN CHANGE

According to Beitman (1987), "The process of change takes place in a number of contexts. . . . The psychotherapeutic contexts include the strength of the therapeutic alliance and the specificity of the patterns identified for change" (p. 173). This quotation serves as a reminder that counseling is a cyclic process, not a linear one. You do not "achieve" rapport, graduate to pattern search and goal setting, and then move on to change. Instead, each element builds and feeds the others. As the move toward change quickens, two important concepts emerge: *responsibility* and *practice.*

Responsibility

Every counseling theory since the time of Freud includes personal responsibility as a major philosophical underpinning. From a basic standpoint, human beings have the capacity to be aware of their responsibility for their own thoughts, feelings, and behavior. As a result, people are ultimately accountable for the choice to change those aspects of the self. Clients intuitively understand this notion. Just watch the multitude of heads nodding when the television therapist Dr. Phil says, "You cannot change what you do not acknowledge." Consider the two following case examples and assess which client will have the better chance of producing a positive change.

Case 1

Nicole is a 15-year-old student who entered counseling at the urging of her parents. Nicole is not doing well in school. In fact, over the past 6 months, her grades have dropped considerably. During the session, although she is initially hesitant, she discloses that she has been struggling both socially and academically. Her best friend moved about 8 months ago, and that loss has left her feeling isolated. She reports that she is having trouble focusing on her schoolwork and feels very sad. She states, "School is my job, and I know I am not working up to my potential. I feel bad that my parents are so confused about what's going on with me. I want to try to get over this and do better."

Case 2

Jeff is a 40-year-old physician in counseling due to relationship problems with his wife of 15 years. Jeff reports that he works long hours and has a very demanding job. He seems proud that he provides financially for his family and keeps them in a comfortable lifestyle. He resents the fact that his wife is so unhappy after all he does for her and the kids. He admits that the nature of his work keeps him away from the family almost every day and sometimes he just sleeps at the hospital when he is on call, which is every other week. He understands that his absence is "not ideal" but chalks it up to the "trade-off for the type of life I am giving them." Jeff states, "I don't see what the problem is. If you ask me, she needs to learn to quit spending money, and then maybe I wouldn't have to work so hard."

After carefully considering each case, you deduced, we hope, that Nicole has a much better probability of changing than Jeff does. Even though both clients entered counseling at the request of a third party, Nicole has the awareness and willingness to accept responsibility for change. Jeff is too busy blaming others and rationalizing the issues. While the end of Nicole's case provides hope for the next step in the counseling process, the end of Jeff's case is met with feelings of hopelessness and stagnation.

Practice

Once the client assumes responsibility for change, practicing the change must occur on a consistent basis. Often, the practicing of new ways of thinking, feeling, and behaving take place within the safety of the counseling session. As the change becomes more comfortable, the client may begin to experiment with the change in other relationships, bringing the feedback to counseling to process. This "fine-tuning" is essential to the change process because it solidifies the change by encouraging continued practice and adapting the change to meet the unique needs of the client's world.

Changes in Cognition, Affect, and Behavior

An examination of the major theories of counseling will highlight the fact that change through counseling is viewed as occurring in three primary spheres: *cognition* (thoughts), *affect* (feelings), and *behavior.* Depending on the theory, one sphere may be more strongly emphasized than the others. It is the human equivalent of the chicken-and-egg conundrum. If you change your thoughts, will that produce change in feeling and behavior? Can you enjoy lasting improvements in your behavior without modifying your thoughts? Does moderating the intensity of your emotional state have an impact on the way you think or behave? All of these questions, and more, are the same queries about how best to help people change. We believe the "correct" answer is a holistic approach. The best guess is that all three spheres are important in the change process, and competent counselors focus on the consistency among all three within the movement of the client. The following sections explore some ways to facilitate change in each of the spheres while providing commentary on how emphasizing one sphere also impacts the others.

Focus on Cognitive Change

The basic premise of therapies that focus on cognitive change is that thoughts greatly influence how we feel and behave. Theories that emphasize cognitive restructuring or changes in belief systems view thoughts as the primary mediating variable in the change process. Figure 8.1 on the following page depicts a simple cognitive cycle, and Figure 8.2 on p. 127 illustrates a model from rational emotive behavior therapy (REBT) that pinpoints beliefs rather than thoughts. Both models represent the idea that cognitions and their modification are the most effective pathways to change. In each of the figures, you can see the impact that thoughts have on the other spheres of feelings and behavior.

Figure 8.1 A Cognitive Cycle

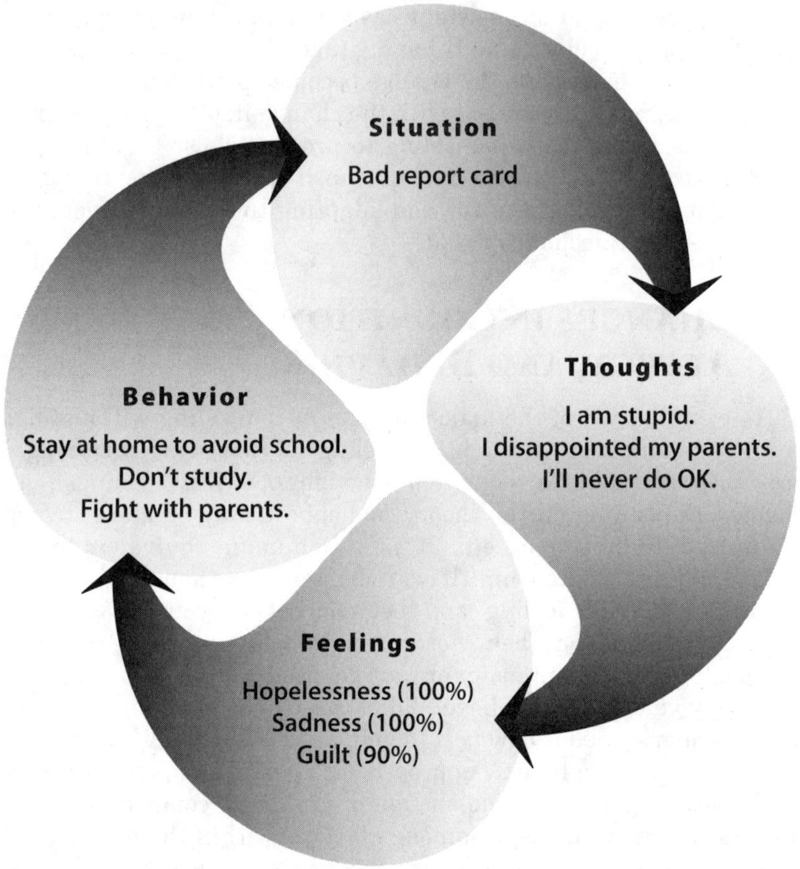

Cognitive change occurs when we challenge the way we think about situations. In counseling, strategies such as cognitive restructuring, disputing, confrontation, and teaching clients self-talk techniques are all examples of some cognitive change strategies. Figures 8.3 (on p. 128) and 8.4 (on p. 129) take the examples used in the previous figures and illustrate both cognitive interventions and the change produced.

Focus on Affective Change

In chapter 6, we discussed the importance of the therapeutic relationship and the role of empathy. Provided that the counselor has forged an alliance with the client, the relationship can be the foundation for continued emotional exploration and growth. Throughout the change process, empathy should be fostered to maintain the relationship and help the client connect with emotional content. In addition to empathy as a method for affective change, two other skills, *normalization* and *working through,* are common methods for helping clients facilitate a new way of experiencing feelings.

Figure 8.2 ABC Model

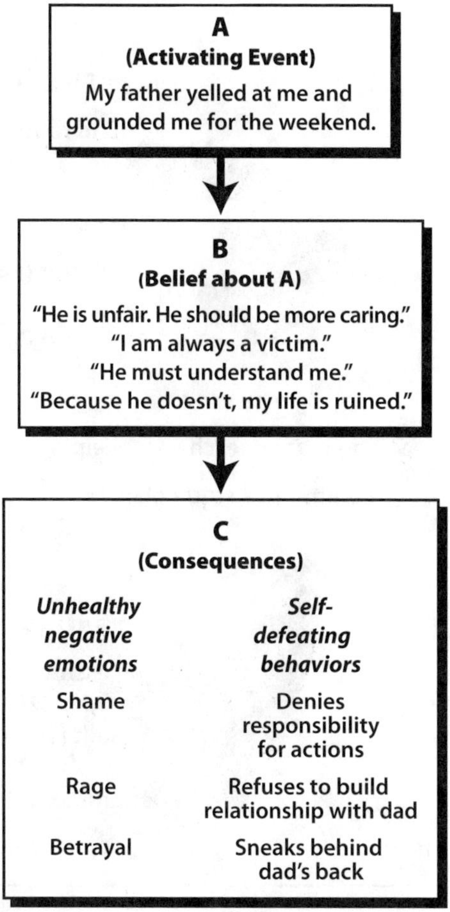

Example from Fall, Holden, & Marquis (2004).

Normalization. Any change is, by definition, a new experience, and new is not always comfortable. In fact, it is often awkward and painful. As new feelings emerge, the client may experience the surfacing emotions as alien or "not normal" and may try to ignore them or make them go away. Counselors can facilitate the client's integration of the changes in affect by helping the client accept the new feelings as "normal." Consider the following case dialogue:

CLIENT: As I have explored my relationship with my sister, I realize that I have been protecting her all these years by not telling her what I really think and how I really feel.

COUNSELOR: You realize that you haven't been genuine with her.

CLIENT: Right! I haven't been myself.

COUNSELOR: I understand that you chose not to share your feelings with her out of an effort to protect her and that maybe you felt it wasn't safe, but I wonder if you, as a first step, might be willing to share those true feelings here?

CLIENT: I think I can do that . . . um . . . I guess when I think about it, I feel a lot of anger toward her . . . frustration.

COUNSELOR: Yes, some anger, and I also sense some resentment.

Figure 8.3 Cognitive Cycle with Change

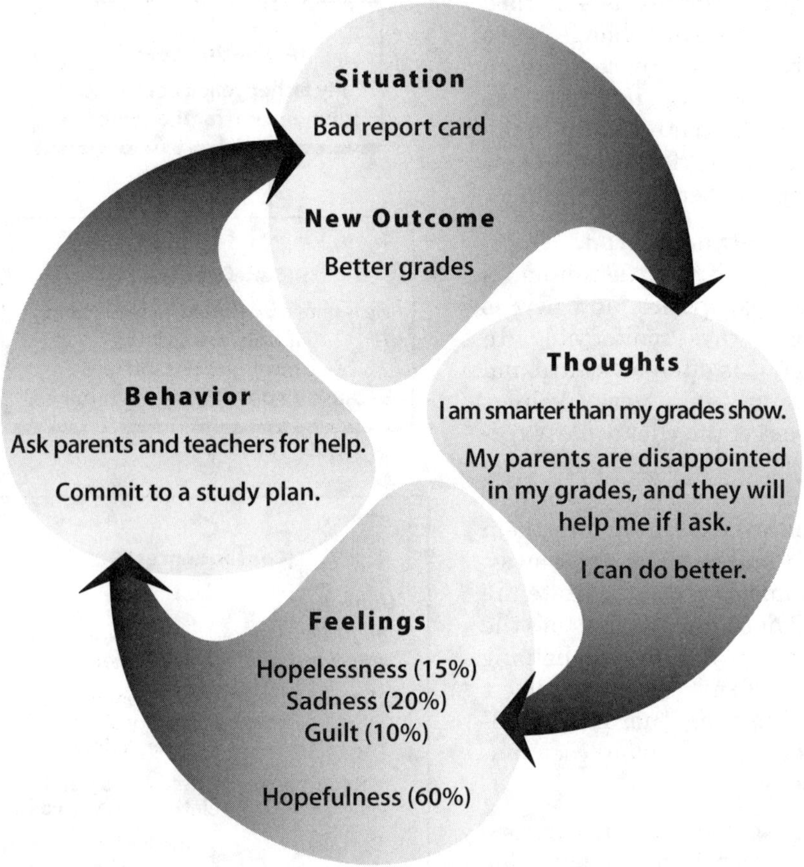

CLIENT: Yes! That's it. Resentment. Wow, that feels really weird to me. I want to push it back.

COUNSELOR: That desire to lock the feeling up again is completely natural considering your competing desire to protect you sister. You are afraid your resentment will hurt her.

CLIENT: Yeah, that's why I don't show it. But when I lock it up, it just gets worse.

COUNSELOR: Because the resentment represents your true feelings at the moment, and the pattern of stuffing those feelings is very natural for you, maybe we can practice experiencing the resentment and work on ways for you to disclose those feelings in a way that is comfortable to you.

CLIENT: That sounds good.

Figure 8.4 ABC Model of Intervention

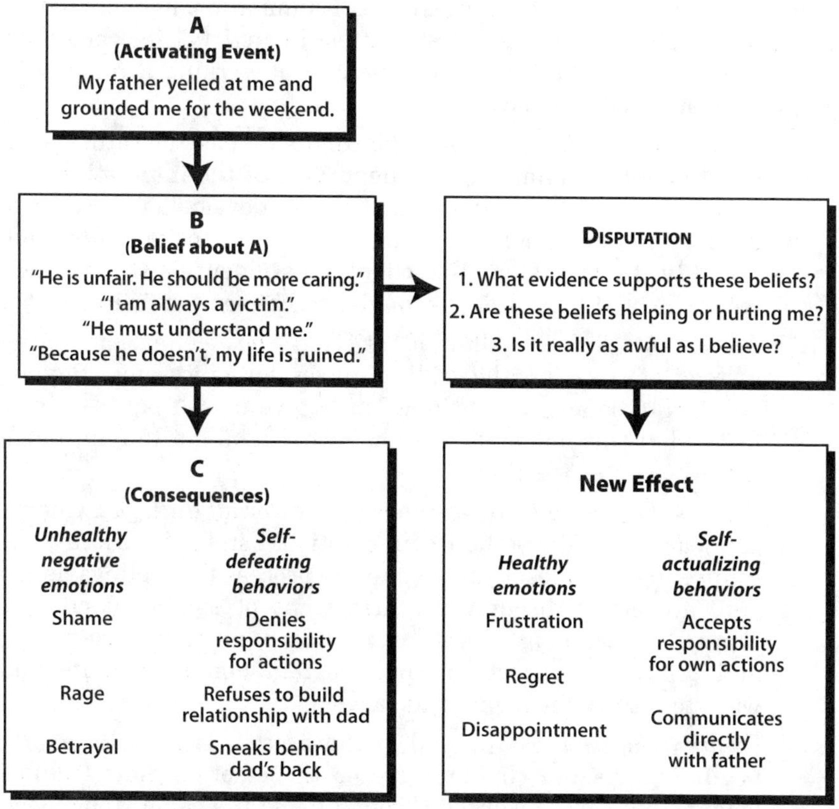

Example from Fall, Holden, & Marquis (2004).

In this example, the client is getting in touch with a new emotion. The counselor has done an effective job of exploring the patterns in the client's life, and as the new emotion emerges, both client and counselor make sense of it based on the pattern. In this case, the new feeling of resentment has been buried as a result of the client's pattern of protecting her sister. As the new feeling surfaces, the client wants to respond based on the old pattern and submerge the emotion, but the counselor illuminates the pattern and normalizes, or legitimates, the feeling in order to facilitate a new way of experiencing the emotion. In the end, the counselor uses the normalizing and pattern identification as a way to encourage and invite the client to practice working through the resentment.

Working through. In working through one's emotions, people get a sense of the process of emotional regulation. Anxiety and its associated problems are a good example of this dynamic. Anxiety is a natural part of existence and in and of itself is not dysfunctional. However, when clients get stuck in anxiety, rumination and escalation occur. As one client mentioned, "getting lost in anxiety" does not allow for working through the feeling. The process of working through feelings can be outlined as follows:

1. *Identify the feeling.* This may be relatively easy or rather difficult to do, depending on the client. One of the interesting outcomes of emotional change is that clients develop a new sense of comfort and an expanded awareness of the continuum of emotionality. In this step, the client must identify the emotion before he or she can work through and change the feeling state.
2. *Accept the feeling.* After identifying the feeling, accepting instead of resisting the feeling allows for processing. Saying, "It's OK to be angry right now," or "I give myself permission to feel sad at this moment," may help the client get fully in touch with the current feeling.
3. *Process the feeling through internal or external dialogue.* Clients can learn to mediate their own emotional states internally, but counseling provides a safe avenue to process the feelings as clients are going through the first steps of emotional change. Through processing, clients can explore emotional, cognitive, and behavioral aspects of their current emotional state and ways to modify the feelings as needed.
4. *Identify the feeling.* The end of the process is actually a new beginning. As the client processes the emotion, new feelings emerge and can be worked through using the same steps. Seen this way, working through is a growth model of change that is cyclic and layered.

Focus on Behavioral Change

Behavioral change refers to adaptations in the client's actions. Modifying behavior can be seen as a pathway to change, such as a client gaining relief from a paralyzing fear of snakes through being in the presence of snakes (the change was the decrease in fear, and the behavior of exposure was the necessary step), or as the element needing the change, as with a client who cannot find a job because he or she lacks some specific social skills. In either instance, the importance of *doing* something different becomes a vital part of the change process.

Behavioral rehearsal allows clients to practice with new sets of skills and deal with the coexisting cognitions and feelings that may arise but are often representative of the old patterns. Cormier and Hackney (1999, p. 143) note that rehearsal is most often used in three main ways:

1. The client possesses a skills deficit ("response acquisition").
2. The client possesses the requisite skills but has difficulty discerning between appropriate and inappropriate times to use the skills ("response facilitation").
3. The client's emotional or cognitive responses are interfering with the productive application of the new skills ("response disinhibition").

Each of these types of behavioral rehearsal domains requires different, but sometimes overlapping, counseling strategies. For example, response acquisition may include techniques that impart information and expose the client to new skill sets. In addition to a more active teaching component, the counselor may also process cognitive and affective responses to the new skills.

In response facilitation, the counselor may use the uncovered patterns to provide the client with insight as to why the client is misapplying the skills. Within this approach the counselor may use empathy, confrontation, and hypothesizing about alternative strategies as a way of working through the issue. Consider the case of the woman who is seeking help with forming a satisfactory relationship. She complains that she finds only men who are controlling and dominating. Through the counseling process, she realizes that in the foundational portion of the relationship, she acts dumb and submissive. Her underlying belief is that "men won't like me if I have an opinion." She possesses the skills to connect with people, but her method is faulty. A behavioral intervention would consider the cognitive and emotional issues surrounding the old and new strategy of connecting with possible partners.

In response disinhibition, counselors will process in depth the emotional and cognitive factors associated with the problematic behavior. Using operant and classical conditioning techniques, the behavior change will be used to moderate the intense emotional and cognitive reactions. Common examples of this form of rehearsal include treatment for anxiety disorders such as panic disorder and simple phobia.

A Model Tying It All Together

Based on your practical experience and formal education, you probably understand that change is not an easy dynamic to sum up in a few pages. In fact, you will spend a great deal of your professional life trying to answer the question, "Why did Client A change, but Client B did not?" We believe that focusing on the basic elements we have discussed in this chapter will provide you with some guidance in facilitating change. Prochaska and colleagues have developed one of the most comprehensive and practical transtheoretical models of change (see Prochaska, DiClemente, & Norcross, 1992; Prochaska et al., 1994; Prochaska & Norcross, 2002). You likely have already been exposed to this model, but if you have not, it should be a good method of integrating the elements of change.

In the transtheoretical model, change progresses through six stages: precontemplation, contemplation, preparation, action, maintenance, and termination. Each stage requires different methods to produce change. This process honors the progression that we have discussed in chapters 6 and 7 and will continue in chapter 9. The unique and attractive element of this model is that it not only emphasizes the emotional, cognitive, and behavioral aspects of change but also helps explain why clients get stuck in the change process. In the most primary sense, stagnation or resistance arises from two primary sources:

1. The client is not personally convinced (emotionally, cognitively, and/or behaviorally) that change is as beneficial as not changing.
2. The counselor is not functioning at the same stage as the client. Remember the old counseling adage, "Meet the client where the client is." Counselors who are interacting with a client with action stage elements when the client is functioning at the precontemplation stage will encounter a lot of resistance. At the same time, a counselor who is moving too slowly, performing at contemplation when the client is ready for action stage change, will experience frustration on the part of the client.

As a way to summarize the change process, we have included Table 8.1 to outline the stages of change and provide some concrete examples of how to match counselor activity to client readiness for change.

Table 8.1 Stages of Change

Stage of Change	Counselor Strategies	Typical Resistance
Precontemplation		
Client is not fully acknowledging need for change. Client may not feel the capacity or desire for change.	Initiate rapport building. Practice active listening: reflection of feeling and content. Focus on gaining an empathic connection and understanding of the client. Begin information gathering. Elicit client's perspective on what he/she views as problem areas in current living.	Because the client does not see a reason to change, the client may prematurely leave counseling. Counselor may get frustrated with the client at this level and may attempt to confront and push the client to the next stage.

Stage of Change	Counselor Strategies	Typical Resistance
Contemplation		
Client is identifying areas for change but expresses ambivalence about the need and/or desire to change.	Continue to focus on rapport building and empathy. Begin pattern search utilizing open and directed exploration of identified issues. Incorporate assessment and diagnosis to further illuminate patterns. *Emotional Sphere:* Continue to reflect feelings, normalize the ambivalence. *Cognitive Sphere*: Explore thoughts related to ambivalence, create a cost-benefit analysis of changing and not changing. *Behavioral Sphere*: Explore behavioral elements of changing, emphasize aspects of personal responsibility to stay or move.	Client may view own ambivalence as a sign of not being ready for change and may leave counseling. Client may decide that the benefits of not changing outweigh the benefits of changing. Counselor may view ambivalence as a negative emotion and may ignore the advantages of not changing or the disadvantages of changing. This could lead to the client feeling misunderstood, which could produce empathic failure and increased chance of client dropout.
Preparation		
Client assumes responsibility for the issues and patterns identified but is unsure about how the change will take place.	Continue rapport building. Use information gathered at this stage to confirm/strengthen identified patterns or identify new patterns. *Emotional Sphere:* Continue empathic understanding, encourage the client to begin to work through the emotional change process, usually first by identifying emotions and allowing self to feel; ambivalence will expand to include other feelings related to the possibility of changing or remaining the same. *Cognitive Sphere*: Begin to identify the thoughts that will promote change; delve deep into the thoughts that produce dysfunction and learn primary methods for modifying those thoughts.	Client may confuse the inherent anxiety associated with change with an alarm signal of impending danger. This confusion may lead the client to conclude that change is "doing the wrong thing." Counselor may get so excited that the client is demonstrating a willingness to change that counselor pushes for change too quickly without fully exploring the stage. Moving too quickly may result in a lack of goal attainment, which often leads to discouragement on the part of both the counselor and the client.

(continued)

Stage of Change	Counselor Strategies	Typical Resistance
	Behavioral Sphere: Develop specific goals for change; identify collection of new actions that are distinct from the old behaviors; hypothesize what might be needed in terms of skill to make the proposed change.	
Action		
Client begins to practice the new ways of feeling, thinking, and behaving.	Continue rapport building. Use your knowledge of client patterns to assess whether the client is really moving in a different direction. Assess external threats and supports for the client's change. Use homework to allow the client to work on and document changes outside of the counseling hour. *Emotional Sphere*: Fully engage the client in normalizing and working through emotions as they emerge in counseling. *Cognitive Sphere*: Help the client challenge unhealthy cognitions and create and reinforce change-related thoughts. *Behavioral Sphere*: Provide opportunity for appropriate use of the methods of rehearsal, beginning first in counseling and branching out into the "real world."	Client may not get change "fast enough" and may feel like it is too much work. This is viewed as a move back to an earlier stage in the model. Although it is common for ambivalence to temporarily increase, the counselor can track the client back, apply the stage-appropriate strategy, and facilitate movement. Counselor must make sure to set specific and appropriate goals. If the goal was vague or too complex, the action can stall.
Maintenance		
Client is working on making the change the new consistent way of being.	Support emotional, cognitive, and behavioral change. Troubleshoot problems that arise. Review goals and prepare for termination.	Counselor may see this as an "easy" stage of counseling with regard to resistance. Client may feel "I'm done" and leave counseling without terminating.

SUMMARY

Change is a complex dynamic. It is not a static stage but is instead a function of how well the counselor-client team prepared for change based on the quality of the therapeutic relation, identified patterns, and goal setting. Once the momentum for change builds, counselor and client can infuse the process with a sense of personal responsibility and desire to make the change consistent through practice. Although how and why people change is an elusive concept, considering and promoting change through the spheres of cognition, emotion, and behavior provide both counselor and client with a holistic view of the change process. We also encourage you to consider the model discussed as a way to conceptualize where the client is in the change process and as a reminder that identifying the client's stage in the process is often the most important element in facilitating change.

REFLECTION QUESTIONS

1. Discuss your own personal experience with change. What are some aspects of your life that were easy to change? Why? What are some areas of your life that have been difficult to change? Why?
2. What does *responsibility* mean to you? How will you help facilitate responsibility in your clients?
3. Many practitioners emphasize one sphere of change over the others. Which sphere or spheres of change do you feel are more conducive to change? What does your theory of counseling emphasize?

Chapter 9

TERMINATION

Throughout the course of your training, you have learned a great deal about the process of counseling. How to build rapport, set goals, and facilitate attainment of the client's goals are all part of the natural flow of counseling. You have also spent some time learning about the process of *termination,* that is, the portion of the counseling when goals have been achieved and counseling is "over." In a sense, you learned the traditional "story line" of counseling: Client enters counseling, client connects with counselor, client works toward change, change occurs, and counseling ends. Although you will experience natural modifications in that story line due to client factors, the structure of the internship experience creates a plot twist at the termination phase that many students and clients do not anticipate.

Internships are limited-time contract jobs that seem to structurally contradict what you learned about the importance of the counseling relationship; namely, that the relationship should find its own flow with a mutually created process that ends when goals have been identified and achieved. The reality for most interns is that they leave when the internship is over, often leaving the clients to pursue their mental health needs with the next wave of interns that are placed at that site. In settings that have a high counselor turnover rate, perhaps due to one-semester commitments, clients may endure several counselor transitions during their time of self-growth and healing. These transitions may be a normal function of receiving treatment in a teaching facility, but the impact on the clientele needs careful attention by the counselor interns and supervisors.

Keeping in mind that the primary responsibility of any clinician is the well-being of the client, termination is viewed as an important part of the therapeutic process. Termination emphasizes the growth that has occurred, the areas of concern that still exist, and the methods of future support. Balancing classroom learning about the termination process and clinical reality can often be confusing. One student commented:

> During our classroom training, we always discussed termination from the perspective that the client was terminating. Most of my clients needed further counseling, so it was weird to leave them. It felt like abandonment in many ways, even though I knew that I had done a good job of referring them to other counselors.

To make these transitions as ethical and as client focused as possible, this chapter emphasizes steps you can take to ensure appropriate termination and referral. To make sense of the elements of termination, this chapter will address termination issues related to clients, supervision, and self.

Facilitating Termination: When Does It Begin?

Let us cover the nonpersonal, structural issues of termination first as a way to ease you into the termination process. One question that seems to come up for most students is, "I understand the importance of termination, but when is a good time to start the discussion?" Most counselors are competent in the assessment of changes in their clients as a way to evaluate appropriateness of termination, but we must also be aware of counselor factors in termination, such as the end of an internship.

As an intern, you should inform all clients of your student status and any time limitations that status may have on the counseling process. Informing clients allows the client to give informed consent for counseling, but it also begins the dialogue about termination. Once the initial parameters are discussed, termination becomes a process issue. Although technically you could continue to discuss termination from the first session, we believe the best guideline is to make sure you discuss termination with enough time for both you and the client to process the relevant issues involved. Clients with issues of loss or abandonment may need more time to process the change, whereas other clients may do well with an advance discussion three or four weeks before the termination date. In other words, the artificial relationship parameter of time may be more integrally woven into the counseling issues for some clients than for others.

During the termination phase, it is important to process all the important elements necessary for a healthy good-bye. Marx and Gelso (1987, p. 7) researched client-initiated termination and outlined a complete termination as covering three main themes: "looking back (reviewing counseling and goal attainment), looking ahead (setting an ending date and discussing future plans), and saying good-bye (sharing feelings about ending)." The same themes will be present in counselor-initiated termination, but the feelings of the client may be slightly different and provide a unique therapeutic challenge. The following section will discuss typical client reactions and possible counselor responses.

Client Reactions and Counselor Responses

Research on the topic of termination reports that this phase is a critical time for both client and counselor (Gelso & Woodhouse, 2002; Paniagua, 2002; Roe, Dekel, Harel, Fennig, & Fennig, 2006). Intense feelings, both positive and negative, emerge as treatment comes to an end. Learning about the possible dynamics inherent in termination can help the counselor process internal struggles and thereby enhance this stage as well as anticipate possible client reactions to ending counseling. Unfortunately, most of the past research has dealt specifically with the traditional story line of termination: client has achieved goals and promotes the idea of termination. Internship adds a unique wrinkle to termination, and thus we need to consider the associated feelings at a slightly different angle.

Clients may experience counselor-initiated termination in a variety of ways. In fact, the same client may cycle through many emotions as the themes of change, loss, and growth resonate with the client's own experiences and ways of perceiving the world. We believe it is important to honor all possible client emotions and provide enough time for the various feelings to emerge. In this section we will cover the common client reactions to termination and provide tips on how the counselor can respond. Once again, keep in mind that clients may experience one, some, or all of these responses, so the counselor must be prepared to process whatever occurs.

Indifference, or "I Don't Care if You Leave"

Clients may respond with indifference for a variety of reasons; maybe they were not invested deeply in the relationship, maybe they approach all relationships with a sense of superficiality, or it could be a way to safeguard themselves from the pain associated with saying good-bye. For clients who have experienced difficulty sharing feelings, the unexpected emotions surrounding termination can be confusing and scary. The easiest way for them to manage the discomfort is to act as though the feelings do not exist.

Counselors confronted with indifference need to first check their internal response to the client. You may feel hurt by the client's lack of caring and therefore may feel the need to make the client care or, worse, may withdraw from the client and assume that the issue of termination no longer needs to be addressed. Understanding that the client's response is both reflective of the feelings regarding termination *and* the client's own issues can help the counselor facilitate exploration of the feeling at both levels. Consider the following dialogue as an example of multilevel processing.

> COUNSELOR: It seems like you feel disconnected from me and the notion of me leaving.
>
> CLIENT: Yeah, I mean, it's not like you cared about me anyway.
>
> COUNSELOR: I'm wondering if you would be willing to talk about that feeling a little more. It seems like it wouldn't feel good to think someone didn't care.
>
> CLIENT: No, I guess it doesn't.
>
> COUNSELOR: Good-byes are difficult. I'm wondering about other good-byes in your life and what they have been like for you.
>
> CLIENT: Pretty awful, I guess. Usually people leave without even saying good-bye . . . like my mom when she died.
>
> COUNSELOR: Yes, I know that was particularly painful for you and how you protect yourself from the pain by pretending to not care. I can also see how important it is for you to be able to say good-bye in a healthy or different way. Maybe that's something we can work on in the next few weeks.

The counselor in this dialogue used basic empathic statements to move between present and past feelings regarding termination. It is rare for indifference to be the real emotion regarding termination. Instead, it is the "safe" emotion; one that protects the client from experiencing the deeper feeling. Creating an open space for reflective dialogue can help the client process and may help facilitate other feelings about termination.

Anger, or "I Hate You for Leaving Me"

Some clients erupt in anger over the notion that you are leaving. Anger can be a method for controlling others (trying to get you to stay), a way of controlling self (inhibiting emotions underlying the anger, such as fear or pain), or a genuine commentary on the counselor's lack of information about the termination process. Penn (1990) notes that the anger can be expressed as hostility toward counseling and the counselor, such as stating, "I should have known better than to accept a trainee. Maybe next time I'll get a real counselor."

Most often, it seems that clients who respond with anger have experienced abandonment and hoped that you would be different. Counselors must pay attention to their own reactions to anger. In our discussions with supervisees, fear of anger always tops the list of supervisee concerns. Responding to the client with fear or anger can shut down the process and inhibit proper resolution. Once again, blending the two levels (counseling issues and personal issues) is indicated, as demonstrated in the following dialogue.

> CLIENT: Well, that's just great! You're going to leave just when I was beginning to open up. This sucks. I can't believe you're doing this to me.
>
> COUNSELOR: I can see you are very angry about this. Can you tell me more about what you said about opening up?
>
> CLIENT: It just seems like I was sharing deep stuff about me . . . and now you are just leaving.
>
> COUNSELOR: So, it's like you trusted me enough to share and it seems like my leaving is disrespecting that. Almost like a betrayal.
>
> CLIENT: Yes! That's exactly it. I never thought of it as betrayal, but that is what it feels like. It's like I invested in something and you are just walking away like it doesn't even matter.
>
> COUNSELOR: It reminds me quite a bit of the feelings you had during your divorce.
>
> CLIENT: No . . . not really. Well, maybe. I do remember feeling betrayed and blindsided by my spouse.
>
> COUNSELOR: And you feel blindsided by me.
>
> CLIENT: Well, no. I knew this was coming, but I guess I still felt like you might stay.
>
> COUNSELOR: Although I can't stay, maybe we can keep working on this issue to come to a better understanding of the feelings involved.

In the dialogue, the counselor responds to the anger in an open, nondefensive way, which allows the client to explore not only the anger but also the additional feelings of surprise and betrayal. The acceptance of the anger and the processing of the underlying emotions create a separate layer of learning, whereby the client can experience the healthy expression of anger that fosters relational growth rather than acting as a destructive force. The open processing also helps tie in personal issues that parallel the counseling issues involving termination.

Hopelessness, or "I Will Never Get Better if You Leave"

Hopelessness is a common client response to termination that leaves both the client and the counselor in a precarious situation. Clients who present with hopelessness will often intensify their symptoms as a way to prolong the therapeutic relationship. The exacerbation of symptoms is bad enough, but it is often accompanied with a stated or implied feeling that the client is not in control or responsible for change but is instead in the hands of the counselor. Counselors are particularly vulnerable to this dynamic, as it kicks in our natural desire to help. If counselors do not monitor their reactions to hopelessness, they risk committing a number of therapeutic mistakes, from taking responsibility for the client's symptoms to prolonging the therapy. The following dialogue illustrates how counselors can address the issues of hopelessness and facilitate responsibility in the client.

COUNSELOR: You are feeling hopeless, like your change will stop if this relationship ends.

CLIENT: Yeah . . . I just feel like I won't be able to keep the momentum going.

COUNSELOR: Tell me more about the loss of momentum.

CLIENT: You have been so instrumental in helping me change, pushing me to do things differently. I just feel like with you not there, I'll just fall back. I am already starting to feel worse and you aren't even gone.

COUNSELOR: I can understand how you might feel like this change will impact you, but I'm wondering about the part you've played in your change process. Where do you see yourself in the momentum?

CLIENT: I really don't know.

COUNSELOR: I see this as a two-person team. You do your part and I do mine. I can see that you are paying attention to my part, but where are you in the process?

CLIENT: Well, since you put it that way, I do work in here. I think about the things we talk about outside of therapy and I use them.

COUNSELOR: I agree. It seems like although my part may change, your part can stay the same. Even more, your role is the more active of the two, the real "workhorse," if you will . . . (both laugh).

CLIENT: I see your point, but I still feel sad that you're leaving.

COUNSELOR: The sadness and ways to manage the change are certainly some things we can continue to talk about.

Hopefulness, or "I Think It's Time for Me to Do This on My Own"

We all hope that our clients will respond with hopefulness to termination, and occasionally it occurs. However, most often we must work through other feelings such as those discussed previously, and if we process those effectively, then perhaps hopefulness will be the counselor and client reward. Hopefulness is characterized by a sense that the client has a firm grasp on the reins of personal change. If the client is able to be accountable for change, forward movement is possible, and it also opens the dialogue to possible future areas of work and how to access counseling when needed. The following example illuminates the feeling of hopefulness.

COUNSELOR: So, you feel like this might be a good place for you to stop as well.

CLIENT: Yeah, I mean, I knew you were leaving at the end of the semester, and I've been preparing for it. I tried to make good use of my time in here.

COUNSELOR: Right. You recognized the boundary and responded to it in a way that was helpful to you. Is that approach different for you?

CLIENT: Absolutely! Before, I think I would have just given up halfway through. I would have blamed you.

COUNSELOR: It must feel empowering to do something different, to recognize that your past patterns weren't working and decide to change.

CLIENT: I think so. I definitely think I can take that and use it in other areas of my life.

COUNSELOR: Tell me about the ways you see it applying.

CLIENT: Oh sure . . . like with my relationship with my son. To realize that we both have responsibilities to maintain the relationship. If I don't like something that's going on with us, I can always blame him, but it's healthier for me to voice my concerns and be willing to make some changes myself.

COUNSELOR: I know that insight took a lot of work on your part. What are some means of support you can access if you feel in a bind again?

CLIENT: I think I'm feeling so strong now that I won't ever go back to where I was.

COUNSELOR: I can appreciate that. I'm not talking about finding yourself in the same place, but more about what supports that you can access so you don't go to a similar or completely different uncomfortable space.

In this example, the counselor validates the client's sense of hope while also exploring avenues for future help. The process allows the client to feel a sense of responsibility for change and also works to address the possibility that the hope may diminish at times, but the client still has access to support.

As the feelings associated with termination are explored, both counselor and client can look ahead to the options available to the client after the counselor leaves. The next section provides an overview of the steps of a well-balanced referral system.

STAGES AND ISSUES OF SUCCESSFUL REFERRAL

As the time to terminate nears, one important consideration is whether a referral is indicated for each of your clients. Referral is a vital aspect of termination and represents your ethical responsibility to not abandon your clients. This section outlines three distinct steps to ensure a responsible approach to referral: (a) deciding which clients need a referral and why, (b) making the referral for those who need it, and (c) easing the referred client's transition.

Determining Need for Referral

Not all of your clients will require or desire a referral. For some clients, adequately processing the feelings associated with termination will result in the client feeling that it is time for a break from counseling. We advocate for the referral decision to be a collaborative process that includes counselor assessment, client assessment of self, and an exploration of alternatives.

The counselor must assess the client's strengths and progress as well as areas of concern. Counselors can review progress toward stated goals, symptom intensity, and social support as elements that might help the counselor decide whether a referral is needed. Having done this assessment, the counselor should be prepared to discuss the findings with the client.

The counselor should also ask the client to self-evaluate progress and what work is left to be done. Clients can provide keen insight into issues that still remain and can be helpful in planning additional care. We think that the more involved they are in the process, the more commitment they will have to the referral process.

Differences in assessment between counselor and client should be discussed and worked through. In the end, four outcomes are possible:

1. Client and counselor agree that no referral is needed.
2. Client and counselor agree that a referral is needed.
3. Client and counselor disagree because client wants a referral, but counselor does not think it is needed.
4. Client and counselor disagree because counselor wants to refer, but client does not think referral is needed.

The first two outcomes are not a problem, and although a possibility, the third one is highly unlikely. The only problematic outcome is when the counselor assesses the client as needing further help, but the client refuses. Although it is awkward, the counselor should explore the underlying feelings related to the client's position. If the client refuses help and the counselor continues to believe a referral is necessary, the ethical strategy is to inform the client of the referral options and let the client know that it is his or her choice to follow up or not. Make sure you document the referral.

If you both agree that a referral is not needed, then you are free to work through termination of treatment. If you both feel a referral is needed, you must then discuss referral options. During this part, the counselor collaborates with the client to find a good match. If other counselors are available at the current placement, explore whether your client is comfortable with that option. Due to limits of availability or other factors, you may have to consider other sites. Discuss this option with your client along with the associated factors of travel time, cost, and any scheduling differences. Once you have a site, elements of the counselor that may influence client comfort include age, gender, counseling style, and specialty areas. Do not assume that any of these factors are unimportant to the client; instead, engage the client in a dialogue about what the client needs in a counselor. Once you have explored these issues, you can move to the next step, making the referral.

Making a Referral

The first step required an in-depth consideration of the need for referral, collaborating with the client on that assessment, and then discussing and exploring possible avenues and characteristics of a good referral. Although it is the responsibility of the client to follow through on the referral, it is the responsibility of the counselor to provide the client with competent referral sources. Although many referrals are based on the factor of availability, we would not advocate for that to be the primary factor. Instead, we expect our supervisees to make each referral based on the client's individual needs. Using that factor as your guiding principle allows you to scan available resources and find the best counselor for that specific client. For example, a client who is struggling with an eating disorder may benefit more from a counselor with experience in treating that issue, whereas a highly intellectual client may prefer a cognitive approach to therapy. Not recognizing these issues that should have been discovered in the first step will diminish the potential of the referral.

We assume here a key component of the second step: You *must* know your referral sources. You cannot facilitate a good fit between counselor and client if you know only half of the puzzle. The following story from a supervisee illustrates what may happen if you are not adequately acquainted with your referral sources:

> It was time for me to leave my internship, so I was busy making appropriate referrals for my clients. We ran out of space in the agency, so I started considering other options for some of my clients. I had attended a workshop the previous week on Gestalt therapy with adolescents. The presenter was so dynamic and seemed so effective. I don't know if she was just on my mind or if I was still moved by her presentation or both, but I referred two adolescent clients to her. The next week I received calls from both clients' parents, angry at me for sending their children to such a "wack job." I asked one parent what happened, and she said the person's office was actually a room in her house. When the clients arrived for the session, they were greeted at the door by the therapist's teenage son, who showed them through the very messy

> house, past bedrooms, to the "office"; a cluttered guest room. The therapist arrived ten minutes late and was dressed like she had been out in the garden. It just got worse from there. I had no idea it was going to be like that, and the clients were so angry at me. That mother was right, it was my responsibility to check these things out. It was like all our hard work went down the drain because I had been so careless.

By the end of this second step, you should feel fairly confident that the issues of referral have been collaboratively explored and, if warranted, that the referrals were the best options available to the client. In many cases, this step is the last one in the process. However, some sources suggest that consulting with the new counselor and providing joint sessions to smooth the transition may be indicated. We include this option as a third step.

Transition Considerations

Once the client has decided on the new counselor, it is common practice for that individual to consult with the preceding counselor to discuss treatment. You can ease this part of the transition by informing your client of this practice, explaining the benefits, and getting the client to sign a form of consent to disclose confidential information to the new counselor once the individual is identified. When contacted by the new counselor, it will be helpful to have information ready about your treatment of the client including conceptualization of the problem, important background information, identified goals, progress toward the goals, and identified areas of growth. In some cases, the new counselor may ask for copies of the client's treatment records. In our practice, both in asking and receiving, we have found it more helpful to have a summary of treatment rather than the entire record. This form is usually one or two pages summarizing the important facets of treatment.

Another method of consultation is to arrange joint sessions with the new counselor. This arrangement allows the client to get a feel for the new counselor while retaining some of the comfort associated with the old. The first session can be a short meet and greet followed by a session where the old counselor facilitates the session while the new counselor acts as process observer. Processing time at the end of the session can help set the agenda for the next session, where open discussion of future treatment among all parties may occur. The advantages of this process include the gradual nature of the transition and the new counselor getting to see the manner of the client in a therapeutic setting. It also bypasses the suspicion associated with "backroom consultations" whereby the client wonders what the counselors are saying in private.

Once the referral has been made and, if used, the last transition session completed, the only aspect of termination left is the final goodbye. Although this part may sound easy compared to all of the other pieces that have been processed, the final step poses some unique struggles. One that you may not have considered is that as you say good-bye to your clients, you must also prepare to terminate with your supervisor. The next two sections provide an overview of how to work through the last step in the termination phase.

Saying Good-Bye to Clients

The process of termination, although much more complicated than just saying "Good-bye," always must eventually end with the final farewell. The goal of the termination process is to provide enough time to discuss pertinent issues so that both parties (counselor and client) understand the purpose of the forced termination and the possible next steps. As you approach the final good-bye, your clients should understand that your leaving has nothing to do with them personally and that you have kept their future counseling needs at the forefront of discussion.

Even when clients are left with a satisfied feeling surrounding the termination, confusion may remain regarding the nature of future relationships with the counselor. In an effort to maintain contact, the client may covertly or overtly push for social contact with the counselor. After all, if counseling is over, why not? When approached by the client to extend the relationship past termination, therapists must make it clear that future contact of any kind is not possible. Penn (1990) cites the inherent power differential within the therapeutic relationship as the main reason posttermination relationships are not wise. She also notes that continuing the relationship informally could interfere with the client's rapport with the new therapist and thus have a detrimental effect on the client's continued counseling.

Saying good-bye to your clients may bring up several emotions in you, as we have discussed. These emotions, if not carefully processed, may interfere with your ability to facilitate the final session. We encourage you to consult with your supervisor and discuss your struggles and feelings as openly as possible. Supervision is an appropriate place to explore your internal reactions to termination, and it can allow a safe working through of the issues so termination can be enhanced.

Terminating with a Supervisor

Most interns are so focused on the anxiety surrounding terminating with clients that they forget that ending one's internship also means an end to the supervisory relationship. The relationship with your supervisor has the potential of being one of the most vital relationships you form as you grow as a counselor, so terminating with a supervisor is just as important as terminating with clients.

Termination should be discussed and processed in much the same way as your work with clients. For example, your supervisor may broach the subject three to four weeks before the final session to get you to start thinking about how you want to close this experience. Each week, you may touch on the various issues until you reach the final session. Ideally, time will be provided for both evaluative and personal reflection.

Evaluation is an important aspect of the supervisory process. Throughout your time in supervision, you have received formative evaluations through feedback on your cases and the ways you comport yourself in the professional environment. During your last supervision session, you receive *summative evaluation,* that is, an overall critique of your work. Some supervisors provide your final evaluation orally, but others prefer a written format. We like the written format because it allows you to review the evaluation at a later time for deeper reflection. Regardless of the format, you should receive comprehensive feedback on topics such as:

- Strengths: theory integration, techniques, rapport building, clientele with whom you work well, knowledge gained, skills attained
- Areas for growth
- Professional issues: ethical behavior, ability to work with others
- Goals for the future

People handle evaluation in various ways; some relish the opportunity for continued self-growth, yet others bristle at the perceived slight of constructive criticism. Also, keep in mind that the confluence of a comprehensive evaluation and termination of a significant relationship can make for an emotionally intense situation. We encourage you to self-reflect before the final evaluation to mentally move yourself into a space where you can hear the opportunities for growth as well as the aspects of your professional self that deserve recognition.

Although doing so is not required or requested by all supervisors, you may also wish to ask if you may evaluate the supervisor and the supervision process. Taking time to reflect on the supervisory experience will help you understand which aspects have been helpful as well as what problematic components to keep in mind when selecting future supervisors. This is also an important opportunity for your supervisor to receive feedback. Form 9.1 provides an example of a written evaluation form.

Making time for more personal reflections on the nature of the supervisory relationship is also an important aspect of the termination session. It is impossible to characterize a universal nature of all supervisory relationships. Some are intense and emotional, while others operate at a safe professional distance. We believe the essence of the good-bye is often congruent with the type of relationship that was

Form 9.1 Sample Evaluation Form

Supervisor's Name: ______________________ Supervision Site: ________________

Faculty Supervisor: _____________________________ Date: _____________

Supervisee's Evaluation of Supervisor and Supervision Site

	Poor						Outstanding
1. Involvement							
A. Demonstrates seriousness and involvement about being a supervisor.	1	2	3	4	5	6	7
B. Is aware and involved in the issues being discussed.	1	2	3	4	5	6	7
2. Growth							
A. Uses personal experiences with clients to further your development.	1	2	3	4	5	6	7
B. Uses personal feelings and insights to further your development.	1	2	3	4	5	6	7
3. Rapport							
A. Makes it easy for you to initiate dialogue with him/her.	1	2	3	4	5	6	7
B. Makes it easy to share your counseling strengths and weaknesses with him/her.	1	2	3	4	5	6	7
4. Facilitation							
A. Initiates helpful discussions of your strengths and competencies with you.	1	2	3	4	5	6	7
B. Initiates helpful discussions with you of your areas for growth.	1	2	3	4	5	6	7
5. Climate and Relationship							
A. Is open and flexible to your wants and style.	1	2	3	4	5	6	7
B. Is accessible between sessions.	1	2	3	4	5	6	7
C. Shares and negotiates expectations of supervision.	1	2	3	4	5	6	7
6. Implementation							
A. Models specific interventions.	1	2	3	4	5	6	7
B. Presents alternative interventions.	1	2	3	4	5	6	7
C. Helps you identify movement in the client.	1	2	3	4	5	6	7
D. Helps you identify lack of movement in the client.	1	2	3	4	5	6	7
E. Aids in your conceptualization of the client's behavior.	1	2	3	4	5	6	7
F. Focuses on content of counseling session.	1	2	3	4	5	6	7
G. Focuses on process of counseling session.	1	2	3	4	5	6	7

(continued)

7. Site Critique

A. Provides accessible office space for interns.	1	2	3	4	5	6	7
B. Provides opportunities to fulfill the client contact requirement.	1	2	3	4	5	6	7
C. Provides opportunities to work with a variety of clientele.	1	2	3	4	5	6	7
D. Provides helpful group supervision.	1	2	3	4	5	6	7
E. Office staff support and help interns.	1	2	3	4	5	6	7
F. Provides adequate orientation of new interns.	1	2	3	4	5	6	7

Suggestions for Supervisor:

Suggestions for Site:

---

formed. This congruence is normal, although both parties should use this time to summarize the relationship and note any aspects that could have been improved.

During the final session, it is also wise to discuss the future of the supervisory relationship. We see the supervisory relationship as one that can continue to exist but one that is transformed through the supervision process. The intern, as a result of all the growth and hard work, can continue to enjoy the benefits of a relationship with the supervisor as a professional resource and support. The supervisor, as an outcome of quality supervision, can reap the benefits of the continued relationship with the intern who represents a competent professional contact. The end of the process merely gives way to a new beginning in which each party gains a new consultant and a new colleague. However, not all supervisors or supervisees desire a future relationship with each other. Regardless of the nature of the future relationship, it is something that can and should be discussed during the termination session.

Summary

You may have noticed the similarities in the process of termination with clients and supervisors. This is one additional example of the power of parallel process. We note the similarities because you have the power to influence and change the process, but you must recognize the dynamic before you can impact it. For example, interns who are struggling with personal fears over terminating with clients will avoid termination discussions with their supervisor. The intern and supervisor have two opportunities to pick up on the problematic feelings surrounding termination. Just as the problems exist in a parallel fashion, the positive patterns also work across the two relationships. Confronting the struggle of termination within the supervision relationship can then lead to improvements in discussing the issue with clients.

Reflection Questions

1. Think about the major terminations in your life. What were they like? How were they resolved? What impact do your personal experiences with termination have on your counseling?
2. Which typical client reaction to termination would be most difficult for you and why? Which client reaction would be easiest for you to handle and why?
3. Act as if you were your supervisor and create a summative evaluation for your work as an intern. What are your strengths? What are your areas for growth?

PART 3

ENTERING THE COUNSELING PROFESSION

The two chapters that form this final part of the book describe the administrative steps and developmental milestones that pave the route to your entry into the counseling profession, provide recommendations about how to complete this stage of your training, and offer suggestions that respond to the rigors of clinical work. Practice is governed by state laws that grant licensed professional counselors (LPCs) rights and a range of professional responsibilities. A license allows you to make the formal transition from the status of student or counselor intern to that of mental health professional. The clinical and academic experiences that make you eligible for licensure also introduce you to a way of comporting yourself as a counseling professional. Spruill and Benshoff (1996) concluded, "Professionalism in counseling is developed through a variety of formal and informal experiences provided by counselor educators, counseling supervisors, professional counselors, and professional organizations" (p. 470). In the following chapters we will offer suggestions not only about how to proceed through the licensing process but what it means to be a counseling professional and what you can do to continue your professional development. To begin we offer additional suggestions (see Part 1) from "What Every Graduate Student Needs to Know" (Connelly, 2005):

6. A degree in counseling doesn't guarantee licensure. Find out what the requirements are for the state in which you intend to practice and make sure you are meeting all of the requirements as you pursue your degree.
7. You're probably going to have to find a supervisor on your own, and you may have to pay her or him. Start networking NOW.

8. Licensure portability (a.k.a. reciprocity) is a work in progress. If you plan to relocate (or even if you don't PLAN to relocate), keep thorough (and duplicate) records of your supervision and stay in touch with your supervisor(s) for the foreseeable future. (A greeting card during the holidays is a nice touch.)
9. A degree in counseling doesn't guarantee a job in counseling. You will have to write a resume or vita and apply for positions. Figure out how to differentiate yourself from every other counseling student to make yourself marketable upon graduation.
10. We don't advise that you launch your private practice the month after you graduate, pass the NCE, or gain licensure. Get some experience first. (But when you're ready, be sure to take advantage of ACA's Private Practice Initiative. Read ahead if you're caught up on your coursework.)

(Reprinted from Connelly, A. R., 2005. What every graduate student needs to know. *Counseling Today, 48*(3), 22. The American Counseling Association. Reprinted with permission. No further reproduction authorized without written permission from the American Counseling Association.)

Chapter 10

Post-Master's Supervised Clinical Experience, Licensure, and Employment

Very early in this text, we suggested that the term *counselor training* oversimplified a process that is larger and broader than the words convey. To us, *counselor formation* seemed a better way to title the process that brings novices to a level of professional competence in a field as personally challenging and involved as counseling can be. The aspect of the counselor formation process presented in this chapter deals with how you obtain a license, pursue employment, and continue to grow as a practicing clinician. As graduate students, we saw licensure as the important and ultimate goal. As practicing clinicians, we now recognize that this journey has no real end point. Getting licensed is a critical step, but it is just that—a step. Continuing education requirements coupled with a personal drive to remain current in a rapidly changing field guarantee that licensed professionals engage in many of the activities that we list in this chapter throughout the course of their professional lives. Spruill and Benshoff (1996) confirm this point: "Professional development roles for practicing counselors include active participation in professional organizations, obtaining professional credentials, and involvement in continuing education, research, and publishing" (p. 469). Continuous professional development is the only responsible, ethical, and legal way to honor your professional obligations in a rapidly evolving branch of the mental health service delivery system.

Participation in the noted range of activities not only helps you remain current but also guarantees that you will network with other professionals. One important truth about clinical practice is that it can be very isolating. Unmitigated, such isolation cripples counselors professionally and personally. According to Kottler (1986),

> The marriage between the personal and the professional in the life of a therapist not only provides an enriched form of work but some special hardships. The clinician's life is fraught with draining days, intense pressures, and personal risks. Those who become too involved with their work pay a dear price in giving up leisure time and a private life; those who too assertively distance themselves from therapeutic sessions risk emotional sterility in other relationships. (p. 43)

Striking the correct balance ensures stability and effectiveness. That balance occurs when you develop and rely upon a network of lay people (family and friends) for social and personal needs while depending on professional colleagues (peers, consultants, specialists) for profession-related concerns. Those who delude themselves into believing that all they need is their work and their time in sessions with their clients embark upon a perilous journey—dangerous not only to themselves but also to their clients.

Clinical supervisors are equally important at this stage of your professional development. We have stressed the importance of such supervisory relationships, so you will not be surprised when we suggest that one comforting aspect of entering the counseling profession is the fact that you can retain the important relationships that helped you become a counselor. Once counselors terminate their work with clients, they will have no contact with them unless the client returns for continued treatment. Termination in supervision is different. We often keep these relationships, and although they may transform into consultative rather than supervisory, thankfully they continue. Wachowiak, Bauer, and Simono (1979) point out that

> For some students, leaving graduate school often involves giving up the mentor before the student is psychologically ready. In actuality many of these mentor/mentee relationships do not end when students leave the graduate school but continue for some time, even though the new Ph.D.s may have moved far from their graduate school base. For other graduates, a new mentor/mentee relationship is established on the entry-level job site. (pp. 724–725)

Professional Associations and Organizations

According to VanZandt (1990), "It is difficult to comprehend how a counselor can 'grow' with the profession without belonging to professional organizations and taking advantage of their resources and services" (p. 244). We would certainly agree. Professional associations offer a vital source of profession-specific information, a community of like-minded counseling professionals, a route to improving the quality of care for clients, an influential force for making sure that mental health concerns are considered in legal and legislative activities, and a method for adding important clinical credentials. Given the range of activities and benefits accrued from membership in such organizations, you will find the need to be involved in a number of them. Some are narrowly focused while others would best be termed *umbrella* organizations.

Most would agree that the largest and arguably most important umbrella organization for counselors is the American Counseling Association (ACA). During orientation, we urge our students to become student members. We also expect them to continue their membership throughout their work life. As clinical interests become more focused, ACA members commonly join one or more of the divisions that deal with specific aspects or types of counseling. The Association for Specialists in Group Work (ASGW) and Counselors for Social Justice (CSJ) are but two examples of the 19 chartered divisions of ACA. A quick visit to the ACA Web site noted at the end of this chapter reveals the wide range of services offered, the number of divisions available to members, and the critical role the organization plays in the profession.

Of course state and regional counseling associations are equally important. They offer similar services on a smaller scale with a tighter focus on the needs and concerns particular to a given state or region. Such associations also contain divisions identical to those offered by the national organization.

Finally, you may also be interested in joining and participating in an honorary society. These organizations limit membership to those who have achieved a specified level of academic success. They seek to recognize and reward outstanding students and clinicians. Chi Sigma Iota has 290 chapters and more than 11,000 active members. According to its Web site,

> *Chi Sigma Iota* is the international honor society for students, professional counselors, and counselor educators established at Ohio University in 1985. Our *mission* is to promote scholarship, research, professionalism, leadership, and excellence in counseling, and to recognize high attainment in the pursuit of academic and clinical excellence in the profession of counseling.

At Loyola University New Orleans, the Chi Sigma Iota chapter often sponsors professional meetings, guest speakers, and socials at which student members meet with graduates of the counseling program. Training and networking opportunities produce many benefits for the membership and the counseling program.

NATIONAL CERTIFICATION

The National Board for Certified Counselors (NBCC) states on its Web site that it "is the nation's premiere professional certification board devoted to credentialing counselors who meet standards for the general and specialty practices of professional counseling." The Web site also contains a wealth of important information for both counselor license applicants and practicing clinicians. NBCC's National Counselor Exam (NCE) is the test used by nearly every state licensing board. We urge all of our students to apply for NBCC certification as soon as they are eligible.

One additional national certification board is the Commission on Rehabilitation Counselor Certification (CRCC). If rehabilitation counseling is a professional interest, consider obtaining the CRCC credential of certified rehabilitation counselor (CRC). Much like the NBCC Web site, the CRCC Web site contains application information, a certification-specific code of ethics, continuing education requirements, continuing education provider information, and published lists of counselors who are currently certified.

STATE LICENSING

To be considered a professional counselor and to practice independently, you will need to obtain a license. Because this is a capstone of professional achievement, we provide licensing information to our students during orientation, in select content courses, and early in the clinical training component of their graduate program. We are most familiar with the Louisiana and Texas laws, so it is an easy matter for us to guide students who plan to obtain licenses in either of these two states. For students planning to pursue licenses in other states, we direct them to the ACA Web site, where they can find information under "Licensure & Certification—State Professional Counselor Licensure Boards." The site contains information about the type of license or certification offered, e-mail and mailing addresses, and Web links for each state's licensing board. ACA also publishes *Licensure Requirements for Professional Counselors: A State by State Report* (American Counseling Office of Professional Affairs, 2007). This text includes detailed licensing requirements and descriptions of the scope of practice for each state, along with portability and reciprocity information.

As a new counselor, you may find it surprising that what counselors are licensed to do varies from one state to another. These differences exist because state counselor licensure laws are a compromise between and among other mental health professions as well as mental health related constituencies within the state. Some states allow counselors to do testing, others may not, and some may restrict the types of tests they would be allowed to do. Psychiatric diagnosis is another area where state-to-state differences in laws are common. Although the scope of practice is a fixed entity, it can be changed through amendments to the state laws that govern clinical practice. Such changes are subject to the political processes and entities that guide and influence this type of legislation. Many counselors become involved in the legislative aspect of the profession. They work to ensure that counselors are allowed to offer a range of services to clients, maintain the integrity of the counseling profession, and to guarantee that clients receive care from licensed professionals. If you have an interest in this aspect of the profession, you can easily identify like-minded professionals who would be happy to introduce you to this important part of the counseling profession.

Reciprocity and portability are significant concerns, especially if you are planning to pursue employment in a state other than the one in which you completed your graduate coursework. *Reciprocity* refers to an agreement between two or more states whereby the licensing boards of those states have agreed to accept the credentials of counselors licensed in the other state or states. Some states have such agreements; others offer no reciprocity whatsoever. This patchwork quilt propels, to some extent, the need for a national response to the issue. The American Association of State Counseling Boards (AASCB) is in a unique position regarding this problem because it works cooperatively with all of the state licensing boards. According to its Web site, "AASCB continues to work with states in their efforts to establish licensing, develop common standards, and nationwide portability of licenses. In addition, AASCB has established the National Credentials Registry as a perpetual holding site for documents related to licensing and portability." Both of these efforts will likely lead to some type of national credential that will ensure *portability,* that is, it will make counseling licenses transferable among all 50 states. Given how mobile we are as a nation, such portability is important. Portability is also helpful because it tends to nationalize the identity of the profession and organize counseling professionals beyond state or regional boundaries. You can expect a number of further advances in this area. In the meantime, it would be wise to at least review the AASCB Counselor Portability Brochure referenced in the Internet Resources section at the end of this chapter.

Obtaining State Licensure Requirements

Understanding how state licensing requirements come into being will help as you review the laws and regulations governing counseling practice in the state where you will become licensed. Once the legislature ratifies a particular bill and it is signed into law by the governor, a licensing board is formed. The board has the responsibility of taking the law and creating a set of rules that, among other things, defines counseling practice and determines how an individual becomes licensed, how licenses are renewed, and the conditions under which licenses may be suspended or revoked. Of course the process is far more involved than this oversimplified sequence of events would suggest. It took many years of work before legislators would even sponsor bills aimed at licensing counselors. In any case, licensing board Web sites usually contain copies of the law, copies of the rules, and all of the forms that are required to carry out the law, so you can obtain a more complete picture of the complexities by reviewing this information. It may not look like much fun to read, but it really does help you understand the profession you are about to enter, and it offers clues to how the legislative process negotiated its way through constituencies that can at times be at odds with one another.

State licensing requirements are easily obtained from licensing board Web sites or by writing directly to the licensing board secretary. Regardless of how you obtain the forms, it is also a good idea to ask if any major or minor changes to the existing law are being considered. In most jurisdictions, you are held to the rules that were in place at the time your application was accepted. People who graduate and then delay applying often find themselves with a laundry list of additional requirements to complete. We receive one or two calls each year from students who graduated but unfortunately opted not to pursue their license immediately. One student had to complete 15 additional hours of coursework (five more courses) before she was allowed to begin the application process. And not one single hour of clinical work that she did during the years between graduation and license application could be counted toward the 3,000-hour supervised clinical experience. Her work in a local school was permitted under the laws of the state, but had she applied at the time of graduation and registered her supervision, it could have also been used to meet the supervised clinical experience requirement.

Rather than just describing general requirements, we offer as an abridged example the Louisiana Licensing Board's application form (see Form 10.1). Other states' applications will differ, but all will require confirmation of your education, prior work experience, verification of supervised clinical experience, examination scores, criminal history, licensing history, and recommendations.

Sections of this application call for the completion and submission of additional forms and supporting documents (see item B-13 or item E). As an applicant, you may also be required to show how the graduate courses in your program met each of the specific concentration areas

Form 10.1 Abridged Example of Louisiana Licensing Board's Application

STATE OF LOUISIANA:
LICENSED PROFESSIONAL COUNSELORS BOARD OF EXAMINERS

License No. ______________________ Issue Date ______________________

B. GENERAL INFORMATION

Dr.
1. Name: Mr. ______________________________________
Ms.
2. Current Residence: ______________________________________

____

City/State ______________________________ Zip ______________
3. Place of Employment ______________________________________

Address______________________________________

City/State ______________________________ Zip______________
4. Which address do you prefer be used for correspondence? ____ Home ____ Work

Which address do you prefer be put on the LPC Website? _____ Home _____ Work
5. E-mail Address ______________________________________
6. Home Telephone: (____) _____-______ Business Telephone: (____) _____-______
7. Exam Score: ____________ 8. Date Exam was taken: ____________ MO/DA/YR

10. Social Security Number: ______________________________________
11. Date of Birth: ________________________
12. Place of Birth: ______________________________
13. A Registration of Supervision form is on file at the LPC Board office?

_____ Yes, _____ No.
14. Employer or Place of Business: ______________________________
15. Have you ever applied for this license before? _____ Yes, _____ No.
16. Have you ever been denied a professional license and/or certificate?

_____ Yes, _____ No. If Yes, state reasons on an attached sheet.
17. Are you certified by a national counseling certifying agency? _____ Yes,_____ No. If Yes, give certification numbers and name and address of the certifying agencies.

____

____

____

(continued)

18. Do you possess or have you ever possessed a professional license(s) or certificate(s) to practice counseling or related profession by Louisiana and/or any other state? _____ Yes, _____ No. If Yes, give license or certificate number(s), title(s), and state(s) issuing the license(s) or certificate(s).

____

____

____

19. Has action been taken to suspend/revoke your license/certificate? _____ Yes, _____ No. If Yes, state date and type of action; name and address of entity taking such action.____

____

____

20. Have you ever been convicted of a felony? _____ Yes, _____ No. If Yes, state the felony, date of conviction, name, location of court (City, County/Parish, State) on a separate attached sheet. Also, if conviction was set aside, give date and explain using the separate attached sheet.

C. EDUCATION

Official transcripts must be sent directly to the Board from the granting institution to validate the information in this section. Only those transcripts containing the degree and coursework used to meet the licensure requirement need be sent. If more space is needed, use additional sheets supplying the same type of information.

Name on transcript if different from B.1: ______________________________

University/College: ____

Location: ______________________ Accredited By: ______________________

Dates Attended: ______________________ Date of Graduation: ______________

Degree: ________________ Major: ________________ Hours in Degree: _________

D. PROFESSIONAL COUNSELING EXPERIENCE

List below the experience you claim as qualifying experience for obtaining a license. If more space is needed, use additional sheets supplying the same type of information.

Name of Employing Agency or Person: ________________________________

Address of employer: ____

____

Immediate Supervisor: ____

Employment Date: From ______________ To______________ Hours per week _____

Your Employment / Job Title: _______________________________________

Brief Description of Your Job Duties: __________________________________

____

____

E. NBCC EXAM SCORES

All applicants must provide an NCE score sent directly from NBCC. (Unless exam was taken through the LPC Board office.)

F. PHOTOGRAPH

All applicants must provide a recent 2″ × 3″ photograph. Picture must be a frontal view showing the applicant's head and shoulders. Sign name on back of picture.

G. LICENSE LETTERING

Please type or print your name below how you would like for it to appear on your license, should you be approved by the Board. Degrees, titles, honors or other information will not be added.

____

H. AFFIDAVIT

Must be signed in presence of notary.

I, the below named applicant, being duly sworn, do hereby affirm that I am the person referred to in this application for a license to practice mental health counseling as a Licensed Professional Counselor in the State of Louisiana, and that all foregoing statements and enclosures are true in every respect. Should I furnish any false information in this application, I hereby agree that such act shall constitute cause for the denial, suspension, or revocation of the license to practice mental health counseling in the State of Louisiana. The Board of Examiners reserves the right to secure further evidence that it deems reasonable and proper from the sources above.

Enclose the application fee of $200.00 made payable to the Licensed Professional Counselors Board of Examiners, *WHICH IS NON REFUNDABLE*, in the form of a money order, cashier's check, or bank draft. PERSONAL CHECKS ARE NOT ACCEPTED.

State of Louisiana

Parish of ______________________________

Applicant Signature ______________________________ Date: ____________

Subscribed and sworn before me this ______ day of ____________________, 20____

Notary Public Signature ______________________________

Notary Public Name (Typed or printed) ______________________________

Notary Public Seal My Commission Expires ____________

Used with permission of the Louisiana LPC Board of Examiners. Please refer to its Web site, www.lpcboard.org, for the most up-to-date version of this form.

defined in the licensure law. And documentation of the supervised clinical experience is often a separate form completed and submitted by your approved supervisor and sent directly by her or him to the licensing board office. By carefully reviewing the law, the application process, and the application forms, you will be prepared to meet and document all of the specific requirements associated with licensure. Plan to review these documents before you graduate, preferably while completing your practicum and internships. Doing so will give you plenty of time to anticipate potential problems and correct any deficiencies.

SUPERVISED CLINICAL EXPERIENCE

Three thousand hours of supervised, post-master's clinical training is a common, basic licensure requirement. Where and under whom you work as you complete your clinical training can create a dizzying range of possibilities. To make a good decision, you will need to be clear about the type of clients and psychological problems you expect to treat during this clinical experience. Knowing the counseling theory or theories that you rely upon or want to learn more about is also important. Such specificity will allow you to narrow the list of possible sites and supervisors to those whose professional interests and theoretical orientations parallel yours. Take your time, consult with others, and make wise choices about each of these options. While our students often discuss these choices with us, they also solicit information from their peers and other professionals with whom they have worked. The general information offered in the next few paragraphs helps, but you should tap into all of your trusted information sources.

Selecting a Site

You will want to narrow your choices to sites that work with the types of clients in which you have a professional interest. The field sites where you completed practicum and internship are good starting points, but do not confine yourself to only those facilities. And if you do find a place that is a good match but discover that it is no longer hiring or accepting additional counselors working under supervision, be sure to ask there for the names of other sites that treat similar clients.

If you were to ask us to help you select a place to complete your supervised clinical experience, we would probably begin by discussing best- to worst-case scenarios with you. The ideal, best-case situation would be for you to obtain a paid position at a site that matches your career interests and where supervision is offered at no charge by an employee of the site who is both licensed and an approved supervisor. This "all supervision expenses paid" alternative does happen, though you will need to be motivated and skillful in landing the job with paid or covered supervision.

Our second, next-best-case alternative is also the most common one. You would obtain a paid position in an agency or school that matches your career interests and then contract for supervision with someone outside of the setting. This alternative calls for you to personally pay for supervision, but you do have the benefit of being in a paid position as well as selecting your own supervisor. Also, sometimes agencies may decide to pay all or part of your supervision costs if you ask them to do so.

The last option, the worst-case scenario, is also the most financially costly. In this scenario, you would complete your hours as a volunteer (unpaid) at an agency and pay for your own outside supervision. Receiving no income and paying supervision costs can produce a difficult financial burden. However, we do know of one volunteer agency that had the insight and good fortune to recruit several approved supervisors to its volunteer staff. Our students who volunteered with that agency were supervised by the agency's volunteer supervisors. This arrangement remains a popular option for students who can delay obtaining gainful employment because in addition to volunteer supervision, the agency offers a rich assortment of counselor training activities (in-service skills training, expanded case consultations, etc.) and an interesting client population with which to work.

Although options in your city may not be identical to what we offer here, it helps to be familiar with the range of alternatives presented. We urge you to check as many different settings as you can and ask about options even if they do not already exist. Your suggestions may spark new alternatives for agencies that they had not previously considered, which might ultimately prove beneficial to them and to you.

Selecting a Post-Master's Clinical Supervisor

In comparison to practicum and internship site supervision, selecting a clinical supervisor is a different and more complicated process. In making this choice, you confront (a) a larger group of field sites, (b) a larger pool of counselor supervisors from which to choose, (c) the prospect of working for a much longer period of time with the same supervisor, and (d) ultimate responsibility for the choice. Fortunately, what you have learned from working under one or more site supervisors can be used to help guide you through this decision.

You know from your practicum and internship experiences that finding someone with whom you can form a strong supervisor-supervisee relationship is critical. But how is it possible to predict the type of professional relationship you will have with someone you barely know? The short answer to the question: Arm yourself with the most complete and up-to-date information obtainable. Two sources are immediately available to you: (a) personal interviews with the supervisor and (b) talks with others who have been or are currently being supervised by the person whom you are considering. Personal interviews with potential supervisors provide factual and subjective information. These interviews yield the most useful data when you work off of a carefully developed list of questions prepared in advance. You will need to know about the person's theoretical orientation, background, and experience, theoretical model of supervision, and estimate how he or she might react to the common situations that arise in supervision. For example, you would want to know what the supervisor would want you to do in case of an emergency, how the supervisor would tell you that something you are doing is inconsistent with standard practice, and so forth.

Even though no two people will interact in the same way, it does make sense to at least partially rely upon information gained from others who have been or who are being supervised by the person you are considering. At the very least, their experiences may raise potential concerns, illuminate potential strengths, and help you identify issues that would need to be discussed before coming to a final decision. For this reason it is probably better to talk to others before your appointment with the supervisor prospect. Information from other supervisees can help you tailor the questions that you will ask and the issues that will need to be clarified.

A thorough job of researching and interviewing supervisors improves your decision but does not guarantee that you will make a successful choice. If you find that your supervisor-supervisee relationship is not what it needs to be and you have not been able to improve conditions, it is probably wise to consider a transfer. This action must be taken systematically so there is no gap in your supervision, but it can and should be taken when circumstances dictate such a change.

In many states clinical supervisors must be approved by the state licensing board. Supervisor applicants must submit applications and supporting documents to the board for consideration. Once approved by the board, these supervisors are eligible to serve. The state licensing board Web sites contain lists of approved supervisors, or you can obtain the written list from the licensing board office. If you choose to obtain a supervisor who is not approved, you risk being disciplined for working without a license, and the hours you completed under these conditions will not count toward the 3,000-hour requirement. Be sure that the person you select is approved and that the supervision arrangement has been filed and agreed to by the licensing board.

Unlike internship supervisors, clinical supervisors are usually paid for their work with you. Thus your contractual relationship with your supervisor should include the cost of supervision, frequency of meeting, policies for missed supervision sessions, what to do in case of an emergency, and so on. Given the legal and professional nature of the relationship, it is advisable to review the laws and rules governing clinical supervisors and the process of working under supervision for your particular jurisdiction.

EMPLOYMENT

During application interviews to the counseling program, we always ask where prospective students see themselves five or ten years after graduation. Answers vary greatly, but most students have a remarkably clear idea of where they hope to end up employed. Diverse graduate school experiences often cause students to widen their range of employment possibilities, but such options still often include large parts of their original plan.

How can we best help students as they pursue their first paid counseling positions? Our anecdotal evidence mirrors what Wachowiak et al. (1979) concluded: "One of the very real and meaningful forces that have a direct impact on the career direction of many graduate students is the relationship that is often established with a professor, therapy supervisor, or other significant individual" (p. 724). During postgraduation surveys and through informal discussions between program graduates and program faculty, we learned how sharing our ideas, discussing our suggestions, and offering our encouragement help students as they make critical career and post-master's education choices.

We also recognize that students who obtain good jobs do so because they vigorously pursue job prospects, prepare résumés that properly highlight their skills and abilities, meet with and obtain permission from those whom they wish to list as references, practice interview skills, and maintain network connections with a range of mental health professionals, peers, professors, and supervisors. Our university counseling center offers a range of job placement and job application services, so students are urged to meet with vocational and career counselors toward the end of their program. Because our counseling faculty members work closely with many local mental health agencies and schools, we often receive job announcements and less formal requests from local employers. We post these opportunities on the program bulletin boards and contact students directly. And we are impressed by the number of students who are hired at the same field sites where they completed practicum or internship requirements.

Counseling is a field with an almost infinite range of employment possibilities. Our graduates work in an impressive range of settings as counselors as well as agency or school administrators. Availability not withstanding, it would be hard to imagine a graduate who could not identify a setting that meets his or her unique interests and skills. We encourage our students to be creative, motivated, and informed as they apply for work. Also, we reiterate how important all of the professional contacts they have are to the goal of obtaining a job and their work as a counselor.

One final note is worth including. Students often worry that they are not sufficiently qualified to obtain a counseling job. Our survey evidence regarding what practicum and internship supervisors are seeking in a student is probably, with minor changes, equally applicable to hiring criteria for novice counselors. Openness to supervision, knowledge of ethical codes, and being responsible and accountable are probably more important issues to prospective employers than arriving with a fully formed approach to dealing with a specific type of client. Agencies have policies and procedures that they expect and desire to teach new employees. At the risk of being too cryptic, the process concerns (how you comport yourself) are more important at this level than the content (what idiosyncratic information you possess).

PROFESSIONAL NETWORK

Like other topics covered in this chapter, your professional network is vital to you now, and its importance will not diminish. You are even likely to continue these networking relationships beyond the point of your retirement from the profession. Colleagues, consultants, teachers, and professionals from other mental health specialties enrich your work, support you during the inevitable difficult times, and help you make sure that your clients receive quality care.

We have spoken mostly of supervisory and consultative relationships that exist between you and licensed counselors. Your professional network also will include, if it does not already, a host of other mental health professionals. It is virtually impossible to practice counseling without referrals, depending upon client need, to psychiatrists, psychologists, substance abuse counselors, educational specialists, and other mental health experts. Having a cadre of such specialists ensures that your clients will have access to critical services. Having a good working relationship with these professionals makes it much easier to refer when necessary and coordinate such services for your clients. With appropriate releases it becomes an easy matter of consulting with other specialists involved in the clients' care. As you develop these relationships, you also place yourself within the referral network of these other professionals. For example, psychiatrists who restrict their practice to medication management will often refer clients out for counseling. Many LPCs have similar cooperative and mutually beneficial relationships with psychiatrists who do not provide talking therapies to clients. Just as in chapter 1 we emphasized the importance of the relationships that help students become professionals, this section carries that notion forward and broadens the network to include all members of the mental health service delivery system.

SUMMARY

Counseling licensure and national certifications are important landmarks. We discussed the steps that you must take to complete this stage of your training, noting that licensure or certification is but one step in a career-long journey. Many of the processes and activities that are required to become licensed and certified will be needed throughout your professional life.

Active participation in counseling organizations and in personal and professional networks were shown to be equally important for facilitating quality care to clients and your own well-being, given the risk of counseling's tendency to isolate you. We offered some recommendations for obtaining your first counseling job. We noted that the relationships covered in the beginning of the text remain as important at this point as they did when you began your training. We also recognized the need to expand your professional relationships to include other types of mental health professionals. Counselors recognize that the healing force is probably contained in the relationship between counselor and client. As counselor educators, we recognize that the equivalent force for counseling professionals comes from our relationship with the network of professionals with whom we surround ourselves.

REFLECTION QUESTIONS

1. What signs do you see within yourself that would indicate that you are becoming a mental health professional?
2. How do you plan to go about identifying an agency and a supervisor for the 3,000-hour supervised clinical experience portion of your training?
3. Which of the ACA divisions are most interesting to you?
4. What concerns, if any, do you have about forming consultative relationships with other mental health professionals (e.g., psychiatrists, educational specialists)?
5. Under what conditions would you seriously consider changing supervisors?
6. How could your faculty and college best help you as you pursue your first counseling job?

Selected Internet Resources

1. American Counseling Association (ACA): www.aca.org
   Licensure & Certification—State Professional Counselor Licensure Boards:
   www.counseling.org/Counselors/LicensureAndCert/TP/StateRequirements/CT2.aspx
2. American Association of State Counseling Boards (AASCB): http://aascb.org
   AASCB Counselor Portability Brochure: www.counseling.org/Files/FD.ashx?guid=7c55862b-e3a8-4022-bba9-9c98e51afaa3
3. Chi Sigma Iota (CSI) Counseling Honorary Society: www.csi-net.org
4. National Board for Certified Counselors (NBCC): www.nbcc.org
5. Commission on Rehabilitation Counselor Certification (CRCC): www.crccertification.com

Chapter 11

Managing the Personal Challenges of Counseling Clients

Once you have endured the joys and tribulations of the academic courses, supervised clinical experiences, application for licensure, and securing of employment, a sense of relief may rush over you. You may even say to yourself, "I am finally here." We believe it is important to sit back and enjoy your climb to what must feel like the top of the mountain, but we also know that what seems like the apex is only the beginning. Now that you have achieved a degree of professional autonomy, you must face the continuous personal challenges that come with working with clients. Throughout your previous training, you have had the support of supervisors and other colleagues, so the transition to "licensed professional" can feel suddenly isolating and scary, as many new counselors report. This chapter addresses some of the issues that you may confront in this stage of your professional development and some methods for working through the challenges that lie ahead. The issues we will discuss are competency, intimacy, empathy poisoning, and burnout.

Issues of Competency

One of the most maddening ongoing issues mental health professionals face is trying to answer the question, "Am I any good at this?" Rooted in this question are many other concerns related to competency. Ethical guidelines compel us to do good and do no harm, yet if you asked many counselors at any point if they really knew whether they were making a difference in the lives of their clients, you might get a troubled look. Consider this thoughtful remark from one seasoned professional:

> My most nagging doubt about my profession is whether or not I am positively impacting my clients. There are sessions when I feel like I am right on, but I don't really know if the client is getting it. There have also been numerous occasions when I thought the session went horribly wrong and the client comes in the next week and says it was the best session ever. In times like that, I really wonder if I truly understand what works about this process.

Elements of Competency

There are two main elements of competency: internal feelings of inferiority, which are subjective, and measures of competency, which are objective. The internal feelings of inferiority are a normal part of life. Dealt with in a healthy way, these feelings can motivate you to stretch yourself and continue to grow. We hope that in your supervision courses and post-master's experience, you worked with a supervisor who helped you gain a sense of comfort with your areas for growth and to understand that competent practitioners always look for ways to improve. Because your feelings of inferiority are normal, it is not so much a question of whether you have them but what you choose to do with them. That question brings us to the objective measures of competency.

Assessing Competency

Throughout your program of study, we are assuming you have been thoroughly evaluated based on your ability in basic and advanced skills. Formal coursework assessments (both formative and summative), comprehensive exams, and licensing exams all represent methods of competency assessment. When you are out in the "real" world, what do you do? In discussing ways to assess competency, we like to use the *triad of competency* model (see Figure 11.1). To illustrate the model, we will use the case of George. George is a new professional counselor who

Figure 11.1 Triad of Competency

wants to start a group for adolescent girls to discuss issues of forming healthy relationships. How does George know he is competent to facilitate this kind of group?

The first leg of the triad is *formal education*. Formal education includes taking a graduate-level course or an extended workshop on the topic. Formal education activities expose the professional to relevant literature, experiential activities, and opportunities to ask an expert (the instructor) questions to enhance the learning experience. In the example of George, he would consider the courses he has taken in his graduate training. He, like most counselors, took a course in group counseling, so that would meet this aspect of competency for group. He has also taken courses in life span theory, where he learned about adolescent development. He seems to have this leg of the triad under control.

The second leg of the triad is *supervised clinical experience*. Supervised clinical experience means that you have practice working with the modality or population and that your practice has been supervised by someone with more experience than you do with the modality or population. If George had facilitated groups while he was seeking licensure, he might have felt more competent than if he had not, due to the feedback he received during supervision. If George is licensed and has not received any supervised experience related to group (modality) and/or population (adolescent girls), George can work on this leg of the triad in two ways. The first way is to seek a coleader for the group who is competent. Using a coleader can give George some in vivo training and feedback from someone who possesses more expertise. George can participate in pregroup planning and postsession feedback sessions with his coleader to improve his level of competency.

The second way for George to obtain supervised clinical experience is to seek a colleague to supervise his group work. If George is licensed, he may feel embarrassed to seek supervision from a colleague, but it is the ethical and professional thing to do. George can pay attention to his feelings of inferiority ("I am supposed to be competent. What if my colleague thinks I'm an idiot for asking for help?") and handle them in appropriate ways. On a personal note, we have found that our faith in other professionals increases when they ask for help because it is an indication that they know how to access help when they need it. It is those who do not ask for help whom we worry about.

The third leg of the triad is *continuing education*. Dedicating your professional career to continuous growth allows the dynamic of competency to be ever expanding rather than a static process. The exciting part of the field of counseling is that we do not, nor will we ever, know everything there is to know about human behavior. Therefore, competency is always changing, and we must seek out experiences that add depth to our professional knowledge. There are several ways to increase one's competency through continuing education. Licensing boards require a certain number of CEUs (continuing education units) per licensing cycle. CEUs can be obtained by attending conferences at the state, regional, or national level. Conferences provide excellent opportunities to learn a wide array of advanced clinical skills, get a refresher on old skills, and be exposed to new ideas.

You can also attend workshops that are held in your city or area. If you are licensed, you will soon receive countless flyers advertising these workshops. In addition to live continuing education, belonging to professional organizations allows you to receive professional journals filled with the latest research and ideas. Many of the professional journals allow the reader to fill out a form and answer some questions for CEU credit. George can use continuing education to broaden his understanding of groups and adolescent girls. He can attend conferences dedicated to the practice of group work or read journal articles detailing various group protocols when working with adolescents. As George continues to grow, his competency level will grow too, and both George and his clientele will benefit.

Obviously, feeling competent and being competent are two different concepts. Feelings of doubt creep into the minds of even the most seasoned professionals. The presence of those feelings means neither that you are fully competent nor that you lack competence. When you experience those feelings, we hope you consider the triad of competency as a way to assess the meaning behind the emotions. Like George, you now have a method for managing the feelings and when they point to a lack of competency, a way to achieve growth and expand your practice.

Issues of Intimacy

From the moment you began your training, you were taught how to develop rapport with your clients. The core techniques of empathic listening, reflection of feeling and content, summarization, and open-ended questions are all designed to facilitate the client's deeper exploration of self and provide the counselor with the information needed to help with that exploration. Along with these skills you were probably also provided with guidelines and prohibitions against self-disclosure; the theory being that information about the personal life of the counselor impedes the self-exploration of the client. The negative ideas about self-disclosure have their roots in Freud's conceptualization of the need for the analyst to serve as a blank slate in order to foster a clean transference. As the counselor actively listens to the client, the client unfolds his or her inner world, intimacy deepens, and the rapport occurs.

As a result of this process, a relationship develops that is far different from the relationships that form outside the counseling session.

Counseling relationships and traditional relationships vary in three primary ways: (a) flow of communication, (b) depth of sharing, and (c) speed of intimacy development. Traditional relationships develop through mutual sharing; as each person shares meaningful aspects of self, the relationship deepens. In counseling, the flow of information goes only one way, client to counselor, and yet a form of intimacy develops between the two people. As a product of the one-way relationship, a power differential occurs as the counselor comes to know a lot about the client but the client knows little to nothing about the personal life of the counselor.

In addition to the unidirectional flow, counseling relationships also differ from traditional relationships in the depth and speed of sharing as well as in concomitant intimacy development. As you well know from your work with clients, they will share pieces of themselves that are extremely private, and they do so soon within the life span of the therapeutic relationship. As you see more clients, you will be surprised how many times you hear, "I've never told this to anyone . . ." after knowing a client for only a session or two. We tell our students, "Psychological intimacy travels much faster than traditional intimacy," in our attempt to prepare them for the deep connection the client will feel as a result of rapport building.

In the context of this deeply intimate reaction, client and counselor create an atmosphere conducive to growth. However, clients are apt to respond to the felt sense of deep intimacy in ways that the individual normally responds to related intimacy levels in "real-world" relationships. For instance, clients who respond with avoidance or fear of intimacy in their personal relationships will respond in a congruent fashion to the intimacy in counseling. Many clients connect psychological intimacy with physical intimacy. For many people, the idea of responding to psychological closeness with physical closeness is very natural. Regardless of the response, it is the counselor's job to process the feelings and fold them into learning opportunities for the client.

In your time as a professional counselor, you will deal with client-to-counselor attraction on numerous occasions. Equally as frequent, you will also encounter times when you feel an attraction to one of your clients. Counselors are people, and as a function of our humanity, we enjoy the feeling of intimacy generated in the counseling session. We enjoy the fact that clients are willing to trust us, tell us their secrets, and even pay us for our time. We feel important, needed, and respected. For counselors who are not getting these needs met in outside relationships, the tendency to look to clients for fulfillment is strong. Being attracted to a client is not the unethical aspect—in fact, it is very normal. What differentiates unhealthy attraction from healthy attraction is how the counselor handles it. Because most counselors respond to the thought of being attracted to a client with denial and shame, we will first outline some warning signs of a developing yet unnoticed attraction, and then we will discuss some steps to manage the feelings.

Pope, Sonne, and Holroyd (1993, pp. 103–117) list several clues to what they term "unacknowledged sexual feelings." They are:

1. *Dehumanization of the client and/or counselor.* Dehumanization is a way to push the sexual feelings away and gain some emotional distance without actually dealing with the attraction. Dehumanizing clients comes in the form of beginning to see the client as a label, such as their diagnosis. Dehumanizing the counselor is characterized by a movement to a more aloof professional posture, such as being overly cognitive or playing the "expert."
2. *Avoidance.* Sometimes the counselor is so ashamed of the feelings the only thing to do (besides deal with them) is to avoid them by avoiding the client. Counselors can pick up on this clue if they find themselves "forgetting" to return phone calls from the client, or missing or canceling appointments.
3. *Obsession and/or fantasies during sexual activities.* Not being able to get thoughts of your client out of your head is one important sign that something is going on that needs to be explored. An extension of constantly thinking about the client would be when you think about your client as a sexual partner while masturbating or having sexual relations with your partner. Before you say, "That would never happen to me," Pope and Tabachnick (1993) conducted a national survey and noted that half the sample reported having sexual fantasies about their clients on rare occasions and a fourth responded that the fantasies were more frequent than rare.
4. *Isolation of the client and/or counselor.* The counselor may begin to isolate the client from family, friends, and romantic ties by subtly encouraging the client to cut off communication with these individuals. An example would be the counselor stating, "You know, it sounds like you are very unhappy with the way your boyfriend is treating you. You feel he just doesn't listen or respect you. Maybe you are right in trying to disconnect from him for awhile." By doing so, the client may become more reliant on the counselor for emotional support. Another clue to isolating the client would be the atmosphere of secrecy around the relationship or what occurs in counseling. Saying to the client, "I think we should keep this to ourselves because other people wouldn't understand" should be a clear sign that the relationship needs to be reexamined.

   Isolation of the counselor occurs when the counselor knows something is not right, but cannot pinpoint the catalyst for the discomfort (the sexual attraction). Instead the counselor reports feeling "overwhelmed and stressed out" and as a result, often begins to pull away from support networks of colleagues and friends. The isolation may be interpreted as "they don't understand me" or "they would judge me" which in turn, propels the counselor deeper into the bond with the client who does "understand."

When the vigilant counselor notices the clues pointing toward attraction, steps must be taken to ensure that the attraction does not interfere with the counseling process. We are fairly certain that this issue was addressed in your counseling curriculum, but here are a few guidelines that may help you process the feeling as they arise.

1. *Define the scope of the issue.* In this stage, the counselor should explore and define the feelings associated with the attraction. These feelings can run the gamut from excitement and sexual lust to shame and fear. As the counselor examines the emotional landscape of the attraction, he or she can also look at the reasons for the feelings. Counselors can explore the reasons by asking questions such as:
   - What's going on in my intimate relationships right now? Do I feel loved? Do I feel respected? Do I feel needed?
   - What about the client do I find attractive? Is this a physical attraction? Emotional attraction? Intellectual attraction? Spiritual attraction? Often, the emotions detected that are associated with the attraction will be found to be absent in one's current relationships.
2. *Consult.* As mentioned, isolation is not only a clue to attraction but also can push the counselor closer to the client in unhealthy ways. Consulting a colleague about your feelings can give you an ally in preventing destructive contact with your client. The consultant can validate your perspective, give you insight on aspects of the relationship you might miss, and help you manage the feelings in a productive way.
3. *Seek personal counseling.* If the emotional strain is troubling to you, or if through your exploration you find elements missing in your current relationship, you should strongly consider working out those issues in your own counseling. As you know, getting your emotional needs met through your client is inappropriate, but finding ways to get what you want is a perfect arena for your personal counseling.
4. *Continue or refer.* As you move through this process, you will have to make a decision whether to continue seeing the client or refer the client to another mental health professional. Because attraction to clients is fairly common and normal, managing the

feelings with these steps will allow most counselors to continue to work with the client as long as they continue to monitor the boundaries. In cases where the sexual attraction cannot be managed, the feelings will create an obstacle to the counseling and a referral must be made.

So what do you say after you've determined that you can't continue? Well, we believe that sexual attraction that creates an impasse in the counselor will often be felt by both parties as a "stuck place" in the counseling; a perceived lack of movement. The counselor can note the "stuckness" as the reason for referral. For example, "It seems like we are not making progress in our work. Perhaps this is as far as we can go." Getting client feedback is essential, as is reevaluating goals and making appropriate referral based on those goals. The point here is that you can make the referral based on the process of counseling, rather than discussing the reason for the impasse, which is your issue, not the client's.

Issues of Empathy Poisoning

During admission interviews for our university's counseling program, we inform all applicants of this caveat to beginning a course of study in counseling:

> What you are asking to undertake is a serious and in some cases, dangerous, process. Studying counseling is different from other professions. We are not in the business of studying fish or dirt. We do not run numbers or examine molecules. Most other professionals have the luxury of studying external phenomena. We don't have that buffer zone. We study the internal workings of humanity, and as you study counseling, you will be studying your family, your children, and yourself.

When we discuss this issue with applicants, we sometimes get a vision of that sign at the entrance to hell in Dante's *Inferno,* "Abandon hope, all ye who enter here." Very ominous indeed! The purpose of the speech is not to encourage students to abandon hope, however, simply to understand that counseling is a serious proposition. It is the intersection of two lives: one in emotional pain and the other presumably healthy enough to help. It is only when counselors do not take care of themselves that the pain of the client can overwhelm or resonate so deeply with our own pain that we lose objectivity. It is in those two dynamics that *empathy poisoning* takes place.

Strange as it may seem, Freud had an excellent explanation of the process of empathy poisoning in his conceptualization of transference and countertransference. The Freudian version of an empathic connection or understanding of a client's world came in the process known as *transference*. The idea here is that the client would connect (in Freudian terms, "cathect") with the counselor and the issues would flow into the counselor whereas the counselor, ideally, would be a safe holding environment for the processing of those issues (Freudians, bear with us here and give us some latitude). Counselors create a safe holding environment by being "empty buckets" for the client's "stuff" (this is why psychoanalysts undergo years of psychoanalysis; to empty their buckets). If the connection goes as planned, the client gains insight and the transference is complete.

However, the process does not always go so smoothly. If the counselor's bucket is not empty, then it may not have enough space for the client's stuff. As the client transfers issues, they get all mixed up with the counselor's issues, and spillage occurs. This process is known as *countertransference*. Freudian material aside, empathy poisoning occurs when your bucket is too full and your issues get tangled up with the client's issues. Now that we have the bucket metaphor firmly implanted in your mind, we can explore specific examples and discuss how to empty your bucket.

One example of empathy poisoning comes from being overwhelmed by client material. It is indicative of poor processing and compartmentalizing of client material so that as the counselor moves from session to session, remnants of the last client's material are left in the bucket. By the end of the day, the counselor is left with a conglomeration of emotional pain; the leftovers from a day of helping. One counselor summed up the effects of this form of empathy poisoning:

> Every day I would go home and feel like the weight of the world was on my shoulders. So much pain. In one particularly difficult day I saw two kids who had been abused by parents, a woman who lost her son in a traffic accident, and a couple going through a divorce. That's four "working" hours in an eight-hour workday, and I felt demolished. I couldn't even talk to my family. I went straight to bed and cried myself to sleep. That night I dreamed about them, almost playing the sessions over and over again in my mind. I felt haunted.

With this type of empathy poisoning, the counselor must learn appropriate ways to process the client material and distance the self from the process. Empathy is about temporarily entering the client's world, not living there. You are a visitor. It is also about entering the client's world without losing a sense of your own world and how you are separate from the client's life. One practical suggestion is to monitor the types of clients you see and arrange them so you do not see back-to-back clients you experience as challenging. In our clinical work, we try to arrange for diverse groups of clients so that issues do not have a multiplying effect. Counselors often develop rituals to help themselves delineate between sessions and between work and home. For example, one supervisee used the sound of the front door closing and locking as a symbolic way to keep work material at work. One counselor remarked, "You just have to develop a mechanism that works for you. You are training your brain to compartmentalize."

Another type of empathy poisoning occurs when you have unresolved issues in your bucket. As clients dump their issues into you, your bucket overflows. Counselors are people too. In your professional lifetime you will have all sorts of life changes occurring in the same time period as you are seeing clients. Relationship issues, trauma, illness, bad moods, parenting struggles, and work stress are all examples of issues counselors must deal with on a regular basis in their personal lives. The difficult thing is that there is no hard-and-fast rule about how to manage the issues. For example, no one says, "Well, if you are having a fight with your spouse, you shouldn't do couples counseling that day," or "If you were just in a car accident, you must cancel your clients for a week." Absent objective rules, the counselor must be self-aware and self-disciplined to effectively handle both the personal issues and the client.

Issues of Burnout

If you are reading this text as a part of your clinical coursework, we hope boredom and burnout have not yet appeared on your radar of concerns. If you are like most students, you are slightly overwhelmed with the myriad unique situations that occur in the field on a day-to-day basis. When everything is new, it is probably difficult to imagine that you would ever feel bored, and most likely you are so enthusiastic about the work that burnout seems hardly possible as well. Unfortunately, for many mental health professionals, the newness erodes and disillusionment sets in.

Stages of Burnout

As Kessler (1990) described burnout, "Where once there was enthusiasm, conviction, and compassion for helping others, only frustration, apathy, and terrible loneliness remain. Paradoxically, the need to reach out and help is still there, but it is mired in a personal sense of reduced motivation, low energy, and an overwhelming sense of futility and fraud" (p. 301). Edelwich and Brodsky (1980) identified four stages of burnout:

1. *Enthusiasm.* Hopefully every new member of the profession possesses a sense of excitement about the profession and work of counseling. Counselors prone to burnout tend to use the enthusiasm to dump themselves into their work, thus creating a fusing of identity between self and work. This overidentification can manifest in several behavior patterns noted by Gibson and Mitchell (2003): getting to work early and leaving late,

working through lunch, taking work home evenings and weekends, rarely taking vacations, and being unable to say no to extra cases or work around the office. This misuse of enthusiasm can also lead to overidentification for clients (see section on empathy poisoning).

2. *Stagnation.* This stage comes after the counselor can no longer keep up the pace of the enthusiasm stage and a settling occurs. If your professional life is a marathon race, then the enthusiasm stage is like sprinting the first mile, then realizing that you are exhausted and you have 25 miles remaining. The slowing of the work pace can lead the counselor to begin to resent colleagues for "not working as hard" or "not respecting what I do around here."
3. *Frustration.* As the discontent builds, the frustration stage is characterized by growing boredom and resentment. The counselor in this stage may find difficulty in motivating oneself to get work done. Non-counseling duties are usually the first to fall, such as note taking and insurance forms. Soon, others will begin to notice the lack of attention to basic duties and will often comment of the counselor's lack of professionalism. Feedback from others will be interpreted by the counselor as "one more reason this works stinks." It is also at this stage that counselors start secretly wishing their clients would not show up, not because of anxiety, but because they would rather have nothing to do. It is a sinking down into the boredom. Each work task that gets avoided and each client that does not show adds to the avalanche of boredom and restlessness of the counselor.
4. *Apathy.* In the final stage, the counselor may experience hopelessness and helplessness, perhaps even deep depression and anxiety. The counselor at this stage will often exhibit behaviors ranging from unethical (missing appointments, refusing to consult) to unprofessional and lazy (refusing to finish reports and instead spends non-counseling time sleeping or playing on the computer). By this time, the counselor has severed support ties with colleagues and views them as people who "don't understand me." Isolated and hopeless, a counselor at this stage poses serious risk to self and the clients seen.

Managing Boredom and Burnout

Due to the serious nature of burnout, counselors must be vigilant and responsible for managing their own professional development. Boy and Pine (1980) propose some excellent suggestions for mental health professionals to use as they manage issues of boredom and burnout. We will use their suggestions as a three-part model for you to consider as you move forward in your career.

Spend the major portion of the day actually counseling clients. Boy and Pine noticed back in 1980 that counselors spend a lot of time doing noncounseling tasks. Unfortunately, it is as true today as it was in 1980. The counseling laws and accrediting agencies seem to recognize the reality that being a counselor requires more than counseling skills, as evidenced by the fact that indirect hour requirements are always more than direct counseling hour requirements. For example, in Louisiana, our CACREP- accredited program follows the guideline of a 600-hour internship that includes 240 direct client hours and 360 indirect hours. Students report early in their experience that seeing clients is "exciting" whereas the indirect duties such as doing paperwork, writing case notes, and attending meetings are less than invigorating.

Much like the experience of interns, most professionals would not say they entered the counseling field for the love of doing office work or administration. Instead, they would say they pursued their license so they could see clients. Counselors tend to get bored and burn out the more they participate in noncounseling activities. The key is finding a balance that works for you. We understand that your job may necessitate noncounseling activities, but you can be assertive about how you spend your time, especially when it comes to client services. The main idea here is: The more time you spend as a counselor, the more likely you will feel you are doing what you were trained to do, and satisfaction increases. The less time you spend doing counseling, the greater the chance of boredom and burnout. Consider this story from a professional who was faced with the dilemma of noncounseling duties encroaching on counseling clients.

Pat

I thought I had really hit the big time when I was promoted to clinical director of the outpatient treatment program. I had worked so hard to create the type of program that I could be proud of and the administration was rewarding me with the directorship. I soon found that the administrative title meant more time spent doing reports, writing grants, evaluating staff, and attending meetings. Week by week, I found myself handing over my groups and individual clients to other staff. As that happened, I found myself dreading coming to work. This was a feeling I hadn't experienced at work before, so it worried me. I was faced with the realization that promotion was not going to work for me if it meant I had to sacrifice doing counseling for attending meetings. Luckily for me, I was the director, so I set aside a portion of every day to do counseling, and I treated that time as sacred. I also talked with my supervisor to explain that my passion was for counseling and that I could be a more effective director if I kept consistent with my client contact. My supervisor agreed, and I have loved my work even more.

Stay connected with committed and caring colleagues. Once you have graduated, you realize that the world of graduate school was unlike the world of professional clinical practice. Although it does not have to be so isolating, many graduates find that they had no idea they would feel so alone. Graduate school had classes where you met with colleagues to discuss counseling topics. In your clinical courses, you routinely gathered together in group supervision and met with supervisors to discuss cases. In graduate school, you probably felt more connected and supported.

After graduation, you will begin to work on your licensure hours. You will feel some level of support from your supervisor, with whom you will have a close working relationship. However, from your colleagues, you may begin to notice the "I'm tired, I'm busy" attitude that clouds collegial relationships in the "real" world. Everybody is trying to get hours and maintain a semblance of a personal life. This is a prime time to work on balancing your work life and personal life, but many professionals put their head down and try to plow through their experience, using their supervision as a professional lifeline. When they are finally finished with their hours, license obtained, many professionals find themselves isolated from any sense of professional community.

Within this dynamic of isolation, two primary activities can help you avoid this pitfall. First, find a good support network within your professional circle. The easiest place to start is with your group from graduate school. Your cohorts may be in different jobs, but you all are facing that same sense of isolation. Having a preexisting connection makes the process more natural even if the structure has changed due to graduation. The next place to look is at your job site. Developing a support network on-site is a great way to alleviate stress as it develops throughout the day. Once you have a group, what do you do with them? Well, whatever helps you feel more connected and less isolated. You can meet as an informal supervision group to discuss cases or you can meet for dinner. You get to decide, but choose your colleagues well, because your choices can affect the impact (positive or negative) of the group.

Whom you choose is up to you, and this choice is linked to the second helpful activity on which you can focus: Avoid negative professional influences. Surrounding yourself with ethical, competent, and enthusiastic professionals increases your likelihood of feeling the same. Connecting yourself to cynical, bored professionals hastens your feelings of burnout. One of our recent graduates accepted a job at a local high school. She was eager to begin her work and viewed school counseling as a noble profession. During her first few weeks, a senior school counselor took her under her wing as a mentor to orient her to the new position. The new counselor quickly learned that her mentor had a different view of school counseling. The mentor spent her days talking to her boyfriend on the phone and shopping online. She left for lunch off campus at 11 AM and often did not return until after 1 PM. When the new counselor asked if she could start a divorce support group for the ninth-grade class, the mentor said, "Oh, we don't do stuff like that here." Basically, the mentor never saw students, except for scheduling and some advising.

The new counselor was mature enough to realize that her mentor's view of counseling was going to have a negative effect on her own development. It was too late to find another job, so she chose to do two things. First, she created a networking group of new school counselors from area schools. That afforded her some positive support. Second, she interacted with the other school counselor only on an as-needed basis. When she had new ideas, she either enacted them on her own or went though her supervisor. The key is that she recognized the negative influence and took responsibility for her own career growth.

Commit to theory development. We believe that too much emphasis has been placed on theoretical integration and eclecticism. Theory represents a consistent philosophical framework designed to organize the complex information provided by the client. Trying to pick and choose from all the theories leaves the counselor confused as to the method of the picking and choosing. For novice counselors (and many "experts," for that matter) deciding what to do becomes a random process rather than a cohesive one. For this reason, we encourage our students to choose the theory that bests resonates from their own philosophical beliefs about people and how change occurs. Once a congruence has been found between theory and counselor, then expansion, not contraction, can occur.

The advantages of theoretical consistency go beyond clinical impact. Boy and Pine (1980, pp. 162–163) list the following as benefits to the counselor as a developing professional:

- Enables the counselor to review research by others employing the approach and make modifications based on that research.
- Enables the counselor to conduct personal research contributing to the effectiveness of the approach.
- Provides the counselor with a consistent base from which modifications can occur.
- Enables the counselor to contribute to the advancement of knowledge regarding the theory.
- Presents a behavioral consistency influencing the client's pattern of responses.
- Presents the client with a professionally responsible approach possessing goals for which there is supporting research.

In the service of preventing burnout, theory provides not only a road map that decreases the experiences of feeling lost but also a framework for new counselors to grow and contribute to the field through original research. In these two arenas, theory provides a backdrop for personal and professional growth, keys to avoiding boredom and burnout.

Summary

Your path as a professional counselor is probably just beginning. Along the way, you will experience the peaks of joy and confidence and the valleys of confusion and disappointment. This chapter provided some issues for you to consider as you start your journey. In the discussion of competency, we introduced a three-legged model—the triad of competency—to help you assess your level of expertise as you grow. We also introduced the important dynamic of intimacy in counseling. We examined how it can be utilized for rapport building as well as the warning signs of possible unhealthy uses of intimacy by client or counselor. Finally, we discussed burnout, and you learned some of the warning signs and some considerations for maintaining the feeling of vitality in your professional life. The topics covered here are not an exhaustive list of issues you will confront, but they will serve as a reminder that there are issues to attend to as you move forward. Although this chapter is the end of the book, we recognize that it represents only the beginning for you.

Reflection Questions

1. How might you seek to resolve internal feelings of inferiority?
2. What role do you see continuing education playing in your life as a clinician?
3. How could issues in your personal life create intimacy boundary issues between you and your clients?
4. What specific steps will you personally take to prevent counselor burnout?

Appendix A

ACA CODE OF ETHICS

ACA CODE OF ETHICS PREAMBLE

The American Counseling Association is an educational, scientific, and professional organization whose members work in a variety of settings and serve in multiple capacities. ACA members are dedicated to the enhancement of human development throughout the life span. Association members recognize diversity and embrace a cross-cultural approach in support of the worth, dignity, potential, and uniqueness of people within their social and cultural contexts.

Professional values are an important way of living out an ethical commitment. Values inform principles. Inherently held values that guide our behaviors or exceed prescribed behaviors are deeply ingrained in the counselor and developed out of personal dedication, rather than the mandatory requirement of an external organization.

ACA CODE OF ETHICS PURPOSE

The *ACA Code of Ethics* serves five main purposes:

1. The *Code* enables the association to clarify to current and future members, and to those served by members, the nature of the ethical responsibilities held in common by its members.
2. The *Code* helps support the mission of the association.
3. The *Code* establishes principles that define ethical behavior and best practices of association members.
4. The *Code* serves as an ethical guide designed to assist members in constructing a professional course of action that best serves those uti-

lizing counseling services and best promotes the values of the counseling profession.

5. The *Code* serves as the basis for processing of ethical complaints and inquiries initiated against members of the association.

The *ACA Code of Ethics* contains eight main sections that address the following areas:

Section A: The Counseling Relationship
Section B: Confidentiality, Privileged Communication, and Privacy
Section C: Professional Responsibility
Section D: Relationships with Other Professionals
Section E: Evaluation, Assessment, and Interpretation
Section F: Supervision, Training, and Teaching
Section G: Research and Publication
Section H: Resolving Ethical Issues

Each section of the *ACA Code of Ethics* begins with an Introduction. The introductions to each section discuss what counselors should aspire to with regard to ethical behavior and responsibility. The Introduction helps set the tone for that particular section and provides a starting point that invites reflection on the ethical mandates contained in each part of the *ACA Code of Ethics.*

When counselors are faced with ethical dilemmas that are difficult to resolve, they are expected to engage in a carefully considered ethical decision-making process. Reasonable differences of opinion can and do exist among counselors with respect to the ways in which values, ethical principles, and ethical standards would be applied when they conflict. While there is no specific ethical decision-making model that is most effective, counselors are expected to be familiar with a credible model of decision making that can bear public scrutiny and its application.

Through a chosen ethical decision-making process and evaluation of the context of the situation, counselors are empowered to make decisions that help expand the capacity of people to grow and develop.

A brief glossary is given to provide readers with a concise description of some of the terms used in the *ACA Code of Ethics.*

Section A: The Counseling Relationship

Introduction

Counselors encourage client growth and development in ways that foster the interest and welfare of clients and promote formation of healthy relationships. Counselors actively attempt to understand the diverse cultural backgrounds of the clients they serve. Counselors also explore their own cultural identities and how these affect their values and beliefs about the counseling process.

Counselors are encouraged to contribute to society by devoting a portion of their professional activity to services for which there is little or no financial return (pro bono public).

A.1. Welfare of Those Served by Counselors

A.1.a. Primary Responsibility

The primary responsibility of counselors is to respect the dignity and to promote the welfare of clients.

A.1.b. Records

Counselors maintain records necessary for rendering professional services to their clients and as required by laws, regulations, or agency or institution procedures. Counselors include sufficient and timely documentation in their client records to facilitate the delivery and continuity of needed services. Counselors take reasonable steps to ensure that documentation in records accurately reflects client progress and services provided. If errors are made in client records, counselors take steps to properly note the correction of such errors according to agency or institutional policies. *(See A.12.g.7., B.6., B.6.g., G.2.j.)*

A.1.c. Counseling Plans

Counselors and their clients work jointly in devising integrated counseling plans that offer reasonable promise of success and are consistent with abilities and circumstances of clients. Counselors and clients regularly review counseling plans to assess their continued viability and effectiveness, respecting the freedom of choice of clients. *(See A.2.a., A.2.d., A.12.g.)*

A.1.d. Support Network Involvement

Counselors recognize that support networks hold various meanings in the lives of clients and consider enlisting the support, understanding, and involvement of others (e.g., religious/spiritual/community leaders, family members, friends) as positive resources, when appropriate, with client consent.

A.1.e. Employment Needs

Counselors work with their clients considering employment in jobs that are consistent with the overall abilities, vocational limitations, physical restrictions, general temperament, interest and aptitude patterns, social skills, education, general qualifications, and other relevant characteristics and needs of clients. When appropriate, counselors appropriately trained in career development will assist in the placement of clients in positions that are consistent with the interest, culture, and the welfare of clients, employers, and/or the public.

A.2. Informed Consent in the Counseling Relationship

(See A.12.g., B.5., B.6.b., E.3., E.13.b., F.1.c., G.2.a.)

A.2.a. Informed Consent

Clients have the freedom to choose whether to enter into or remain in a counseling relationship and need adequate information about the counseling process and the counselor. Counselors have an obligation to review in writing and verbally with clients the rights and responsibilities of both the counselor and the client. Informed consent is an ongoing part of the counseling process, and counselors appropriately document discussions of informed consent throughout the counseling relationship.

A.2.b. Types of Information Needed

Counselors explicitly explain to clients the nature of all services provided. They inform clients about issues such as, but not limited to, the following: the purposes, goals, techniques, procedures, limitations, potential risks, and benefits of services; the counselor's qualifications, credentials, and relevant experience; continuation of services upon the incapacitation or death of a counselor; and other pertinent information. Counselors take steps to ensure that clients understand the implications of diagnosis, the intended use of tests and reports, fees, and billing arrangements. Clients have the right to confidentiality and to be provided with an explanation of its limitations (including how supervisors and/or treatment team professionals are involved); to obtain clear information about their records to participate in the ongoing counseling plans; and to refuse any services or modality change and to be advised of the consequences of such refusal.

A.2.c. Developmental and Cultural Sensitivity

Counselors communicate information in ways that are both developmentally and culturally appropriate. Counselors use clear and understandable language when discussing issues related to informed consent. When clients have difficulty understanding the language used by counselors, they provide necessary services (e.g., arranging for a qualified interpreter or translator) to ensure comprehension by clients. In collaboration with clients, counselors consider cultural implications of informed consent procedures and, where possible, counselors adjust their practices accordingly.

A.2.d. Inability to Give Consent

When counseling minors or persons unable to give voluntary consent, counselors seek the assent of clients to services, and include them in decision making as appropriate. Counselors recognize the need to balance the ethical rights of clients to make choices, their capacity to give consent or assent to receive services, and parental or familial legal rights and responsibilities to protect these clients and make decisions on their behalf.

A.3. Clients Served by Others

When counselors learn that their clients are in a professional relationship with another mental health professional, they request release from clients to inform the other professionals and strive to establish positive and collaborative professional relationships.

A.4. Avoiding Harm and Imposing Values

A.4.a. Avoiding Harm

Counselors act to avoid harming their clients, trainees, and research participants and to minimize or to remedy unavoidable or unanticipated harm.

A.4.b. Personal Values

Counselors are aware of their own values, attitudes, beliefs, and behaviors and avoid imposing values that are inconsistent with counseling goals. Counselors respect the diversity of clients, trainees, and research participants.

A.5. Roles and Relationships with Clients

(See F.3., F.10., G.3.)

A.5.a. Current Clients

Sexual or romantic counselor–client interactions or relationships with current clients, their romantic partners, or their family members are prohibited.

A.5.b. Former Clients

Sexual or romantic counselor–client interactions or relationships with former clients, their romantic partners, or their family members are prohibited for a period of 5 years following the last professional contact. Counselors, before engaging in sexual or romantic interactions or relationships with clients, their romantic partners, or client family members after 5 years following the last professional contact, demonstrate forethought and document (in written form) whether the interactions or relationship can be viewed as exploitive in some way and/or whether there is still potential to harm the former client; in cases of potential exploitation and/or harm, the counselor avoids entering such an interaction or relationship.

A.5.c. Nonprofessional Interactions or Relationships (Other Than Sexual or Romantic Interactions or Relationships)

Counselor–client nonprofessional relationships with clients, former clients, their romantic partners, or their family members should be avoided, except when the interaction is potentially beneficial to the client. *(See A.5.d.)*

A.5.d. Potentially Beneficial Interactions

When a counselor–client nonprofessional interaction with a client or former client may be potentially beneficial to the client or former client, the counselor must document in case records, prior to the interaction (when feasible), the rationale for such an interaction, the potential benefit, and anticipated consequences for the client or former client and other individuals significantly involved with the client or former client. Such interactions should be initiated with appropriate client consent. Where unintentional harm occurs to the client or former client, or to an individual significantly involved with the client or former client, due to the nonprofessional interaction, the counselor must show evidence of an attempt to remedy such harm. Examples of potentially beneficial interactions include, but are not limited to, attending a formal ceremony (e.g., a wedding/commitment ceremony or graduation); purchasing a service or product provided by a client or former client (excepting unrestricted bartering); hospital visits to an ill family member; mutual membership in a professional association, organization, or community. *(See A.5.c.)*

A.5.e. Role Changes in the Professional Relationship

When a counselor changes a role from the original or most recent contracted relationship, he or she obtains informed consent from the client and explains the right of the client to refuse services related to the change. Examples of role changes include

1. changing from individual to relationship or family counseling, or vice versa;
2. changing from a nonforensic evaluative role to a therapeutic role, or vice versa;
3. changing from a counselor to a researcher role (i.e., enlisting clients as research participants), or vice versa; and
4. changing from a counselor to a mediator role, or vice versa.

Clients must be fully informed of any anticipated consequences (e.g., financial, legal, personal, or therapeutic) of counselor role changes.

A.6. Roles and Relationships at Individual, Group, Institutional, and Societal Levels

A.6.a. Advocacy

When appropriate, counselors advocate at individual, group, institutional, and societal levels to examine potential barriers and obstacles that inhibit access and/or the growth and development of clients.

A.6.b. Confidentiality and Advocacy

Counselors obtain client consent prior to engaging in advocacy efforts on behalf of an identifiable client to improve the provision of services and to work toward removal of systemic barriers or obstacles that inhibit client access, growth, and development.

A.7. Multiple Clients

When a counselor agrees to provide counseling services to two or more persons who have a relationship, the counselor clarifies at the outset which person or persons are clients and the nature of the relationships the counselor will have with each involved person. If it becomes apparent that the counselor may be called upon to perform potentially conflicting roles, the counselor will clarify, adjust, or withdraw from roles appropriately. *(See A.8.a., B.4.)*

A.8. Group Work

(See B.4.a.)

A.8.a. Screening

Counselors screen prospective group counseling/therapy participants. To the extent possible, counselors select members whose needs and goals are compatible with goals of the group, who will not impede the group process, and whose well-being will not be jeopardized by the group experience.

A.8.b. Protecting Clients

In a group setting, counselors take reasonable precautions to protect clients from physical, emotional, or psychological trauma.

A.9. End-of-Life Care for Terminally Ill Clients

A.9.a. Quality of Care

Counselors strive to take measures that enable clients

1. to obtain high-quality end-of-life care for their physical, emotional, social, and spiritual needs;
2. to exercise the highest degree of self-determination possible;
3. to be given every opportunity possible to engage in informed decision making regarding their end-of-life care; and
4. to receive complete and adequate assessment regarding their ability to make competent, rational decisions on their own behalf from a mental health professional who is experienced in end-of-life care practice.

A.9.b. Counselor Competence, Choice, and Referral

Recognizing the personal, moral, and competence issues related to end-of-life decisions, counselors may choose to work or not work with terminally ill clients who wish to explore their end-of-life options. Counselors provide appropriate referral information to ensure that clients receive the necessary help.

A.9.c. Confidentiality

Counselors who provide services to terminally ill individuals who are considering hastening their own deaths have the option of breaking or not breaking confidentiality, depending on applicable laws and the specific circumstances of the situation and after seeking consultation or supervision from appropriate professional and legal parties. *(See B.5.c., B.7.c.)*

A.10. Fees and Bartering

A.10.a. Accepting Fees From Agency Clients

Counselors refuse a private fee or other remuneration for rendering services to persons who are entitled to such services through the counselor's employing agency or institution. The policies of a particular agency may make explicit provisions for agency clients to receive counseling services from members of its staff in private practice. In such instances, the clients must be informed of other options open to them should they seek private counseling services.

A.10.b. Establishing Fees

In establishing fees for professional counseling services, counselors consider the financial status of clients and locality. In the event that the established fee structure is inappropriate for a client, counselors assist clients in attempting to find comparable services of acceptable cost.

A.10.c. Nonpayment of Fees

If counselors intend to use collection agencies or take legal measures to collect fees from clients who do not pay for services as agreed upon, they first inform clients of intended actions and offer clients the opportunity to make payment.

A.10.d. Bartering

Counselors may barter only if the relationship is not exploitive or harmful and does not place the counselor in an unfair advantage, if the client requests it, and if such arrangements are an accepted practice among professionals in the community. Counselors consider the cultural implications of bartering and discuss relevant concerns with clients and document such agreements in a clear written contract.

A.10.e. Receiving Gifts

Counselors understand the challenges of accepting gifts from clients and recognize that in some cultures, small gifts are a token of respect and showing gratitude. When determining whether or not to accept a gift from clients, counselors take into account the therapeutic relationship, the monetary value of the gift, a client's motivation for giving the gift, and the counselor's motivation for wanting or declining the gift.

A.11. Termination and Referral

A.11.a. Abandonment Prohibited

Counselors do not abandon or neglect clients in counseling. Counselors assist in making appropriate arrangements for the continuation of treatment, when necessary, during interruptions such as vacations, illness, and following termination.

A.11.b. Inability to Assist Clients

If counselors determine an inability to be of professional assistance to clients, they avoid entering or continuing counseling relationships. Counselors are knowledgeable about culturally and clinically appropriate referral resources and suggest these alternatives. If clients decline the suggested referrals, counselors should discontinue the relationship.

A.11.c. Appropriate Termination

Counselors terminate a counseling relationship when it becomes reasonably apparent that the client no longer needs assistance, is not likely to benefit, or is being harmed by continued counseling. Counselors may terminate counseling when in jeopardy of harm by the client, or another person with whom the client has a relationship, or when clients do not pay fees as agreed upon. Counselors provide pretermination counseling and recommend other service providers when necessary.

A.11.d. Appropriate Transfer of Services

When counselors transfer or refer clients to other practitioners, they ensure that appropriate clinical and administrative processes are completed and open communication is maintained with both clients and practitioners.

A.12. Technology Applications

A.12.a. Benefits and Limitations

Counselors inform clients of the benefits and limitations of using information technology applications in the counseling process and in business/billing procedures. Such technologies include but are not limited to computer hardware and software, telephones, the World Wide Web, the Internet, online assessment instruments, and other communication devices.

A.12.b. Technology-Assisted Services

When providing technology-assisted distance counseling services, counselors determine that clients are intellectually, emotionally, and physically capable of using the application and that the application is appropriate for the needs of clients.

A.12.c. Inappropriate Services

When technology-assisted distance counseling services are deemed inappropriate by the counselor or client, counselors consider delivering services face to face.

A.12.d. Access

Counselors provide reasonable access to computer applications when providing technology-assisted distance counseling services.

A.12.e. Laws and Statutes

Counselors ensure that the use of technology does not violate the laws of any local, state, national, or international entity and observe all relevant statutes.

A.12.f. Assistance

Counselors seek business, legal, and technical assistance when using technology applications, particularly when the use of such applications crosses state or national boundaries.

A.12.g. Technology and Informed Consent

As part of the process of establishing informed consent, counselors do the following:

1. Address issues related to the difficulty of maintaining the confidentiality of electronically transmitted communications.
2. Inform clients of all colleagues, supervisors, and employees, such as Informational Technology (IT) administrators, who might have authorized or unauthorized access to electronic transmissions.
3. Urge clients to be aware of all authorized or unauthorized users including family members and fellow employees who have access to any technology clients may use in the counseling process.
4. Inform clients of pertinent legal rights and limitations governing the practice of a profession over state lines or international boundaries.
5. Use encrypted Web sites and e-mail communications to help ensure confidentiality when possible.
6. When the use of encryption is not possible, counselors notify clients of this fact and limit electronic transmissions to general communications that are not client specific.
7. Inform clients if and for how long archival storage of transaction records are maintained.

8. Discuss the possibility of technology failure and alternate methods of service delivery.
9. Inform clients of emergency procedures, such as calling 911 or a local crisis hotline, when the counselor is not available.
10. Discuss time zone differences, local customs, and cultural or language differences that might impact service delivery.
11. Inform clients when technology-assisted distance counseling services are not covered by insurance. *(See A.2.)*

A.12.h. Sites on the World Wide Web

Counselors maintaining sites on the World Wide Web (the Internet) do the following:

1. Regularly check that electronic links are working and professionally appropriate.
2. Establish ways clients can contact the counselor in case of technology failure.
3. Provide electronic links to relevant state licensure and professional certification boards to protect consumer rights and facilitate addressing ethical concerns.
4. Establish a method for verifying client identity.
5. Obtain the written consent of the legal guardian or other authorized legal representative prior to rendering services in the event the client is a minor child, an adult who is legally incompetent, or an adult incapable of giving informed consent.
6. Strive to provide a site that is accessible to persons with disabilities.
7. Strive to provide translation capabilities for clients who have a different primary language while also addressing the imperfect nature of such translations.
8. Assist clients in determining the validity and reliability of information found on the World Wide Web and other technology applications.

Section B: Confidentiality, Privileged Communication, and Privacy

Introduction

Counselors recognize that trust is a cornerstone of the counseling relationship. Counselors aspire to earn the trust of clients by creating an ongoing partnership, establishing and upholding appropriate boundaries, and maintaining confidentiality. Counselors communicate the parameters of confidentiality in a culturally competent manner.

B.1. Respecting Client Rights

B.1.a. Multicultural/Diversity Considerations

Counselors maintain awareness and sensitivity regarding cultural meanings of confidentiality and privacy. Counselors respect differing views toward disclosure of information. Counselors hold ongoing discussions with clients as to how, when, and with whom information is to be shared.

B.1.b. Respect for Privacy

Counselors respect client rights to privacy. Counselors solicit private information from clients only when it is beneficial to the counseling process.

B.1.c. Respect for Confidentiality

Counselors do not share confidential information without client consent or without sound legal or ethical justification.

B.1.d. Explanation of Limitations

At initiation and throughout the counseling process, counselors inform clients of the limitations of confidentiality and seek to identify foreseeable situations in which confidentiality must be breached. *(See A.2.b.)*

B.2. Exceptions

B.2.a. Danger and Legal Requirements

The general requirement that counselors keep information confidential does not apply when disclosure is required to protect clients or identified others from serious and foreseeable harm or when legal requirements demand that confidential information must be revealed. Counselors consult with other professionals when in doubt as to the validity of an exception. Additional considerations apply when addressing end-of-life issues. *(See A.9.c.)*

B.2.b. Contagious, Life-Threatening Diseases

When clients disclose that they have a disease commonly known to be both communicable and life threatening, counselors may be justified in disclosing information to identifiable third parties, if they are known to be at demonstrable and high risk of contracting the disease. Prior to making a disclosure, counselors confirm that there is such a diagnosis and assess the intent of clients to inform the third parties about their disease or to engage in any behaviors that may be harmful to an identifiable third party.

B.2.c. Court-Ordered Disclosure

When subpoenaed to release confidential or privileged information without a client's permission, counselors obtain written, informed consent from the client or take steps to prohibit the disclosure or have it limited as narrowly as possible due to potential harm to the client or counseling relationship.

B.2.d. Minimal Disclosure

To the extent possible, clients are informed before confidential information is disclosed and are involved in the disclosure decision-making process. When circumstances require the disclosure of confidential information, only essential information is revealed.

B.3. Information Shared With Others

B.3.a. Subordinates

Counselors make every effort to ensure that privacy and confidentiality of clients are maintained by subordinates, including employees, supervisees, students, clerical assistants, and volunteers. *(See F.1.c.)*

B.3.b. Treatment Teams

When client treatment involves a continued review or participation by a treatment team, the client will be informed of the team's existence and composition, information being shared, and the purposes of sharing such information.

B.3.c. Confidential Settings

Counselors discuss confidential information only in settings in which they can reasonably ensure client privacy.

B.3.d. Third-Party Payers

Counselors disclose information to third-party payers only when clients have authorized such disclosure.

B.3.e. Transmitting Confidential Information

Counselors take precautions to ensure the confidentiality of information transmitted through the use of computers, electronic mail, facsimile machines, telephones, voice mail, answering machines, and other electronic or computer technology. *(See A.12.g.)*

B.3.f. Deceased Clients

Counselors protect the confidentiality of deceased clients, consistent with legal requirements and agency or setting policies.

B.4. Groups and Families

B.4.a. Group Work

In group work, counselors clearly explain the importance and parameters of confidentiality for the specific group being entered.

B.4.b. Couples and Family Counseling

In couples and family counseling, counselors clearly define who is considered "the client" and discuss expectations and limitations of confidentiality. Counselors seek agreement and document in writing such agreement among all involved parties having capacity to give consent concerning each individual's right to confidentiality and any obligation to preserve the confidentiality of information known.

B.5. Clients Lacking Capacity to Give Informed Consent

B.5.a. Responsibility to Clients

When counseling minor clients or adult clients who lack the capacity to give voluntary, informed consent, counselors protect the confidentiality of information received in the counseling relationship as specified by federal and state laws, written policies, and applicable ethical standards.

B.5.b. Responsibility to Parents and Legal Guardians

Counselors inform parents and legal guardians about the role of counselors and the confidential nature of the counseling relationship. Counselors are sensitive to the cultural diversity of families and respect the inherent rights and responsibilities of parents/guardians over the welfare of their children/charges according to law. Counselors work to establish, as appropriate, collaborative relationships with parents/guardians to best serve clients.

B.5.c. Release of Confidential Information

When counseling minor clients or adult clients who lack the capacity to give voluntary consent to release confidential information, counselors seek permission from an appropriate third party to disclose information. In such instances, counselors inform clients consistent with their level of understanding and take culturally appropriate measures to safeguard client confidentiality.

B.6. Records

B.6.a. Confidentiality of Records

Counselors ensure that records are kept in a secure location and that only authorized persons have access to records.

B.6.b. Permission to Record

Counselors obtain permission from clients prior to recording sessions through electronic or other means.

B.6.c. Permission to Observe

Counselors obtain permission from clients prior to observing counseling sessions, reviewing session transcripts, or viewing recordings of sessions with supervisors, faculty, peers, or others within the training environment.

B.6.d. Client Access

Counselors provide reasonable access to records and copies of records when requested by competent clients. Counselors limit the access of clients to their records, or portions of their records, only when there is compelling evidence that such access would cause harm to the client. Counselors document the request of clients and the rationale for withholding some or all of the record in the files of clients. In situations involving multiple clients, counselors provide individual clients with only those parts of records that related directly to them and do not include confidential information related to any other client.

B.6.e. Assistance With Records

When clients request access to their records, counselors provide assistance and consultation in interpreting counseling records.

B.6.f. Disclosure or Transfer

Unless exceptions to confidentiality exist, counselors obtain written permission from clients to disclose or transfer records to legitimate third parties. Steps are taken to ensure that receivers of counseling records are sensitive to their confidential nature. *(See A.3., E.4.)*

B.6.g. Storage and Disposal After Termination

Counselors store records following termination of services to ensure reasonable future access, maintain records in accordance with state and federal statutes governing records, and dispose of client records and other sensitive materials in a manner that protects client confidentiality. When records are of an artistic nature, counselors obtain client (or guardian) consent with regard to handling of such records or documents. *(See A.1.b.)*

B.6.h. Reasonable Precautions

Counselors take reasonable precautions to protect client confidentiality in the event of the counselor's termination of practice, incapacity, or death. *(See C.2.h.)*

B.7. Research and Training

B.7.a. Institutional Approval

When institutional approval is required, counselors provide accurate information about their research proposals and obtain approval prior to conducting their research. They conduct research in accordance with the approved research protocol.

B.7.b. Adherence to Guidelines

Counselors are responsible for understanding and adhering to state, federal, agency, or institutional policies or applicable guidelines regarding confidentiality in their research practices.

B.7.c. Confidentiality of Information Obtained in Research

Violations of participant privacy and confidentiality are risks of participation in research involving human participants. Investigators maintain all research records in a secure manner. They explain to participants the risks of violations of privacy and confidentiality and disclose to participants any limits of confidentiality that reasonably can be expected. Regardless of the degree to which confidentiality will be maintained, investigators must disclose to participants any limits of confidentiality that reasonably can be expected. *(See G.2.e.)*

B.7.d. Disclosure of Research Information

Counselors do not disclose confidential information that reasonably could lead to the identification of a research participant unless they have obtained the prior consent of the person. Use of data derived from counseling relationships for purposes of training, research, or publication is confined to content that is disguised to ensure the anonymity of the individuals involved. *(See G.2.a., G.2.d.)*

B.7.e. Agreement for Identification

Identification of clients, students, or supervisees in a presentation or publication is permissible only when they have reviewed the material and agreed to its presentation or publication. *(See G.4.d.)*

B.8. Consultation

B.8.a. Agreements

When acting as consultants, counselors seek agreements among all parties involved concerning each individual's rights to confidentiality, the obligation of each individual to preserve confidential information, and the limits of confidentiality of information shared by others.

B.8.b. Respect for Privacy

Information obtained in a consulting relationship is discussed for professional purposes only with persons directly involved with the case. Written and oral reports present only data germane to the purposes of the consultation, and every effort is made to protect client identity and to avoid undue invasion of privacy.

B.8.c. Disclosure of Confidential Information

When consulting with colleagues, counselors do not disclose confidential information that reasonably could lead to the identification of a client or other person or organization with whom they have a confidential relationship unless they have obtained the prior consent of the person or organization or the disclosure cannot be avoided. They disclose information only to the extent necessary to achieve the purposes of the consultation. *(See D.2.d.)*

Section C: Professional Responsibility

Introduction

Counselors aspire to open, honest, and accurate communication in dealing with the public and other professionals. They practice in a nondiscriminatory manner within the boundaries of professional and personal competence and have a responsibility to abide by the *ACA Code of Ethics*. Counselors actively participate in local, state, and national associations that foster the development and improvement of counseling. Counselors advocate to promote change at the individual, group, institutional, and societal levels that improves the quality of life for individuals and groups and removes potential barriers to the provision or access of appropriate services being offered. Counselors have a responsibility to the public to engage in counseling practices that are based on rigorous research methodologies. In addition, counselors engage in self-care activities to maintain and promote their emotional, physical, mental, and spiritual well-being to best meet their professional responsibilities.

C.1. Knowledge of Standards

Counselors have a responsibility to read, understand, and follow the *ACA Code of Ethics* and adhere to applicable laws and regulations.

C.2. Professional Competence

C.2.a. Boundaries of Competence

Counselors practice only within the boundaries of their competence, based on their education, training, supervised experience, state and national professional credentials, and appropriate professional experience. Counselors gain knowledge, personal awareness, sensitivity, and skills pertinent to working with a diverse client population. *(See A.9.b., C.4.e., E.2., F.2., F.11.b.)*

C.2.b. New Specialty Areas of Practice

Counselors practice in specialty areas new to them only after appropriate education, training, and supervised experience. While developing skills in new specialty areas, counselors take steps to ensure the competence of their work and to protect others from possible harm. *(See F.6.f.)*

C.2.c. Qualified for Employment

Counselors accept employment only for positions for which they are qualified by education, training, supervised experience, state and national professional credentials, and appropriate professional experience. Counselors hire for professional counseling positions only individuals who are qualified and competent for those positions.

C.2.d. Monitor Effectiveness

Counselors continually monitor their effectiveness as professionals and take steps to improve when necessary. Counselors in private practice take reasonable steps to seek peer supervision as needed to evaluate their efficacy as counselors.

C.2.e. Consultation on Ethical Obligations

Counselors take reasonable steps to consult with other counselors or related professionals when they have questions regarding their ethical obligations or professional practice.

C.2.f. Continuing Education

Counselors recognize the need for continuing education to acquire and maintain a reasonable level of awareness of current scientific and professional information in their fields of activity. They take steps to maintain competence in the skills they use, are open to new procedures, and keep current with the diverse populations and specific populations with whom they work.

C.2.g. Impairment

Counselors are alert to the signs of impairment from their own physical, mental, or emotional problems and refrain from offering or providing professional services when such impairment is likely to harm a client or others. They seek assistance for problems that reach the level of professional impairment, and, if necessary, they limit, suspend, or terminate their professional responsibilities until such time it is determined that they may safely resume their work. Counselors assist colleagues or supervisors in recognizing their own professional impairment and provide consultation and assistance when warranted with colleagues or supervisors showing signs of impairment and intervene as appropriate to prevent imminent harm to clients. *(See A.11.b., F.8.b.)*

C.2.h. Counselor Incapacitation or Termination of Practice

When counselors leave a practice, they follow a prepared plan for transfer of clients and files. Counselors prepare and disseminate to an identified colleague or "records custodian" a plan for the transfer of clients and files in the case of their incapacitation, death, or termination of practice.

C.3. Advertising and Soliciting Clients

C.3.a. Accurate Advertising

When advertising or otherwise representing their services to the public, counselors identify their credentials in an accurate manner that is not false, misleading, deceptive, or fraudulent.

C.3.b. Testimonials

Counselors who use testimonials do not solicit them from current clients nor former clients nor any other persons who may be vulnerable to undue influence.

C.3.c. Statements by Others

Counselors make reasonable efforts to ensure that statements made by others about them or the profession of counseling are accurate.

C.3.d. Recruiting Through Employment

Counselors do not use their places of employment or institutional affiliation to recruit or gain clients, supervisees, or consultees for their private practices.

C.3.e. Products and Training Advertisements

Counselors who develop products related to their profession or conduct workshops or training events ensure that the advertisements concerning these products or events are accurate and disclose adequate information for consumers to make informed choices. *(See C.6.d.)*

C.3.f. Promoting to Those Served

Counselors do not use counseling, teaching, training, or supervisory relationships to promote their products or training events in a manner that is deceptive or would exert undue influence on individuals who may be vulnerable. However, counselor educators may adopt textbooks they have authored for instructional purposes.

C.4. Professional Qualifications

C.4.a. Accurate Representation

Counselors claim or imply only professional qualifications actually completed and correct any known misrepresentations of their qualifications by others. Counselors truthfully represent the qualifications of their professional colleagues. Counselors clearly distinguish between paid and volunteer work experience and accurately describe their continuing education and specialized training. *(See C.2.a.)*

C.4.b. Credentials

Counselors claim only licenses or certifications that are current and in good standing.

C.4.c. Educational Degrees

Counselors clearly differentiate between earned and honorary degrees.

C.4.d. Implying Doctoral-Level Competence

Counselors clearly state their highest earned degree in counseling or closely related field. Counselors do not imply doctoral-level competence when only possessing a master's degree in counseling or a related field by referring to themselves as "Dr." in a counseling context when their doctorate is not in counseling or a related field.

C.4.e. Program Accreditation Status

Counselors clearly state the accreditation status of their degree programs at the time the degree was earned.

C.4.f. Professional Membership

Counselors clearly differentiate between current, active memberships and former memberships in associations. Members of the American Counseling Association must clearly differentiate between professional membership, which implies the possession of at least a master's degree in counseling, and regular membership, which is open to individuals whose interests and activities are consistent with those of ACA but are not qualified for professional membership.

C.5. Nondiscrimination

Counselors do not condone or engage in discrimination based on age, culture, disability, ethnicity, race, religion/spirituality, gender, gender identity, sexual orientation, marital status/partnership, language preference, socioeconomic status, or any basis proscribed by law. Counselors do not discriminate against clients, students, employees, supervisees, or research participants in a manner that has a negative impact on these persons.

C.6. Public Responsibility

C.6.a. Sexual Harassment

Counselors do not engage in or condone sexual harassment. Sexual harassment is defined as sexual solicitation, physical advances, or verbal or nonverbal conduct that is sexual in nature, that occurs in connection with professional activities or roles, and that either

1. is unwelcome, is offensive, or creates a hostile workplace or learning environment, and counselors know or are told this; or
2. is sufficiently severe or intense to be perceived as harassment to a reasonable person in the context in which the behavior occurred.

Sexual harassment can consist of a single intense or severe act or multiple persistent or pervasive acts.

C.6.b. Reports to Third Parties

Counselors are accurate, honest, and objective in reporting their professional activities and judgments to appropriate third parties, including courts, health insurance companies, those who are the recipients of evaluation reports, and others. *(See B.3., E.4.)*

C.6.c. Media Presentations

When counselors provide advice or comment by means of public lectures, demonstrations, radio or television programs, prerecorded tapes, technology-based applications, printed articles, mailed material, or other media, they take reasonable precautions to ensure that

1. the statements are based on appropriate professional counseling literature and practice,
2. the statements are otherwise consistent with the *ACA Code of Ethics*, and
3. the recipients of the information are not encouraged to infer that a professional counseling relationship has been established.

C.6.d. Exploitation of Others

Counselors do not exploit others in their professional relationships. *(See C.3.e.)*

C.6.e. Scientific Bases for Treatment Modalities

Counselors use techniques/procedures/modalities that are grounded in theory and/or have an empirical or scientific foundation. Counselors who do not must define the techniques/procedures as "unproven" or "developing" and explain the potential risks and ethical considerations of using such techniques/procedures and take steps to protect clients from possible harm. *(See A.4.a., E.5.c., E.5.d.)*

C.7. Responsibility to Other Professionals

C.7.a. Personal Public Statements

When making personal statements in a public context, counselors clarify that they are speaking from their personal perspectives and that they are not speaking on behalf of all counselors or the profession.

Section D: Relationships With Other Professionals

Introduction

Professional counselors recognize that the quality of their interactions with colleagues can influence the quality of services provided to clients. They work to become knowledgeable about colleagues within and outside the field of counseling. Counselors develop positive working relationships and systems of communication with colleagues to enhance services to clients.

D.1. Relationships With Colleagues, Employers, and Employees

D.1.a. Different Approaches

Counselors are respectful of approaches to counseling services that differ from their own. Counselors are respectful of traditions and practices of other professional groups with which they work.

D.1.b. Forming Relationships

Counselors work to develop and strengthen interdisciplinary relations with colleagues from other disciplines to best serve clients.

D.1.c. Interdisciplinary Teamwork

Counselors who are members of interdisciplinary teams delivering multifaceted services to clients keep the focus on how to best serve the clients. They participate in and contribute to decisions that affect the well-being of clients by drawing on the perspectives, values, and experiences of the counseling profession and those of colleagues from other disciplines. *(See A.1.a.)*

D.1.d. Confidentiality

When counselors are required by law, institutional policy, or extraordinary circumstances to serve in more than one role in judicial or administrative proceedings, they clarify role expectations and the parameters of confidentiality with their colleagues. *(See B.1.c., B.1.d., B.2.c., B.2.d., B.3.b.)*

D.1.e. Establishing Professional and Ethical Obligations

Counselors who are members of interdisciplinary teams clarify professional and ethical obligations of the team as a whole and of its individual members. When a team decision raises ethical concerns, counselors first attempt to resolve the concern within the team. If they cannot reach resolution among team members, counselors pursue other avenues to address their concerns consistent with client well-being.

D.1.f. Personnel Selection and Assignment

Counselors select competent staff and assign responsibilities compatible with their skills and experiences.

D.1.g. Employer Policies

The acceptance of employment in an agency or institution implies that counselors are in agreement with its general policies and principles. Counselors strive to reach agreement with employers as to acceptable standards of conduct that allow for changes in institutional policy conducive to the growth and development of clients.

D.1.h. Negative Conditions

Counselors alert their employers of inappropriate policies and practices. They attempt to effect changes in such policies or procedures through constructive action within the organization. When such policies are potentially disruptive or damaging to clients or may limit the effectiveness of services provided and change cannot be effected, counselors take appropriate further action. Such action may include referral to appropriate certification, accreditation, or state licensure organizations, or voluntary termination of employment.

D.1.i. Protection From Punitive Action

Counselors take care not to harass or dismiss an employee who has acted in a responsible and ethical manner to expose inappropriate employer policies or practices.

D.2. Consultation

D.2.a. Consultant Competency

Counselors take reasonable steps to ensure that they have the appropriate resources and competencies when providing consultation services. Counselors provide appropriate referral resources when requested or needed. *(See C.2.a.)*

D.2.b. Understanding Consultees

When providing consultation, counselors attempt to develop with their consultees a clear understanding of problem definition, goals for change, and predicted consequences of interventions selected.

D.2.c. Consultant Goals

The consulting relationship is one in which consultee adaptability and growth toward self-direction are consistently encouraged and cultivated.

D.2.d. Informed Consent in Consultation

When providing consultation, counselors have an obligation to review, in writing and verbally, the rights and responsibilities of both counselors and consultees. Counselors use clear and understandable language to inform all parties involved about the purpose of the services to be provided, relevant costs, potential risks and benefits, and the limits of confidentiality. Working in conjunction with the consultee, counselors attempt to develop a clear definition of the problem, goals for change, and predicted consequences of interventions that are culturally responsive and appropriate to the needs of consultees. *(See A.2.a., A.2.b.)*

Section E: Evaluation, Assessment, and Interpretation

Introduction

Counselors use assessment instruments as one component of the counseling process, taking into account the client's personal and cultural context. Counselors promote the well-being of individual clients or groups of clients by developing and using appropriate educational, psychological, and career-assessment instruments.

E.1. General

E.1.a. Assessment

The primary purpose of educational, psychological, and career assessment is to provide measurements that are valid and reliable in either comparative or absolute terms. These include, but are not limited to, measurements of ability, personality, interest, intelligence, achievement, and performance. Counselors recognize the need to interpret the statements in this section as applying to both quantitative and qualitative assessments.

E.1.b. Client Welfare

Counselors do not misuse assessment results and interpretations, and they take reasonable steps to prevent others from misusing the information these techniques provide. They respect the client's right to know the results, the interpretations made, and the bases for counselors' conclusions and recommendations.

E.2. Competence to Use and Interpret Assessment Instruments

E.2.a. Limits of Competence

Counselors utilize only those testing and assessment services for which they have been trained and are competent. Counselors using technology-assisted test interpretations are trained in the construct being measured and the specific instrument being used prior to using its technology-based application. Counselors take reasonable measures to ensure the proper use of psychological and career-assessment techniques by persons under their supervision. *(See A.12.)*

E.2.b. Appropriate Use

Counselors are responsible for the appropriate application, scoring, interpretation, and use of assessment instruments relevant to the needs of the client, whether they score and interpret such assessments themselves or use technology or other services.

E.2.c. Decisions Based on Results

Counselors responsible for decisions involving individuals or policies that are based on assessment results have a thorough understanding of educational, psychological, and career measurement, including validation criteria, assessment research, and guidelines for assessment development and use.

E.3. Informed Consent in Assessment

E.3.a. Explanation to Clients

Prior to assessment, counselors explain the nature and purposes of assessment and the specific use of results by potential recipients. The explanation will be given in the language of the client (or other legally authorized person on behalf of the client), unless an explicit exception has been agreed upon in advance. Counselors consider the client's personal or cultural context, the level of the client's understanding of the results, and the impact of the results on the client. *(See A.2., A.12.g., F.1.c.)*

E.3.b. Recipients of Results

Counselors consider the examinee's welfare, explicit understandings, and prior agreements in determining who receives the assessment results. Counselors include accurate and appropriate interpretations with any release of individual or group assessment results. *(See B.2.c., B.5.)*

E.4. Release of Data to Qualified Professionals

Counselors release assessment data in which the client is identified only with the consent of the client or the client's legal representative. Such data are released only to persons recognized by counselors as qualified to interpret the data. *(See B.1., B.3., B.6.b.)*

E.5. Diagnosis of Mental Disorders

E.5.a. Proper Diagnosis

Counselors take special care to provide proper diagnosis of mental disorders. Assessment techniques (including personal interview) used to determine client care (e.g., locus of treatment, type of treatment, or recommended follow-up) are carefully selected and appropriately used.

E.5.b. Cultural Sensitivity

Counselors recognize that culture affects the manner in which clients' problems are defined. Clients' socioeconomic and cultural experiences are considered when diagnosing mental disorders. *(See A.2.c.)*

E.5.c. Historical and Social Prejudices in the Diagnosis of Pathology

Counselors recognize historical and social prejudices in the misdiagnosis and pathologizing of certain individuals and groups and the role of mental health professionals in perpetuating these prejudices through diagnosis and treatment.

E.5.d. Refraining From Diagnosis

Counselors may refrain from making and/or reporting a diagnosis if they believe it would cause harm to the client or others.

E.6. Instrument Selection

E.6.a. Appropriateness of Instruments

Counselors carefully consider the validity, reliability, psychometric limitations, and appropriateness of instruments when selecting assessments.

E.6.b. Referral Information

If a client is referred to a third party for assessment, the counselor provides specific referral questions and sufficient objective data about the client to ensure that appropriate assessment instruments are utilized. *(See A.9.b., B.3.)*

E.6.c. Culturally Diverse Populations

Counselors are cautious when selecting assessments for culturally diverse populations to avoid the use of instruments that lack appropriate psychometric properties for the client population. *(See A.2.c., E.5.b.)*

E.7. Conditions of Assessment Administration

(See A.12.b, A.12.d.)

E.7.a. Administration Conditions

Counselors administer assessments under the same conditions that were established in their standardization. When assessments are not administered under standard conditions, as may be necessary to accommodate clients with disabilities, or when unusual behavior or irregularities occur during the administration, those conditions are noted in interpretation, and the results may be designated as invalid or of questionable validity.

E.7.b. Technological Administration

Counselors ensure that administration programs function properly and provide clients with accurate results when technological or other electronic methods are used for assessment administration.

E.7.c. Unsupervised Assessments

Unless the assessment instrument is designed, intended, and validated for self-administration and/or scoring, counselors do not permit inadequately supervised use.

E.7.d. Disclosure of Favorable Conditions

Prior to administration of assessments, conditions that produce most favorable assessment results are made known to the examinee.

E.8. Multicultural Issues/Diversity in Assessment

Counselors use with caution assessment techniques that were normed on populations other than that of the client. Counselors recognize the effects of age, color, culture, disability, ethnic group, gender, race, language preference, religion, spirituality, sexual orientation, and socioeconomic status on test administration and interpretation, and place test results in proper perspective with other relevant factors. *(See A.2.c., E.5.b.)*

E.9. Scoring and Interpretation of Assessments

E.9.a. Reporting

In reporting assessment results, counselors indicate reservations that exist regarding validity or reliability due to circumstances of the assessment or the inappropriateness of the norms for the person tested.

E.9.b. Research Instruments

Counselors exercise caution when interpreting the results of research instruments not having sufficient technical data to support respondent results. The specific purposes for the use of such instruments are stated explicitly to the examinee.

E.9.c. Assessment Services

Counselors who provide assessment scoring and interpretation services to support the assessment process confirm the validity of such interpretations. They accurately describe the purpose, norms, validity, reliability, and applications of the procedures and any special qualifications applicable to their use. The public offering of an automated test interpretations service is considered a professional-to-professional consultation. The formal responsibility of the consultant is to the consultee, but the ultimate and overriding responsibility is to the client. *(See D.2.)*

E.10. Assessment Security

Counselors maintain the integrity and security of tests and other assessment techniques consistent with legal and contractual obligations. Counselors do not appropriate, reproduce, or modify published assessments or parts thereof without acknowledgment and permission from the publisher.

E.11. Obsolete Assessments and Outdated Results

Counselors do not use data or results from assessments that are obsolete or outdated for the current purpose. Counselors make every effort to prevent the misuse of obsolete measures and assessment data by others.

E.12. Assessment Construction

Counselors use established scientific procedures, relevant standards, and current professional knowledge for assessment design in the development, publication, and utilization of educational and psychological assessment techniques.

E.13. Forensic Evaluation: Evaluation for Legal Proceedings

E.13.a. Primary Obligations

When providing forensic evaluations, the primary obligation of counselors is to produce objective findings that can be substantiated based on information and techniques appropriate to the evaluation, which may include examination of the individual and/or review of records. Counselors are entitled to form professional opinions based on their professional knowledge and expertise that can be supported by the data gathered in evaluations. Counselors will define the limits of their reports or testimony, especially when an examination of the individual has not been conducted.

E.13.b. Consent for Evaluation

Individuals being evaluated are informed in writing that the relationship is for the purposes of an evaluation and is not counseling in nature, and entities or individuals who will receive the evaluation report are identified. Written consent to be evaluated is obtained from those being evaluated unless a court orders evaluations to be conducted without the written consent of individuals being evaluated. When children or vulnerable adults are being evaluated, informed written consent is obtained from a parent or guardian.

E.13.c. Client Evaluation Prohibited

Counselors do not evaluate individuals for forensic purposes they currently counsel or individuals they have counseled in the past. Counselors do not accept as counseling clients individuals they are evaluating or individuals they have evaluated in the past for forensic purposes.

E.13.d. Avoid Potentially Harmful Relationships

Counselors who provide forensic evaluations avoid potentially harmful professional or personal relationships with family members, romantic partners, and close friends of individuals they are evaluating or have evaluated in the past.

Section F: Supervision, Training, and Teaching

Introduction

Counselors aspire to foster meaningful and respectful professional relationships and to maintain appropriate boundaries with supervisees and students. Counselors have theoretical and pedagogical foundations for their work and aim to be fair, accurate, and honest in their assessments of counselors-in-training.

F.1. Counselor Supervision and Client Welfare

F.1.a. Client Welfare

A primary obligation of counseling supervisors is to monitor the services provided by other counselors or counselors-in-training. Counseling supervisors monitor client welfare and supervisee clinical performance and professional development. To fulfill these obligations, supervisors meet regularly with supervisees to review case notes, samples of clinical work, or live observations. Supervisees have a responsibility to understand and follow the *ACA Code of Ethics*.

F.1.b. Counselor Credentials

Counseling supervisors work to ensure that clients are aware of the qualifications of the supervisees who render services to the clients. *(See A.2.b.)*

F.1.c. Informed Consent and Client Rights

Supervisors make supervisees aware of client rights including the protection of client privacy and confidentiality in the counseling relationship. Supervisees provide clients with professional disclosure information and inform them of how the supervision process influences the limits of confidentiality. Supervisees make clients aware of who will have access to records of the counseling relationship and how these records will be used. *(See A.2.b., B.1.d.)*

F.2. Counselor Supervision Competence

F.2.a. Supervisor Preparation

Prior to offering clinical supervision services, counselors are trained in supervision methods and techniques. Counselors who offer clinical supervision services regularly pursue continuing education activities including both counseling and supervision topics and skills. *(See C.2.a., C.2.f.)*

F.2.b. Multicultural Issues/Diversity in Supervision

Counseling supervisors are aware of and address the role of multiculturalism/diversity in the supervisory relationship.

F.3. Supervisory Relationships

F.3.a. Relationship Boundaries With Supervisees

Counseling supervisors clearly define and maintain ethical professional, personal, and social relationships with their supervisees. Counseling supervisors avoid nonprofessional relationships with current supervisees. If supervisors must assume other professional roles (e.g., clinical and administrative supervisor, instructor) with supervisees, they work to minimize potential conflicts and explain to supervisees the expectations and responsibilities associated with each role. They do not engage in any form of nonprofessional interaction that may compromise the supervisory relationship.

F.3.b. Sexual Relationships

Sexual or romantic interactions or relationships with current supervisees are prohibited.

F.3.c. Sexual Harassment

Counseling supervisors do not condone or subject supervisees to sexual harassment. *(See C.6.a.)*

F.3.d. Close Relatives and Friends

Counseling supervisors avoid accepting close relatives, romantic partners, or friends as supervisees.

F.3.e. Potentially Beneficial Relationships

Counseling supervisors are aware of the power differential in their relationships with supervisees. If they believe nonprofessional relationships with a supervisee may be potentially beneficial to the supervisee, they take precautions similar to those taken by counselors when working with clients. Examples of potentially beneficial interactions or relationships include attending a formal ceremony; hospital visits; providing support during a stressful event; or mutual membership in a professional association, organization, or community. Counseling supervisors engage in open discussions with supervisees when they consider entering into relationships with them outside of their roles as clinical and/or administrative supervisors. Before engaging in nonprofessional relationships, supervisors discuss with supervisees and document the rationale for such interactions, potential benefits or drawbacks, and anticipated consequences for the supervisee. Supervisors clarify the specific nature and limitations of the additional role(s) they will have with the supervisee.

F.4. Supervisor Responsibilities

F.4.a. Informed Consent for Supervision

Supervisors are responsible for incorporating into their supervision the principles of informed consent and participation. Supervisors inform supervisees of the policies and procedures to which they are to adhere and the mechanisms for due process appeal of individual supervisory actions.

F.4.b. Emergencies and Absences

Supervisors establish and communicate to supervisees procedures for contacting them or, in their absence, alternative on-call supervisors to assist in handling crises.

F.4.c. Standards for Supervisees

Supervisors make their supervisees aware of professional and ethical standards and legal responsibilities. Supervisors of postdegree counselors encourage these counselors to adhere to professional standards of practice. *(See C.1.)*

F.4.d. Termination of the Supervisory Relationship

Supervisors or supervisees have the right to terminate the supervisory relationship with adequate notice. Reasons for withdrawal are provided to the other party. When cultural, clinical, or professional issues are crucial to the viability of the supervisory relationship, both parties make efforts to resolve differences. When termination is warranted, supervisors make appropriate referrals to possible alternative supervisors.

F.5. Counseling Supervision Evaluation, Remediation, and Endorsement

F.5.a. Evaluation

Supervisors document and provide supervisees with ongoing performance appraisal and evaluation feedback and schedule periodic formal evaluative sessions throughout the supervisory relationship.

F.5.b. Limitations

Through ongoing evaluation and appraisal, supervisors are aware of the limitations of supervisees that might impede performance. Supervisors assist supervisees in securing remedial assistance when needed. They recommend dismissal from training programs, applied counseling settings, or state or voluntary professional credentialing processes when those supervisees are unable to provide competent professional services. Supervisors seek consultation and document their decisions to dismiss or refer supervisees for assistance. They ensure that supervisees are aware of options available to them to address such decisions. *(See C.2.g.)*

F.5.c. Counseling for Supervisees

If supervisees request counseling, supervisors provide them with acceptable referrals. Counselors do not provide counseling services to supervisees. Supervisors address interpersonal competencies in terms of the impact of these issues on clients, the supervisory relationship, and professional functioning. *(See F.3.a.)*

F.5.d. Endorsement

Supervisors endorse supervisees for certification, licensure, employment, or completion of an academic or training program only when they believe supervisees are qualified for the endorsement. Regardless of qualifications, supervisors do not endorse supervisees whom they believe to be impaired in any way that would interfere with the performance of the duties associated with the endorsement.

F.6. Responsibilities of Counselor Educators

F.6.a. Counselor Educators

Counselor educators who are responsible for developing, implementing, and supervising educational programs are skilled as teachers and practitioners. They are knowledgeable regarding the ethical, legal, and regulatory aspects of the profession, are skilled in applying that knowledge, and make students and supervisees aware of their responsibilities. Counselor educators conduct counselor education and training programs in an ethical manner and serve as role models for professional behavior. *(See C.1., C.2.a., C.2.c.)*

F.6.b. Infusing Multicultural Issues/Diversity

Counselor educators infuse material related to multiculturalism/diversity into all courses and workshops for the development of professional counselors.

F.6.c. Integration of Study and Practice

Counselor educators establish education and training programs that integrate academic study and supervised practice.

F.6.d. Teaching Ethics

Counselor educators make students and supervisees aware of the ethical responsibilities and standards of the profession and the ethical responsibilities of students to the profession. Counselor educators infuse ethical considerations throughout the curriculum. *(See C.1.)*

F.6.e. Peer Relationships

Counselor educators make every effort to ensure that the rights of peers are not compromised when students or supervisees lead counseling groups or provide clinical supervision. Counselor educators take steps to ensure that students and supervisees understand they have the same ethical obligations as counselor educators, trainers, and supervisors.

F.6.f. Innovative Theories and Techniques

When counselor educators teach counseling techniques/procedures that are innovative, without an empirical foundation, or without a well-grounded theoretical foundation, they define the counseling techniques/procedures as "unproven" or "developing" and explain to students the potential risks and ethical considerations of using such techniques/ procedures.

F.6.g. Field Placements

Counselor educators develop clear policies within their training programs regarding field placement and other clinical experiences. Counselor educators provide clearly stated roles and responsibilities for the student or supervisee, the site supervisor, and the program supervisor. They confirm that site supervisors are qualified to provide supervision and inform site supervisors of their professional and ethical responsibilities in this role.

F.6.h. Professional Disclosure

Before initiating counseling services, counselors-in-training disclose their status as students and explain how this status affects the limits of confidentiality. Counselor educators ensure that the clients at field placements are aware of the services rendered and the qualifications of the students and supervisees rendering those services. Students and supervisees obtain client permission before they use any information concerning the counseling relationship in the training process. *(See A.2.b.)*

F.7. Student Welfare

F.7.a. Orientation

Counselor educators recognize that orientation is a developmental process that continues throughout the educational and clinical training of students. Counseling faculty provide prospective students with information about the counselor education program's expectations:

1. the type and level of skill and knowledge acquisition required for successful completion of the training;
2. program training goals, objectives, and mission, and subject matter to be covered;
3. bases for evaluation;
4. training components that encourage self-growth or self-disclosure as part of the training process;

5. the type of supervision settings and requirements of the sites for required clinical field experiences;
6. student and supervisee evaluation and dismissal policies and procedures; and
7. up-to-date employment prospects for graduates.

F.7.b. Self-Growth Experiences

Counselor education programs delineate requirements for self-disclosure or self-growth experiences in their admission and program materials. Counselor educators use professional judgment when designing training experiences they conduct that require student and supervisee self-growth or self-disclosure. Students and supervisees are made aware of the ramifications their self-disclosure may have when counselors whose primary role as teacher, trainer, or supervisor requires acting on ethical obligations to the profession. Evaluative components of experiential training experiences explicitly delineate predetermined academic standards that are separate and do not depend on the student's level of self-disclosure. Counselor educators may require trainees to seek professional help to address any personal concerns that may be affecting their competency.

F.8. Student Responsibilities

F.8.a. Standards for Students

Counselors-in-training have a responsibility to understand and follow the *ACA Code of Ethics* and adhere to applicable laws, regulatory policies, and rules and policies governing professional staff behavior at the agency or placement setting. Students have the same obligations to clients as those required of professional counselors. *(See C.1., H.1.)*

F.8.b. Impairment

Counselors-in-training refrain from offering or providing counseling services when their physical, mental, or emotional problems are likely to harm a client or others. They are alert to the signs of impairment, seek assistance for problems, and notify their program supervisors when they are aware that they are unable to effectively provide services. In addition, they seek appropriate professional services for themselves to remediate the problems that are interfering with their ability to provide services to others. *(See A.1., C.2.d., C.2.g.)*

F.9. Evaluation and Remediation of Students

F.9.a. Evaluation

Counselors clearly state to students, prior to and throughout the training program, the levels of competency expected, appraisal methods, and timing of evaluations for both didactic and clinical competencies. Counselor educators provide students with ongoing performance appraisal and evaluation feedback throughout the training program.

F.9.b. Limitations

Counselor educators, throughout ongoing evaluation and appraisal, are aware of and address the inability of some students to achieve counseling competencies that might impede performance. Counselor educators

1. assist students in securing remedial assistance when needed,
2. seek professional consultation and document their decision to dismiss or refer students for assistance, and

3. ensure that students have recourse in a timely manner to address decisions to require them to seek assistance or to dismiss them and provide students with due process according to institutional policies and procedures. *(See C.2.g.)*

F.9.c. Counseling for Students

If students request counseling or if counseling services are required as part of a remediation process, counselor educators provide acceptable referrals.

F.10. Roles and Relationships Between Counselor Educators and Students

F.10.a. Sexual or Romantic Relationships

Sexual or romantic interactions or relationships with current students are prohibited.

F.10.b. Sexual Harassment

Counselor educators do not condone or subject students to sexual harassment. *(See C.6.a.)*

F.10.c. Relationships With Former Students

Counselor educators are aware of the power differential in the relationship between faculty and students. Faculty members foster open discussions with former students when considering engaging in a social, sexual, or other intimate relationship. Faculty members discuss with the former student how their former relationship may affect the change in relationship.

F.10.d. Nonprofessional Relationships

Counselor educators avoid nonprofessional or ongoing professional relationships with students in which there is a risk of potential harm to the student or that may compromise the training experience or grades assigned. In addition, counselor educators do not accept any form of professional services, fees, commissions, reimbursement, or remuneration from a site for student or supervisee placement.

F.10.e. Counseling Services

Counselor educators do not serve as counselors to current students unless this is a brief role associated with a training experience.

F.10.f. Potentially Beneficial Relationships

Counselor educators are aware of the power differential in the relationship between faculty and students. If they believe a nonprofessional relationship with a student may be potentially beneficial to the student, they take precautions similar to those taken by counselors when working with clients. Examples of potentially beneficial interactions or relationships include, but are not limited to, attending a formal ceremony; hospital visits; providing support during a stressful event; or mutual membership in a professional association, organization, or community. Counselor educators engage in open discussions with students when they consider entering into relationships with students outside of their roles as teachers and supervisors. They discuss with students the rationale for such interactions, the potential benefits and drawbacks, and the anticipated consequences for the student. Educators clarify the specific nature and limitations of the additional role(s) they will have with the student prior to engaging in a nonprofessional relationship. Nonprofessional relationships with students should be time-limited and initiated with student consent.

F.11. Multicultural/Diversity Competence in Counselor Education and Training Programs

F.11.a. Faculty Diversity

Counselor educators are committed to recruiting and retaining a diverse faculty.

F.11.b. Student Diversity

Counselor educators actively attempt to recruit and retain a diverse student body. Counselor educators demonstrate commitment to multicultural/diversity competence by recognizing and valuing diverse cultures and types of abilities students bring to the training experience. Counselor educators provide appropriate accommodations that enhance and support diverse student well-being and academic performance.

F.11.c. Multicultural/Diversity Competence

Counselor educators actively infuse multicultural/diversity competency in their training and supervision practices. They actively train students to gain awareness, knowledge, and skills in the competencies of multicultural practice. Counselor educators include case examples, role-plays, discussion questions, and other classroom activities that promote and represent various cultural perspectives.

Section G: Research and Publication

Introduction

Counselors who conduct research are encouraged to contribute to the knowledge base of the profession and promote a clearer understanding of the conditions that lead to a healthy and more just society. Counselors support efforts of researchers by participating fully and willingly whenever possible. Counselors minimize bias and respect diversity in designing and implementing research programs.

G.1. Research Responsibilities

G.1.a. Use of Human Research Participants

Counselors plan, design, conduct, and report research in a manner that is consistent with pertinent ethical principles, federal and state laws, host institutional regulations, and scientific standards governing research with human research participants.

G.1.b. Deviation From Standard Practice

Counselors seek consultation and observe stringent safeguards to protect the rights of research participants when a research problem suggests a deviation from standard or acceptable practices.

G.1.c. Independent Researchers

When independent researchers do not have access to an Institutional Review Board (IRB), they should consult with researchers who are familiar with IRB procedures to provide appropriate safeguards.

G.1.d. Precautions to Avoid Injury

Counselors who conduct research with human participants are responsible for the welfare of participants throughout the research process and should take reasonable precautions to avoid causing injurious psychological, emotional, physical, or social effects to participants.

G.1.e. Principal Researcher Responsibility

The ultimate responsibility for ethical research practice lies with the principal researcher. All others involved in the research activities share ethical obligations and responsibility for their own actions.

G.1.f. Minimal Interference

Counselors take reasonable precautions to avoid causing disruptions in the lives of research participants that could be caused by their involvement in research.

G.1.g. Multicultural/Diversity Considerations in Research

When appropriate to research goals, counselors are sensitive to incorporating research procedures that take into account cultural considerations. They seek consultation when appropriate.

G.2. Rights of Research Participants

(See A.2., A.7.)

G.2.a. Informed Consent in Research

Individuals have the right to consent to become research participants. In seeking consent, counselors use language that

1. accurately explains the purpose and procedures to be followed,
2. identifies any procedures that are experimental or relatively untried,
3. describes any attendant discomforts and risks,
4. describes any benefits or changes in individuals or organizations that might be reasonably expected,
5. discloses appropriate alternative procedures that would be advantageous for participants,
6. offers to answer any inquiries concerning the procedures,
7. describes any limitations on confidentiality,
8. describes the format and potential target audiences for the dissemination of research findings, and
9. instructs participants that they are free to withdraw their consent and to discontinue participation in the project at any time without penalty.

G.2.b. Deception

Counselors do not conduct research involving deception unless alternative procedures are not feasible and the prospective value of the research justifies the deception. If such deception has the potential to cause physical or emotional harm to research participants, the research is not conducted, regardless of prospective value. When the methodological requirements of a study necessitate concealment or deception, the investigator explains the reasons for this action as soon as possible during the debriefing.

G.2.c. Student/Supervisee Participation

Researchers who involve students or supervisees in research make clear to them that the decision regarding whether or not to participate in research activities does not affect one's academic standing or supervisory relationship. Students or supervisees who choose not to participate in educational research are provided with an appropriate alternative to fulfill their academic or clinical requirements.

G.2.d. Client Participation

Counselors conducting research involving clients make clear in the informed consent process that clients are free to choose whether or not to participate in research activities. Counselors take necessary precautions to protect clients from adverse consequences of declining or withdrawing from participation.

G.2.e. Confidentiality of Information

Information obtained about research participants during the course of an investigation is confidential. When the possibility exists that others may obtain access to such information, ethical research practice requires that the possibility, together with the plans for protecting confidentiality, be explained to participants as a part of the procedure for obtaining informed consent.

G.2.f. Persons Not Capable of Giving Informed Consent

When a person is not capable of giving informed consent, counselors provide an appropriate explanation to, obtain agreement for participation from, and obtain the appropriate consent of a legally authorized person.

G.2.g. Commitments to Participants

Counselors take reasonable measures to honor all commitments to research participants. *(See A.2.c.)*

G.2.h. Explanations After Data Collection

After data are collected, counselors provide participants with full clarification of the nature of the study to remove any misconceptions participants might have regarding the research. Where scientific or human values justify delaying or withholding information, counselors take reasonable measures to avoid causing harm.

G.2.i. Informing Sponsors

Counselors inform sponsors, institutions, and publication channels regarding research procedures and outcomes. Counselors ensure that appropriate bodies and authorities are given pertinent information and acknowledgment.

G.2.j. Disposal of Research Documents and Records

Within a reasonable period of time following the completion of a research project or study, counselors take steps to destroy records or documents (audio, video, digital, and written) containing confidential data or information that identifies research participants. When records are of an artistic nature, researchers obtain participant consent with regard to handling of such records or documents. *(See B.4.a., B.4.g.)*

G.3. Relationships With Research Participants (When Research Involves Intensive or Extended Interactions)

G.3.a. Nonprofessional Relationships

Nonprofessional relationships with research participants should be avoided.

G.3.b. Relationships With Research Participants

Sexual or romantic counselor–research participant interactions or relationships with current research participants are prohibited.

G.3.c. Sexual Harassment and Research Participants

Researchers do not condone or subject research participants to sexual harassment.

G.3.d. Potentially Beneficial Interactions

When a nonprofessional interaction between the researcher and the research participant may be potentially beneficial, the researcher must document, prior to the interaction (when feasible), the rationale for such an interaction, the potential benefit, and anticipated consequences for the research participant. Such interactions should be initiated with appropriate consent of the research participant. Where unintentional harm occurs to the research participant due to the nonprofessional interaction, the researcher must show evidence of an attempt to remedy such harm.

G.4. Reporting Results

G.4.a. Accurate Results

Counselors plan, conduct, and report research accurately. They provide thorough discussions of the limitations of their data and alternative hypotheses. Counselors do not engage in misleading or fraudulent research, distort data, misrepresent data, or deliberately bias their results. They explicitly mention all variables and conditions known to the investigator that may have affected the outcome of a study or the interpretation of data. They describe the extent to which results are applicable for diverse populations.

G.4.b. Obligation to Report Unfavorable Results

Counselors report the results of any research of professional value. Results that reflect unfavorably on institutions, programs, services, prevailing opinions, or vested interests are not withheld.

G.4.c. Reporting Errors

If counselors discover significant errors in their published research, they take reasonable steps to correct such errors in a correction erratum, or through other appropriate publication means.

G.4.d. Identity of Participants

Counselors who supply data, aid in the research of another person, report research results, or make original data available take due care to disguise the identity of respective participants in the absence of specific authorization from the participants to do otherwise. In situations where participants self-identify their involvement in research studies, researchers take active steps to ensure that data is adapted/changed to protect the identity and welfare of all parties and that discussion of results does not cause harm to participants.

G.4.e. Replication Studies

Counselors are obligated to make available sufficient original research data to qualified professionals who may wish to replicate the study.

G.5. Publication

G.5.a. Recognizing Contributions

When conducting and reporting research, counselors are familiar with and give recognition to previous work on the topic, observe copyright laws, and give full credit to those to whom credit is due.

G.5.b. Plagiarism

Counselors do not plagiarize; that is, they do not present another person's work as their own work.

G.5.c. Review/Republication of Data or Ideas

Counselors fully acknowledge and make editorial reviewers aware of prior publication of ideas or data where such ideas or data are submitted for review or publication.

G.5.d. Contributors

Counselors give credit through joint authorship, acknowledgment, footnote statements, or other appropriate means to those who have contributed significantly to research or concept development in accordance with such contributions. The principal contributor is listed first, and minor technical or professional contributions are acknowledged in notes or introductory statements.

G.5.e. Agreement of Contributors

Counselors who conduct joint research with colleagues or students/supervisees establish agreements in advance regarding allocation of tasks, publication credit, and types of acknowledgment that will be received.

G.5.f. Student Research

For articles that are substantially based on students' course papers, projects, dissertations or theses, and on which students have been the primary contributors, they are listed as principal authors.

G.5.g. Duplicate Submission

Counselors submit manuscripts for consideration to only one journal at a time. Manuscripts that are published in whole or in substantial part in another journal or published work are not submitted for publication without acknowledgment and permission from the previous publication.

G.5.h. Professional Review

Counselors who review material submitted for publication, research, or other scholarly purposes respect the confidentiality and proprietary rights of those who submitted it. Counselors use care to make publication decisions based on valid and defensible standards. Counselors review article submissions in a timely manner and based on their scope and competency in research methodologies. Counselors who serve as reviewers at the request of editors or publishers make every effort to only review materials that are within their scope of competency and use care to avoid personal biases.

Section H: Resolving Ethical Issues

Introduction

Counselors behave in a legal, ethical, and moral manner in the conduct of their professional work. They are aware that client protection and trust in the profession depend on a high level of professional conduct. They hold other counselors to the same standards and are willing to take appropriate action to ensure that these standards are upheld.

Counselors strive to resolve ethical dilemmas with direct and open communication among all parties involved and seek consultation with colleagues and supervisors when necessary. Counselors incorporate ethical practice into their daily professional work. They engage in ongoing professional development regarding current topics in ethical and legal issues in counseling.

H.1. Standards and the Law

(See F.9.a.)

H.1.a. Knowledge

Counselors understand the *ACA Code of Ethics* and other applicable ethics codes from other professional organizations or from certification and licensure bodies of which they are members. Lack of knowledge or misunderstanding of an ethical responsibility is not a defense against a charge of unethical conduct.

H.1.b. Conflicts Between Ethics and Laws

If ethical responsibilities conflict with law, regulations, or other governing legal authority, counselors make known their commitment to the *ACA Code of Ethics* and take steps to resolve the conflict. If the conflict cannot be resolved by such means, counselors may adhere to the requirements of law, regulations, or other governing legal authority.

H.2. Suspected Violations

H.2.a. Ethical Behavior Expected

Counselors expect colleagues to adhere to the *ACA Code of Ethics*. When counselors possess knowledge that raises doubts as to whether another counselor is acting in an ethical manner, they take appropriate action. *(See H.2.b., H.2.c.)*

H.2.b. Informal Resolution

When counselors have reason to believe that another counselor is violating or has violated an ethical standard, they attempt first to resolve the issue informally with the other counselor if feasible, provided such action does not violate confidentiality rights that may be involved.

H.2.c. Reporting Ethical Violations

If an apparent violation has substantially harmed or is likely to substantially harm a person or organization and is not appropriate for informal resolution or is not resolved properly, counselors take further action appropriate to the situation. Such action might include referral to state or national committees on professional ethics, voluntary national certification bodies, state licensing boards, or to the appropriate institutional authorities. This standard does not apply when an intervention would violate confidentiality rights or when counselors have been retained to review the work of another counselor whose professional conduct is in question.

H.2.d. Consultation

When uncertain as to whether a particular situation or course of action may be in violation of the *ACA Code of Ethics*, counselors consult with other counselors who are knowledgeable about ethics and the *ACA Code of Ethics*, with colleagues, or with appropriate authorities.

H.2.e. Organizational Conflicts

If the demands of an organization with which counselors are affiliated pose a conflict with the *ACA Code of Ethics*, counselors specify the nature of such conflicts and express to their supervisors or other responsible officials their commitment to the *ACA Code of Ethics*. When possible, counselors work toward change within the organization to allow full adherence to the *ACA Code of Ethics*. In doing so, they address any confidentiality issues.

H.2.f. Unwarranted Complaints

Counselors do not initiate, participate in, or encourage the filing of ethics complaints that are made with reckless disregard or willful ignorance of facts that would disprove the allegation.

H.2.g. Unfair Discrimination Against Complainants and Respondents

Counselors do not deny persons employment, advancement, admission to academic or other programs, tenure, or promotion based solely upon their having made or their being the subject of an ethics complaint. This does not preclude taking action based upon the outcome of such proceedings or considering other appropriate information.

H.3. Cooperation With Ethics Committees

Counselors assist in the process of enforcing the *ACA Code of Ethics*. Counselors cooperate with investigations, proceedings, and requirements of the ACA Ethics Committee or ethics committees of other duly constituted associations or boards having jurisdiction over those charged with a violation.

Counselors are familiar with the ACA Policies and Procedures for Processing Complaints of Ethical Violations and use it as a reference for assisting in the enforcement of the *ACA Code of Ethics*.

Glossary of Terms

Advocacy—promotion of the well-being of individuals and groups and the counseling profession within systems and organizations. Advocacy seeks to remove barriers and obstacles that inhibit access, growth, and development.

Assent—to demonstrate agreement, when a person is otherwise not capable or competent to give formal consent (e.g., informed consent) to a counseling service or plan.

Client—an individual seeking or referred to the professional services of a counselor for help with problem resolution or decision making.

Counselor—a professional (or a student who is a counselor-in-training) engaged in a counseling practice or other counseling-related services. Counselors fulfill many roles and responsibilities such as counselor educators, researchers, supervisors, practitioners, and consultants.

Counselor Educator—a professional counselor engaged primarily in developing, implementing, and supervising the educational preparation of counselors-in-training.

Counselor Supervisor—a professional counselor who engages in a formal relationship with a practicing counselor or counselor-in-training for the purpose of overseeing that individual's counseling work or clinical skill development.

Culture—membership in a socially constructed way of living, which incorporates collective values, beliefs, norms, boundaries, and lifestyles that are cocreated with others who share similar world views comprising biological, psychosocial, historical, psychological, and other factors.

Diversity—the similarities and differences that occur within and across cultures, and the intersection of cultural and social identities.

Documents—any written, digital, audio, visual, or artistic recording of the work within the counseling relationship between counselor and client.

Examinee—a recipient of any professional counseling service that includes educational, psychological, and career appraisal utilizing qualitative or quantitative techniques.

Forensic Evaluation—any formal assessment conducted for court or other legal proceedings.

Multicultural/Diversity Competence—a capacity whereby counselors possess cultural and diversity awareness and knowledge about self and others, and how this awareness and knowledge is applied effectively in practice with clients and client groups.

Multicultural/Diversity Counseling—counseling that recognizes diversity and embraces approaches that support the worth, dignity, potential, and uniqueness of individuals within their historical, cultural, economic, political, and psychosocial contexts.

Student—an individual engaged in formal educational preparation as a counselor-in-training.

Supervisee—a professional counselor or counselor-in-training whose counseling work or clinical skill development is being overseen in a formal supervisory relationship by a qualified trained professional.

Supervisor—counselors who are trained to oversee the professional clinical work of counselors and counselors-in-training.

Teaching—all activities engaged in as part of a formal educational program designed to lead to a graduate degree in counseling.

Training—the instruction and practice of skills related to the counseling profession. Training contributes to the ongoing proficiency of students and professional counselors.

Appendix B

APA Code of Ethics

Introduction and Applicability

The American Psychological Association's (APA's) Ethical Principles of Psychologists and Code of Conduct (hereinafter referred to as the Ethics Code) consists of an Introduction, a Preamble, five General Principles (A–E), and specific Ethical Standards. The Introduction discusses the intent, organization, procedural considerations, and scope of application of the Ethics Code. The Preamble and General Principles are aspirational goals to guide psychologists toward the highest ideals of psychology. Although the Preamble and General Principles are not themselves enforceable rules, they should be considered by psychologists in arriving at an ethical course of action. The Ethical Standards set forth enforceable rules for conduct as psychologists. Most of the Ethical Standards are written broadly, in order to apply to psychologists in varied roles, although the application of an Ethical Standard may vary depending on the context. The Ethical Standards are not exhaustive. The fact that a given conduct is not specifically addressed by an Ethical Standard does not mean that it is necessarily either ethical or unethical.

This Ethics Code applies only to psychologists' activities that are part of their scientific, educational, or professional roles as psychologists. Areas covered include but are not limited to the clinical, counseling, and school practice of psychology; research; teaching; supervision of trainees; public service; policy development; social intervention; development of assessment instruments; conducting assessments; educational counseling; organizational consulting; forensic activities; program design and evaluation; and administration. This Ethics Code applies to these activities across a variety of contexts, such as in person, postal, telephone, Internet, and other electronic transmissions. These activities shall be distinguished from the purely private conduct of psychologists, which is not within the purview of the Ethics Code.

Membership in the APA commits members and student affiliates to comply with the standards of the APA Ethics Code and to the rules and procedures used to enforce them. Lack of awareness or misunderstanding of an Ethical Standard is not itself a defense to a charge of unethical conduct.

The procedures for filing, investigating, and resolving complaints of unethical conduct are described in the current Rules and Procedures of the APA Ethics Committee. APA may impose sanctions on its members for violations of the standards of the Ethics Code, including termination of APA membership, and may notify other bodies and individuals of its actions. Actions that violate the standards of the Ethics Code may also lead to the imposition of sanctions on psychologists or students whether or not they are APA members by bodies other than APA, including state psychological associations, other professional groups, psychology boards, other state or federal agencies, and payors for health services. In addition, APA may take action against a member after his or her conviction of a felony, expulsion or suspension from an affiliated state psychological association, or suspension or loss of licensure. When the sanction to be imposed by APA is less than expulsion, the 2001 Rules and Procedures do not guarantee an opportunity for an in-person hearing, but generally provide that complaints will be resolved only on the basis of a submitted record.

The Ethics Code is intended to provide guidance for psychologists and standards of professional conduct that can be applied by the APA and by other bodies that choose to adopt them. The Ethics Code is not intended to be a basis of civil liability. Whether a psychologist has violated the Ethics Code standards does not by itself determine whether the psychologist is legally liable in a court action, whether a contract is enforceable, or whether other legal consequences occur.

The modifiers used in some of the standards of this Ethics Code (e.g., *reasonably, appropriate, potentially*) are included in the standards when they would (1) allow professional judgment on the part of psychologists, (2) eliminate injustice or inequality that would occur without the modifier, (3) ensure applicability across the broad range of activities conducted by psychologists, or (4) guard against a set of rigid rules that might be quickly outdated. As used in this Ethics Code, the term *reasonable* means the prevailing professional judgment of psychologists engaged in similar activities in similar circumstances, given the knowledge the psychologist had or should have had at the time.

In the process of making decisions regarding their professional behavior, psychologists must consider this Ethics Code in addition to applicable laws and psychology board regulations. In applying the Ethics Code to their professional work, psychologists may consider other materials and guidelines that have been adopted or endorsed by scientific and professional psychological organizations and the dictates of their own conscience, as well as consult with others within the field. If this Ethics Code establishes a higher standard of conduct than is required by law, psychologists must meet the higher ethical standard. If psychologists' ethical responsibilities conflict with law, regulations, or other governing legal authority, psychologists make known their commitment to this Ethics Code and take steps to resolve the conflict in a responsible manner. If the conflict is unresolvable via such means, psychologists may adhere to the requirements of the law, regulations, or other governing authority in keeping with basic principles of human rights.

PREAMBLE

Psychologists are committed to increasing scientific and professional knowledge of behavior and people's understanding of themselves and others and to the use of such knowledge to improve the condition of individuals, organizations, and society. Psychologists respect and protect civil and human rights and the central importance of freedom of inquiry and expression in research, teaching, and publication. They strive to help the public in developing informed judgments and choices concerning human behavior. In doing so, they perform many roles, such as researcher, educator, diagnostician, therapist, supervisor, consultant, administrator, social interventionist, and expert witness. This Ethics Code provides a common set of principles and standards upon which psychologists build their professional and scientific work.

This Ethics Code is intended to provide specific standards to cover most situations encountered by psychologists. It has as its goals the welfare and protection of the individuals and groups with whom psychologists work and the education of members, students, and the public regarding ethical standards of the discipline.

The development of a dynamic set of ethical standards for psychologists' work-related conduct requires a personal commitment and lifelong effort to act ethically; to encourage ethical behavior by students, supervisees, employees, and colleagues; and to consult with others concerning ethical problems.

GENERAL PRINCIPLES

This section consists of General Principles. General Principles, as opposed to Ethical Standards, are aspirational in nature. Their intent is to guide and inspire psychologists toward the very highest ethical ideals of the profession. General Principles, in contrast to Ethical Standards, do not represent obligations and should not form the basis for imposing sanctions. Relying upon General Principles for either of these reasons distorts both their meaning and purpose.

Principle A: Beneficence and Nonmaleficence

Psychologists strive to benefit those with whom they work and take care to do no harm. In their professional actions, psychologists seek to safeguard the welfare and rights of those with whom they interact professionally and other affected persons, and the welfare of animal subjects of research. When conflicts occur among psychologists' obligations or concerns, they attempt to resolve these conflicts in a responsible fashion that avoids or minimizes harm. Because psychologists' scientific and professional judgments and actions may affect the lives of others, they are alert to and guard against personal, financial, social, organizational, or political factors that might lead to misuse of their influence. Psychologists strive to be aware of the possible effect of their own physical and mental health on their ability to help those with whom they work.

Principle B: Fidelity and Responsibility

Psychologists establish relationships of trust with those with whom they work. They are aware of their professional and scientific responsibilities to society and to the specific communities in which they work. Psychologists uphold professional standards of conduct, clarify their professional roles and obligations, accept appropriate responsibility for their behavior, and seek to manage conflicts of interest that could lead to exploitation or harm. Psychologists consult with, refer to, or cooperate with other professionals and institutions to the extent needed to serve the best interests of those with whom they work. They are concerned about the ethical compliance of their colleagues' scientific and professional conduct. Psychologists strive to contribute a portion of their professional time for little or no compensation or personal advantage.

Principle C: Integrity

Psychologists seek to promote accuracy, honesty, and truthfulness in the science, teaching, and practice of psychology. In these activities psychologists do not steal, cheat, or engage in fraud, subterfuge, or intentional misrepresentation of fact. Psychologists strive to keep their promises and to avoid unwise or unclear commitments. In situations in which deception may be ethically justifiable to maximize benefits and minimize harm, psychologists have a serious obligation to consider the need for, the possible consequences of, and their responsibility to correct any resulting mistrust or other harmful effects that arise from the use of such techniques.

Principle D: Justice

Psychologists recognize that fairness and justice entitle all persons to access to and benefit from the contributions of psychology and to equal quality in the processes, procedures, and services being conducted by psychologists. Psychologists exercise reasonable judgment and take precautions to ensure that their potential biases, the boundaries of their competence, and the limitations of their expertise do not lead to or condone unjust practices.

Principle E: Respect for People's Rights and Dignity

Psychologists respect the dignity and worth of all people, and the rights of individuals to privacy, confidentiality, and self-determination. Psychologists are aware that special safeguards may be necessary to protect the rights and welfare of persons or communities whose vulnerabilities impair autonomous decision making. Psychologists are aware of and respect cultural, individual, and role differences, including those based on age, gender, gender identity, race, ethnicity, culture, national origin, religion, sexual orientation, disability, language, and socioeconomic status and consider these factors when working with members of such groups. Psychologists try to eliminate the effect on their work of biases based on those factors, and they do not knowingly participate in or condone activities of others based upon such prejudices.

Ethical Standards

1. Resolving Ethical Issues

1.01 Misuse of Psychologists' Work

If psychologists learn of misuse or misrepresentation of their work, they take reasonable steps to correct or minimize the misuse or misrepresentation.

1.02 Conflicts Between Ethics and Law, Regulations, or Other Governing Legal Authority

If psychologists' ethical responsibilities conflict with law, regulations, or other governing legal authority, psychologists make known their commitment to the Ethics Code and take steps to resolve the conflict. If the conflict is unresolvable via such means, psychologists may adhere to the requirements of the law, regulations, or other governing legal authority.

1.03 Conflicts Between Ethics and Organizational Demands

If the demands of an organization with which psychologists are affiliated or for whom they are working conflict with this Ethics Code, psychologists clarify the nature of the conflict, make known their commitment to the Ethics Code, and to the extent feasible, resolve the conflict in a way that permits adherence to the Ethics Code.

1.04 Informal Resolution of Ethical Violations

When psychologists believe that there may have been an ethical violation by another psychologist, they attempt to resolve the issue by bringing it to the attention of that individual, if an informal resolution appears appropriate and the intervention does not violate any confidentiality rights that may be involved. (See also Standards 1.02, Conflicts Between Ethics and Law, Regulations, or Other Governing Legal Authority, and 1.03, Conflicts Between Ethics and Organizational Demands.)

1.05 Reporting Ethical Violations

If an apparent ethical violation has substantially harmed or is likely to substantially harm a person or organization and is not appropriate for informal resolution under Standard 1.04, Informal Resolution of Ethical Violations, or is not resolved properly in that fashion, psychologists take further action appropriate to the situation. Such action might include referral to state or national committees on professional ethics, to state licensing boards, or to the appropriate institutional authorities. This standard does not apply when an intervention would violate confidentiality rights or when psychologists have been retained to review the work of another psychologist whose professional conduct is in question. (See also Standard 1.02, Conflicts Between Ethics and Law, Regulations, or Other Governing Legal Authority.)

1.06 Cooperating With Ethics Committees

Psychologists cooperate in ethics investigations, proceedings, and resulting requirements of the APA or any affiliated state psychological association to which they belong. In doing so, they address any confidentiality issues. Failure to cooperate is itself an ethics violation. However, making a request for deferment of adjudication of an ethics complaint pending the outcome of litigation does not alone constitute noncooperation.

1.07 Improper Complaints

Psychologists do not file or encourage the filing of ethics complaints that are made with reckless disregard for or willful ignorance of facts that would disprove the allegation.

1.08 Unfair Discrimination Against Complainants and Respondents

Psychologists do not deny persons employment, advancement, admissions to academic or other programs, tenure, or promotion, based solely upon their having made or their being the subject of an ethics complaint. This does not preclude taking action based upon the outcome of such proceedings or considering other appropriate information.

2. Competence

2.01 Boundaries of Competence

(a) Psychologists provide services, teach, and conduct research with populations and in areas only within the boundaries of their competence, based on their education, training, supervised experience, consultation, study, or professional experience.

(b) Where scientific or professional knowledge in the discipline of psychology establishes that an understanding of factors associated with age, gender, gender identity, race, ethnicity, culture, national origin, religion, sexual orientation, disability, language, or socioeconomic status is essential for effective implementation of their services or research, psychologists have or obtain the training, experience, consultation, or supervision necessary to ensure the competence of their services, or they make appropriate referrals, except as provided in Standard 2.02, Providing Services in Emergencies.

(c) Psychologists planning to provide services, teach, or conduct research involving populations, areas, techniques, or technologies new to them undertake relevant education, training, supervised experience, consultation, or study.

(d) When psychologists are asked to provide services to individuals for whom appropriate mental health services are not available and for which psychologists have not obtained the competence necessary, psychologists with closely related prior training or experience may provide such services in order to ensure that services are not denied if they make a reasonable effort to obtain the competence required by using relevant research, training, consultation, or study.

(e) In those emerging areas in which generally recognized standards for preparatory training do not yet exist, psychologists nevertheless take reasonable steps to ensure the competence of their work and to protect clients/patients, students, supervisees, research participants, organizational clients, and others from harm.

(f) When assuming forensic roles, psychologists are or become reasonably familiar with the judicial or administrative rules governing their roles.

2.02 Providing Services in Emergencies

In emergencies, when psychologists provide services to individuals for whom other mental health services are not available and for which psychologists have not obtained the necessary training, psychologists may provide such services in order to ensure that services are not denied. The services are discontinued as soon as the emergency has ended or appropriate services are available.

2.03 Maintaining Competence

Psychologists undertake ongoing efforts to develop and maintain their competence.

2.04 Bases for Scientific and Professional Judgments

Psychologists' work is based upon established scientific and professional knowledge of the discipline. (See also Standards 2.01e, Boundaries of Competence, and 10.01b, Informed Consent to Therapy.)

2.05 Delegation of Work to Others

Psychologists who delegate work to employees, supervisees, or research or teaching assistants or who use the services of others, such as interpreters, take reasonable steps to (1) avoid delegating such work to persons who have a multiple relationship with those being served that would likely lead to exploitation or loss of objectivity; (2) authorize only those responsibilities that such persons can be expected to perform competently on the basis of their education, training, or experience, either independently or with the level of supervision being provided; and (3) see that such persons perform these services competently. (See also Standards 2.02, Providing Services in Emergencies; 3.05, Multiple Relationships; 4.01, Maintaining Confidentiality; 9.01, Bases for Assessments; 9.02, Use of Assessments; 9.03, Informed Consent in Assessments; and 9.07, Assessment by Unqualified Persons.)

2.06 Personal Problems and Conflicts

(a) Psychologists refrain from initiating an activity when they know or should know that there is a substantial likelihood that their personal problems will prevent them from performing their work-related activities in a competent manner.

(b) When psychologists become aware of personal problems that may interfere with their performing work-related duties adequately, they take appropriate measures, such as obtaining professional consultation or assistance, and determine whether they should limit, suspend, or terminate their work-related duties. (See also Standard 10.10, Terminating Therapy.)

3. Human Relations

3.01 Unfair Discrimination

In their work-related activities, psychologists do not engage in unfair discrimination based on age, gender, gender identity, race, ethnicity, culture, national origin, religion, sexual orientation, disability, socioeconomic status, or any basis proscribed by law.

3.02 Sexual Harassment

Psychologists do not engage in sexual harassment. Sexual harassment is sexual solicitation, physical advances, or verbal or nonverbal conduct that is sexual in nature, that occurs in connection with the psychologist's activities or roles as a psychologist, and that either (1) is unwelcome, is offensive, or creates a hostile workplace or educational environment, and the psychologist knows or is told this or (2) is sufficiently severe or intense to be abusive to a reasonable person in the context. Sexual harassment can consist of a single intense or severe act or of multiple persistent or pervasive acts. (See also Standard 1.08, Unfair Discrimination Against Complainants and Respondents.)

3.03 Other Harassment

Psychologists do not knowingly engage in behavior that is harassing or demeaning to persons with whom they interact in their work based on factors such as those persons' age, gender, gender identity, race, ethnicity, culture, national origin, religion, sexual orientation, disability, language, or socioeconomic status.

3.04 Avoiding Harm

Psychologists take reasonable steps to avoid harming their clients/patients, students, supervisees, research participants, organizational clients, and others with whom they work, and to minimize harm where it is foreseeable and unavoidable.

3.05 Multiple Relationships

(a) A multiple relationship occurs when a psychologist is in a professional role with a person and (1) at the same time is in another role with the same person, (2) at the same time is in a relationship with a person closely associated with or related to the person with whom the psychologist has the professional relationship, or (3) promises to enter into another relationship in the future with the person or a person closely associated with or related to the person.

A psychologist refrains from entering into a multiple relationship if the multiple relationship could reasonably be expected to impair the psychologist's objectivity, competence, or effectiveness in performing his or her functions as a psychologist, or otherwise risks exploitation or harm to the person with whom the professional relationship exists.

Multiple relationships that would not reasonably be expected to cause impairment or risk exploitation or harm are not unethical.

(b) If a psychologist finds that, due to unforeseen factors, a potentially harmful multiple relationship has arisen, the psychologist takes reasonable steps to resolve it with due regard for the best interests of the affected person and maximal compliance with the Ethics Code.

(c) When psychologists are required by law, institutional policy, or extraordinary circumstances to serve in more than one role in judicial or administrative proceedings, at the outset they clarify role expectations and the extent of confidentiality and thereafter as changes occur. (See also Standards 3.04, Avoiding Harm, and 3.07, Third-Party Requests for Services.)

3.06 Conflict of Interest

Psychologists refrain from taking on a professional role when personal, scientific, professional, legal, financial, or other interests or relationships could reasonably be expected to (1) impair their objectivity, competence, or effectiveness in performing their functions as psychologists or (2) expose the person or organization with whom the professional relationship exists to harm or exploitation.

3.07 Third-Party Requests for Services

When psychologists agree to provide services to a person or entity at the request of a third party, psychologists attempt to clarify at the outset of the service the nature of the relationship with all individuals or organizations involved. This clarification includes the role of the psychologist (e.g., therapist, consultant, diagnostician, or expert witness), an identification of who is the client, the probable uses of the services provided or the information obtained, and the fact that there may be limits to confidentiality. (See also Standards 3.05, Multiple Relationships, and 4.02, Discussing the Limits of Confidentiality.)

3.08 Exploitative Relationships

Psychologists do not exploit persons over whom they have supervisory, evaluative, or other authority such as clients/patients, students, supervisees, research participants, and employees. (See also Standards 3.05, Multiple Relationships; 6.04, Fees and Financial Arrangements; 6.05, Barter With Clients/Patients; 7.07, Sexual Relationships With Students and Supervisees; 10.05, Sexual Intimacies With Current Therapy Clients/Patients; 10.06, Sexual Intimacies With Relatives or Significant Others of Current Therapy Clients/Patients; 10.07, Therapy With Former Sexual Partners; and 10.08, Sexual Intimacies With Former Therapy Clients/Patients.)

3.09 Cooperation With Other Professionals

When indicated and professionally appropriate, psychologists cooperate with other professionals in order to serve their clients/patients effectively and appropriately. (See also Standard 4.05, Disclosures.)

3.10 Informed Consent

(a) When psychologists conduct research or provide assessment, therapy, counseling, or consulting services in person or via electronic transmission or other forms of communication, they obtain the informed consent of the individual or individuals using language that is reasonably understandable to that person or persons except when conducting such activities without consent is mandated by law or governmental regulation or as otherwise provided in this Ethics Code. (See also Standards 8.02, Informed Consent to Research; 9.03, Informed Consent in Assessments; and 10.01, Informed Consent to Therapy.)

(b) For persons who are legally incapable of giving informed consent, psychologists nevertheless (1) provide an appropriate explanation, (2) seek the individual's assent, (3) consider such persons' preferences and best interests, and (4) obtain appropriate permission from a legally authorized person, if such substitute consent is permitted or required by law. When consent by a legally authorized person is not permitted or required by law, psychologists take reasonable steps to protect the individual's rights and welfare.

(c) When psychological services are court ordered or otherwise mandated, psychologists inform the individual of the nature of the anticipated services, including whether the services are court ordered or mandated and any limits of confidentiality, before proceeding.

(d) Psychologists appropriately document written or oral consent, permission, and assent. (See also Standards 8.02, Informed Consent to Research; 9.03, Informed Consent in Assessments; and 10.01, Informed Consent to Therapy.)

3.11 Psychological Services Delivered to or Through Organizations

(a) Psychologists delivering services to or through organizations provide information beforehand to clients and when appropriate those directly affected by the services about (1) the nature and objectives of the services, (2) the intended recipients, (3) which of the individuals are clients, (4) the relationship the psychologist will have with each person and the organization, (5) the probable uses of services provided and information obtained, (6) who will have access to the information, and (7) limits of confidentiality. As soon as feasible, they provide information about the results and conclusions of such services to appropriate persons.

(b) If psychologists will be precluded by law or by organizational roles from providing such information to particular individuals or groups, they so inform those individuals or groups at the outset of the service.

3.12 Interruption of Psychological Services

Unless otherwise covered by contract, psychologists make reasonable efforts to plan for facilitating services in the event that psychological services are interrupted by factors such as the psychologist's illness, death, unavailability, relocation, or retirement or by the client's/patient's relocation or financial limitations. (See also Standard 6.02c, Maintenance, Dissemination, and Disposal of Confidential Records of Professional and Scientific Work.)

4. Privacy and Confidentiality

4.01 Maintaining Confidentiality

Psychologists have a primary obligation and take reasonable precautions to protect confidential information obtained through or stored in any medium, recognizing that the extent and limits of confidentiality may be regulated by law or established by institutional rules or professional or scientific relationship. (See also Standard 2.05, Delegation of Work to Others.)

4.02 Discussing the Limits of Confidentiality

(a) Psychologists discuss with persons (including, to the extent feasible, persons who are legally incapable of giving informed consent and their legal representatives) and organizations with whom they establish a scientific or professional relationship (1) the relevant limits of confidentiality and (2) the foreseeable uses of the information generated through their psychological activities. (See also Standard 3.10, Informed Consent.)

(b) Unless it is not feasible or is contraindicated, the discussion of confidentiality occurs at the outset of the relationship and thereafter as new circumstances may warrant.

(c) Psychologists who offer services, products, or information via electronic transmission inform clients/patients of the risks to privacy and limits of confidentiality.

4.03 Recording

Before recording the voices or images of individuals to whom they provide services, psychologists obtain permission from all such persons or their legal representatives. (See also Standards 8.03, Informed Consent for Recording Voices and Images in Research; 8.05, Dispensing with Informed Consent for Research; and 8.07, Deception in Research.)

4.04 Minimizing Intrusions on Privacy

(a) Psychologists include in written and oral reports and consultations, only information germane to the purpose for which the communication is made.

(b) Psychologists discuss confidential information obtained in their work only for appropriate scientific or professional purposes and only with persons clearly concerned with such matters.

4.05 Disclosures

(a) Psychologists may disclose confidential information with the appropriate consent of the organizational client, the individual client/patient, or another legally authorized person on behalf of the client/patient unless prohibited by law.

(b) Psychologists disclose confidential information without the consent of the individual only as mandated by law, or where permitted by law for a valid purpose such as to (1) provide needed professional services; (2) obtain appropriate professional consultations; (3) protect the client/patient, psychologist, or others from harm; or (4) obtain payment for services from a client/patient, in which instance disclosure is limited to the minimum that is necessary to achieve the purpose. (See also Standard 6.04e, Fees and Financial Arrangements.)

4.06 Consultations

When consulting with colleagues, (1) psychologists do not disclose confidential information that reasonably could lead to the identification of a client/patient, research participant, or other person or organization with whom they have a confidential relationship unless they have obtained the prior consent of the person or organization or the disclosure cannot be avoided, and (2) they disclose information only to the extent necessary to achieve the purposes of the consultation. (See also Standard 4.01, Maintaining Confidentiality.)

4.07 Use of Confidential Information for Didactic or Other Purposes

Psychologists do not disclose in their writings, lectures, or other public media, confidential, personally identifiable information concerning their clients/patients, students, research participants, organizational clients, or other recipients of their services that they obtained during the course of their work, unless (1) they take reasonable steps to disguise the person or organization, (2) the person or organization has consented in writing, or (3) there is legal authorization for doing so.

5. Advertising and Other Public Statements

5.01 Avoidance of False or Deceptive Statements

(a) Public statements include but are not limited to paid or unpaid advertising, product endorsements, grant applications, licensing applications, other credentialing applications, brochures, printed matter, directory listings, personal resumes or curricula vitae, or comments for use in media such as print or electronic transmission, statements in legal proceedings, lectures and public oral presentations, and published materials. Psychologists do not knowingly make public statements that are false, deceptive, or fraudulent concerning their research, practice, or other work activities or those of persons or organizations with which they are affiliated.

(b) Psychologists do not make false, deceptive, or fraudulent statements concerning (1) their training, experience, or competence; (2) their academic degrees; (3) their credentials; (4) their institutional or association affiliations; (5) their services; (6) the scientific or clinical basis for, or results or degree of success of, their services; (7) their fees; or (8) their publications or research findings.

(c) Psychologists claim degrees as credentials for their health services only if those degrees (1) were earned from a regionally accredited educational institution or (2) were the basis for psychology licensure by the state in which they practice.

5.02 Statements by Others

(a) Psychologists who engage others to create or place public statements that promote their professional practice, products, or activities retain professional responsibility for such statements.

(b) Psychologists do not compensate employees of press, radio, television, or other communication media in return for publicity in a news item. (See also Standard 1.01, Misuse of Psychologists' Work.)

(c) A paid advertisement relating to psychologists' activities must be identified or clearly recognizable as such.

5.03 Descriptions of Workshops and Non-Degree-Granting Educational Programs

To the degree to which they exercise control, psychologists responsible for announcements, catalogs, brochures, or advertisements describing workshops, seminars, or other non-degree-granting educational programs ensure that they accurately describe the audience for which the program is intended, the educational objectives, the presenters, and the fees involved.

5.04 Media Presentations

When psychologists provide public advice or comment via print, Internet, or other electronic transmission, they take precautions to ensure that statements (1) are based on their professional knowledge, training, or experience in accord with appropriate psychological literature and practice; (2) are otherwise consistent with this Ethics Code; and (3) do not indicate that a professional relationship has been established with the recipient. (See also Standard 2.04, Bases for Scientific and Professional Judgments.)

5.05 Testimonials

Psychologists do not solicit testimonials from current therapy clients/patients or other persons who because of their particular circumstances are vulnerable to undue influence.

5.06 In-Person Solicitation

Psychologists do not engage, directly or through agents, in uninvited in-person solicitation of business from actual or potential therapy clients/patients or other persons who because of their particular circumstances are vulnerable to undue influence. However, this prohibition does not preclude (1) attempting to implement appropriate collateral contacts for the purpose of benefiting an already engaged therapy client/patient or (2) providing disaster or community outreach services.

6. Record Keeping and Fees

6.01 Documentation of Professional and Scientific Work and Maintenance of Records

Psychologists create, and to the extent the records are under their control, maintain, disseminate, store, retain, and dispose of records and data relating to their professional and scientific work in order to (1) facilitate provision of services later by them or by other professionals, (2) allow for replication of research design and analyses, (3) meet institutional requirements, (4) ensure accuracy of billing and payments, and (5) ensure compliance with law. (See also Standard 4.01, Maintaining Confidentiality.)

6.02 Maintenance, Dissemination, and Disposal of Confidential Records of Professional and Scientific Work

(a) Psychologists maintain confidentiality in creating, storing, accessing, transferring, and disposing of records under their control, whether these are written, automated, or in any other medium. (See also Standards 4.01, Maintaining Confidentiality, and 6.01, Documentation of Professional and Scientific Work and Maintenance of Records.)

(b) If confidential information concerning recipients of psychological services is entered into databases or systems of records available to persons whose access has not been consented to by the recipient, psychologists use coding or other techniques to avoid the inclusion of personal identifiers.

(c) Psychologists make plans in advance to facilitate the appropriate transfer and to protect the confidentiality of records and data in the event of psychologists' withdrawal from positions or practice. (See also Standards 3.12, Interruption of Psychological Services, and 10.09, Interruption of Therapy.)

6.03 Withholding Records for Nonpayment

Psychologists may not withhold records under their control that are requested and needed for a client's/patient's emergency treatment solely because payment has not been received.

6.04 Fees and Financial Arrangements

(a) As early as is feasible in a professional or scientific relationship, psychologists and recipients of psychological services reach an agreement specifying compensation and billing arrangements.

(b) Psychologists' fee practices are consistent with law.

(c) Psychologists do not misrepresent their fees.

(d) If limitations to services can be anticipated because of limitations in financing, this is discussed with the recipient of services as early as is feasible. (See also Standards 10.09, Interruption of Therapy, and 10.10, Terminating Therapy.)

(e) If the recipient of services does not pay for services as agreed, and if psychologists intend to use collection agencies or legal measures to collect the fees, psychologists first inform the person that such measures will be taken and provide that person an opportunity to make prompt payment. (See also Standards 4.05, Disclosures; 6.03, Withholding Records for Nonpayment; and 10.01, Informed Consent to Therapy.)

6.05 Barter With Clients/Patients

Barter is the acceptance of goods, services, or other nonmonetary remuneration from clients/patients in return for psychological services. Psychologists may barter only if (1) it is not clinically contraindicated, and (2) the resulting arrangement is not exploitative. (See also Standards 3.05, Multiple Relationships, and 6.04, Fees and Financial Arrangements.)

6.06 Accuracy in Reports to Payors and Funding Sources

In their reports to payors for services or sources of research funding, psychologists take reasonable steps to ensure the accurate reporting of the nature of the service provided or research conducted, the fees, charges, or payments, and where applicable, the identity of the provider, the findings, and the diagnosis. (See also Standards 4.01, Maintaining Confidentiality; 4.04, Minimizing Intrusions on Privacy; and 4.05, Disclosures.)

6.07 Referrals and Fees

When psychologists pay, receive payment from, or divide fees with another professional, other than in an employer-employee relationship, the payment to each is based on the services provided (clinical, consultative, administrative, or other) and is not based on the referral itself. (See also Standard 3.09, Cooperation with Other Professionals.)

7. Education and Training

7.01 Design of Education and Training Programs

Psychologists responsible for education and training programs take reasonable steps to ensure that the programs are designed to provide the appropriate knowledge and proper experiences, and to meet the requirements for licensure, certification, or other goals for which claims are made by the program. (See also Standard 5.03, Descriptions of Workshops and Non-Degree-Granting Educational Programs.)

7.02 Descriptions of Education and Training Programs

Psychologists responsible for education and training programs take reasonable steps to ensure that there is a current and accurate description of the program content (including participation in required course- or program-related counseling, psychotherapy, experiential groups, consulting projects, or community service), training goals and objectives, stipends and benefits, and requirements that must be met for satisfactory completion of the program. This information must be made readily available to all interested parties.

7.03 Accuracy in Teaching

(a) Psychologists take reasonable steps to ensure that course syllabi are accurate regarding the subject matter to be covered, bases for evaluating progress, and the nature of course experiences. This standard does not preclude an instructor from modifying course content or requirements when the instructor considers it pedagogically necessary or desirable, so long as students are made aware of these modifications in a manner that enables them to fulfill course requirements. (See also Standard 5.01, Avoidance of False or Deceptive Statements.)

(b) When engaged in teaching or training, psychologists present psychological information accurately. (See also Standard 2.03, Maintaining Competence.)

7.04 Student Disclosure of Personal Information

Psychologists do not require students or supervisees to disclose personal information in course- or program-related activities, either orally or in writing, regarding sexual history, history of abuse and neglect, psychological treatment, and relationships with parents, peers, and spouses or significant others except if (1) the program or training facility has clearly identified this requirement in its admissions and program materials or (2) the information is necessary to evaluate or obtain assistance for students whose personal problems could reasonably be judged to be preventing them from performing their training or professionally related activities in a competent manner or posing a threat to the students or others.

7.05 Mandatory Individual or Group Therapy

(a) When individual or group therapy is a program or course requirement, psychologists responsible for that program allow students in undergraduate and graduate programs the option of selecting such therapy from practitioners unaffiliated with the program. (See also Standard 7.02, Descriptions of Education and Training Programs.)

(b) Faculty who are or are likely to be responsible for evaluating students' academic performance do not themselves provide that therapy. (See also Standard 3.05, Multiple Relationships.)

7.06 Assessing Student and Supervisee Performance

(a) In academic and supervisory relationships, psychologists establish a timely and specific process for providing feedback to students and supervisees. Information regarding the process is provided to the student at the beginning of supervision.

(b) Psychologists evaluate students and supervisees on the basis of their actual performance on relevant and established program requirements.

7.07 Sexual Relationships With Students and Supervisees

Psychologists do not engage in sexual relationships with students or supervisees who are in their department, agency, or training center or over whom psychologists have or are likely to have evaluative authority. (See also Standard 3.05, Multiple Relationships.)

8. Research and Publication

8.01 Institutional Approval

When institutional approval is required, psychologists provide accurate information about their research proposals and obtain approval prior to conducting the research. They conduct the research in accordance with the approved research protocol.

8.02 Informed Consent to Research

(a) When obtaining informed consent as required in Standard 3.10, Informed Consent, psychologists inform participants about (1) the purpose of the research, expected duration, and procedures; (2) their right to decline to participate and to withdraw from the research once participation has begun; (3) the foreseeable consequences of declining or withdrawing; (4) reasonably foreseeable factors that may be expected to influence their willingness to participate such as potential risks, discomfort, or adverse effects; (5) any prospective research benefits; (6) limits of confidentiality; (7) incentives for participation; and (8) whom to contact for questions about the research and research participants' rights. They provide opportunity for the prospective participants to ask questions and receive answers. (See also Standards 8.03, Informed Consent for Recording Voices and Images in Research; 8.05, Dispensing With Informed Consent for Research; and 8.07, Deception in Research.)

(b) Psychologists conducting intervention research involving the use of experimental treatments clarify to participants at the outset of the research (1) the experimental nature of the treatment; (2) the services that will or will not be available to the control group(s) if appropriate; (3) the means by which assignment to treatment and control groups will be made; (4) available treatment alternatives if an individual does not wish to participate in the research or wishes to withdraw once a study has begun; and (5) compensation for or monetary costs of participating including, if appropriate, whether reimbursement from the participant or a third-party payor will be sought. (See also Standard 8.02a, Informed Consent to Research.)

8.03 Informed Consent for Recording Voices and Images in Research

Psychologists obtain informed consent from research participants prior to recording their voices or images for data collection unless (1) the research consists solely of naturalistic observations in public places, and it is not anticipated that the recording will be used in a manner that could cause personal identification or harm, or (2) the research design includes deception, and consent for the use of the recording is obtained during debriefing. (See also Standard 8.07, Deception in Research.)

8.04 Client/Patient, Student, and Subordinate Research Participants

(a) When psychologists conduct research with clients/patients, students, or subordinates as participants, psychologists take steps to protect the prospective participants from adverse consequences of declining or withdrawing from participation.

(b) When research participation is a course requirement or an opportunity for extra credit, the prospective participant is given the choice of equitable alternative activities.

8.05 Dispensing With Informed Consent for Research

Psychologists may dispense with informed consent only (1) where research would not reasonably be assumed to create distress or harm and involves (a) the study of normal educational practices, curricula, or classroom management methods conducted in educational settings; (b) only anonymous questionnaires, naturalistic observations, or archival research for which disclosure of responses would not place participants at risk of criminal or civil liability or damage their financial standing, employability, or reputation, and confidentiality is protected; or (c) the study of factors related to job or organization effectiveness conducted in organizational settings for which there is no risk to participants' employability, and confidentiality is protected or (2) where otherwise permitted by law or federal or institutional regulations.

8.06 Offering Inducements for Research Participation

(a) Psychologists make reasonable efforts to avoid offering excessive or inappropriate financial or other inducements for research participation when such inducements are likely to coerce participation.

(b) When offering professional services as an inducement for research participation, psychologists clarify the nature of the services, as well as the risks, obligations, and limitations. (See also Standard 6.05, Barter With Clients/Patients.)

8.07 Deception in Research

(a) Psychologists do not conduct a study involving deception unless they have determined that the use of deceptive techniques is justified by the study's significant prospective scientific, educational, or applied value and that effective nondeceptive alternative procedures are not feasible.

(b) Psychologists do not deceive prospective participants about research that is reasonably expected to cause physical pain or severe emotional distress.

(c) Psychologists explain any deception that is an integral feature of the design and conduct of an experiment to participants as early as is feasible, preferably at the conclusion of their participation, but no later than at the conclusion of the data collection, and permit participants to withdraw their data. (See also Standard 8.08, Debriefing.)

8.08 Debriefing

(a) Psychologists provide a prompt opportunity for participants to obtain appropriate information about the nature, results, and conclusions of the research, and they take reasonable steps to correct any misconceptions that participants may have of which the psychologists are aware.

(b) If scientific or humane values justify delaying or withholding this information, psychologists take reasonable measures to reduce the risk of harm.

(c) When psychologists become aware that research procedures have harmed a participant, they take reasonable steps to minimize the harm.

8.09 Humane Care and Use of Animals in Research

(a) Psychologists acquire, care for, use, and dispose of animals in compliance with current federal, state, and local laws and regulations, and with professional standards.

(b) Psychologists trained in research methods and experienced in the care of laboratory animals supervise all procedures involving animals and are responsible for ensuring appropriate consideration of their comfort, health, and humane treatment.

(c) Psychologists ensure that all individuals under their supervision who are using animals have received instruction in research methods and in the care, maintenance, and handling of the species being used, to the extent appropriate to their role. (See also Standard 2.05, Delegation of Work to Others.)

(d) Psychologists make reasonable efforts to minimize the discomfort, infection, illness, and pain of animal subjects.

(e) Psychologists use a procedure subjecting animals to pain, stress, or privation only when an alternative procedure is unavailable and the goal is justified by its prospective scientific, educational, or applied value.

(f) Psychologists perform surgical procedures under appropriate anesthesia and follow techniques to avoid infection and minimize pain during and after surgery.

(g) When it is appropriate that an animal's life be terminated, psychologists proceed rapidly, with an effort to minimize pain and in accordance with accepted procedures.

8.10 Reporting Research Results

(a) Psychologists do not fabricate data. (See also Standard 5.01a, Avoidance of False or Deceptive Statements.)

(b) If psychologists discover significant errors in their published data, they take reasonable steps to correct such errors in a correction, retraction, erratum, or other appropriate publication means.

8.11 Plagiarism

Psychologists do not present portions of another's work or data as their own, even if the other work or data source is cited occasionally.

8.12 Publication Credit

(a) Psychologists take responsibility and credit, including authorship credit, only for work they have actually performed or to which they have substantially contributed. (See also Standard 8.12b, Publication Credit.)

b) Principal authorship and other publication credits accurately reflect the relative scientific or professional contributions of the individuals involved, regardless of their relative status. Mere possession of an institutional position, such as department chair, does not justify authorship credit. Minor contributions to the research or to the writing for publications are acknowledged appropriately, such as in footnotes or in an introductory statement.

(c) Except under exceptional circumstances, a student is listed as principal author on any multiple-authored article that is substantially based on the student's doctoral dissertation. Faculty advisors discuss publication credit with students as early as feasible and throughout the research and publication process as appropriate. (See also Standard 8.12b, Publication Credit.)

8.13 Duplicate Publication of Data

Psychologists do not publish, as original data, data that have been previously published. This does not preclude republishing data when they are accompanied by proper acknowledgment.

8.14 Sharing Research Data for Verification

(a) After research results are published, psychologists do not withhold the data on which their conclusions are based from other competent professionals who seek to verify the substantive claims through reanalysis and who intend to use such data only for that purpose, provided that the confidentiality of the participants can be protected and unless legal rights concerning proprietary data preclude their release. This does not preclude psychologists from requiring that such individuals or groups be responsible for costs associated with the provision of such information.

(b) Psychologists who request data from other psychologists to verify the substantive claims through reanalysis may use shared data only for the declared purpose. Requesting psychologists obtain prior written agreement for all other uses of the data.

8.15 Reviewers

Psychologists who review material submitted for presentation, publication, grant, or research proposal review respect the confidentiality of and the proprietary rights in such information of those who submitted it.

9. Assessment

9.01 Bases for Assessments

(a) Psychologists base the opinions contained in their recommendations, reports, and diagnostic or evaluative statements, including forensic testimony, on information and techniques sufficient to substantiate their findings. (See also Standard 2.04, Bases for Scientific and Professional Judgments.)

(b) Except as noted in 9.01c, psychologists provide opinions of the psychological characteristics of individuals only after they have conducted an examination of the individuals adequate to support their statements or conclusions. When, despite reasonable efforts, such an examination is not practical, psychologists document the efforts they made and the result of those efforts, clarify the probable impact of their limited information on the reliability and validity of their opinions, and appropriately limit the nature and extent of their conclusions or recommendations. (See also Standards 2.01, Boundaries of Competence, and 9.06, Interpreting Assessment Results.)

(c) When psychologists conduct a record review or provide consultation or supervision and an individual examination is not warranted or necessary for the opinion, psychologists explain this and the sources of information on which they based their conclusions and recommendations.

9.02 Use of Assessments

(a) Psychologists administer, adapt, score, interpret, or use assessment techniques, interviews, tests, or instruments in a manner and for purposes that are appropriate in light of the research on or evidence of the usefulness and proper application of the techniques.

(b) Psychologists use assessment instruments whose validity and reliability have been established for use with members of the population tested. When such validity or reliability has not been established, psychologists describe the strengths and limitations of test results and interpretation.

(c) Psychologists use assessment methods that are appropriate to an individual's language preference and competence, unless the use of an alternative language is relevant to the assessment issues.

9.03 Informed Consent in Assessments

(a) Psychologists obtain informed consent for assessments, evaluations, or diagnostic services, as described in Standard 3.10, Informed Consent, except when (1) testing is mandated by law or governmental regulations; (2) informed consent is implied because testing is conducted as a routine educational, institutional, or organizational activity (e.g., when participants voluntarily agree to assessment when applying for a job); or (3) one purpose of the testing is to evaluate decisional capacity. Informed consent includes an explanation of the nature and purpose of the assessment, fees, involvement of third parties, and limits of confidentiality and sufficient opportunity for the client/patient to ask questions and receive answers.

(b) Psychologists inform persons with questionable capacity to consent or for whom testing is mandated by law or governmental regulations about the nature and purpose of the proposed assessment services, using language that is reasonably understandable to the person being assessed.

(c) Psychologists using the services of an interpreter obtain informed consent from the client/patient to use that interpreter, ensure that confidentiality of test results and test security are maintained, and include in their recommendations, reports, and diagnostic or evaluative statements, including forensic testimony, discussion of any limitations on the data obtained. (See also Standards 2.05, Delegation of Work to Others; 4.01, Maintaining Confidentiality; 9.01, Bases for Assessments; 9.06, Interpreting Assessment Results; and 9.07, Assessment by Unqualified Persons.)

9.04 Release of Test Data

(a) The term *test data* refers to raw and scaled scores, client/patient responses to test questions or stimuli, and psychologists' notes and recordings concerning client/patient statements and behavior during an examination. Those portions of test materials that include client/patient responses are included in the definition of *test data*. Pursuant to a client/patient release, psychologists provide test data to the client/patient or other persons identified in the release. Psychologists may refrain from releasing test data to protect a client/patient or others from substantial harm or misuse or misrepresentation of the data or the test, recognizing that in many instances release of confidential information under these circumstances is regulated by law. (See also Standard 9.11, Maintaining Test Security.)

(b) In the absence of a client/patient release, psychologists provide test data only as required by law or court order.

9.05 Test Construction

Psychologists who develop tests and other assessment techniques use appropriate psychometric procedures and current scientific or professional knowledge for test design, standardization, validation, reduction or elimination of bias, and recommendations for use.

9.06 Interpreting Assessment Results

When interpreting assessment results, including automated interpretations, psychologists take into account the purpose of the assessment as well as the various test factors, test-taking abilities, and other characteristics of the person being assessed, such as situational, personal, linguistic, and cultural differences, that might affect psychologists' judgments or reduce the accuracy of their interpretations. They indicate any significant limitations of their interpretations. (See also Standards 2.01b and c, Boundaries of Competence, and 3.01, Unfair Discrimination.)

9.07 Assessment by Unqualified Persons

Psychologists do not promote the use of psychological assessment techniques by unqualified persons, except when such use is conducted for training purposes with appropriate supervision. (See also Standard 2.05, Delegation of Work to Others.)

9.08 Obsolete Tests and Outdated Test Results

(a) Psychologists do not base their assessment or intervention decisions or recommendations on data or test results that are outdated for the current purpose.

(b) Psychologists do not base such decisions or recommendations on tests and measures that are obsolete and not useful for the current purpose.

9.09 Test Scoring and Interpretation Services

(a) Psychologists who offer assessment or scoring services to other professionals accurately describe the purpose, norms, validity, reliability, and applications of the procedures and any special qualifications applicable to their use.

(b) Psychologists select scoring and interpretation services (including automated services) on the basis of evidence of the validity of the program and procedures as well as on other appropriate considerations. (See also Standard 2.01b and c, Boundaries of Competence.)

(c) Psychologists retain responsibility for the appropriate application, interpretation, and use of assessment instruments, whether they score and interpret such tests themselves or use automated or other services.

9.10 Explaining Assessment Results

Regardless of whether the scoring and interpretation are done by psychologists, by employees or assistants, or by automated or other outside services, psychologists take reasonable steps to ensure that explanations of results are given to the individual or designated representative unless the nature of the relationship precludes provision of an explanation of results (such as in some organizational consulting, preemployment or security screenings, and forensic evaluations), and this fact has been clearly explained to the person being assessed in advance.

9.11 Maintaining Test Security

The term *test materials* refers to manuals, instruments, protocols, and test questions or stimuli and does not include *test data* as defined in Standard 9.04, Release of Test Data. Psychologists make reasonable efforts to maintain the integrity and security of test materials and other assessment techniques consistent with law and contractual obligations, and in a manner that permits adherence to this Ethics Code.

10. Therapy

10.01 Informed Consent to Therapy

(a) When obtaining informed consent to therapy as required in Standard 3.10, Informed Consent, psychologists inform clients/patients as early as is feasible in the therapeutic relationship about the nature and anticipated course of therapy, fees, involvement of third parties, and limits of confidentiality and provide sufficient opportunity for the client/patient to ask questions and receive answers. (See also Standards 4.02, Discussing the Limits of Confidentiality, and 6.04, Fees and Financial Arrangements.)

(b) When obtaining informed consent for treatment for which generally recognized techniques and procedures have not been established, psychologists inform their clients/patients of the developing nature of the treatment, the potential risks involved, alternative treatments that may be available, and the voluntary nature of their participation. (See also Standards 2.01e, Boundaries of Competence, and 3.10, Informed Consent.)

(c) When the therapist is a trainee and the legal responsibility for the treatment provided resides with the supervisor, the client/patient, as part of the informed consent procedure, is informed that the therapist is in training and is being supervised and is given the name of the supervisor.

10.02 Therapy Involving Couples or Families

(a) When psychologists agree to provide services to several persons who have a relationship (such as spouses, significant others, or parents and children), they take reasonable steps to clarify at the outset (1) which of the individuals are clients/patients and (2) the relationship the psychologist will have with each person. This clarification includes the psychologist's role and the probable uses of the services provided or the information obtained. (See also Standard 4.02, Discussing the Limits of Confidentiality.)

(b) If it becomes apparent that psychologists may be called on to perform potentially conflicting roles (such as family therapist and then witness for one party in divorce proceedings), psychologists take reasonable steps to clarify and modify, or withdraw from, roles appropriately. (See also Standard 3.05c, Multiple Relationships.)

10.03 Group Therapy

When psychologists provide services to several persons in a group setting, they describe at the outset the roles and responsibilities of all parties and the limits of confidentiality.

10.04 Providing Therapy to Those Served by Others

In deciding whether to offer or provide services to those already receiving mental health services elsewhere, psychologists carefully consider the treatment issues and the potential client's/patient's welfare. Psychologists discuss these issues with the client/patient or another legally authorized person on behalf of the client/patient in order to minimize the risk of confusion and conflict, consult with the other service providers when appropriate, and proceed with caution and sensitivity to the therapeutic issues.

10.05 Sexual Intimacies With Current Therapy Clients/Patients

Psychologists do not engage in sexual intimacies with current therapy clients/patients.

10.06 Sexual Intimacies With Relatives or Significant Others of Current Therapy Clients/Patients

Psychologists do not engage in sexual intimacies with individuals they know to be close relatives, guardians, or significant others of current clients/patients. Psychologists do not terminate therapy to circumvent this standard.

10.07 Therapy With Former Sexual Partners

Psychologists do not accept as therapy clients/patients persons with whom they have engaged in sexual intimacies.

10.08 Sexual Intimacies With Former Therapy Clients/Patients

(a) Psychologists do not engage in sexual intimacies with former clients/patients for at least two years after cessation or termination of therapy.

(b) Psychologists do not engage in sexual intimacies with former clients/patients even after a two-year interval except in the most unusual circumstances. Psychologists who engage in such activity after the two years following cessation or termination of therapy and of having no sexual contact with the former client/patient bear the burden of demonstrating that there has been no exploitation, in light of all relevant factors, including (1) the amount of time that has passed since therapy terminated; (2) the nature, duration, and intensity of the therapy; (3) the circumstances of termination; (4) the client's/patient's personal history; (5) the client's/patient's current mental status; (6) the likelihood of adverse impact on the client/patient; and (7) any statements or actions made by the therapist during the course of therapy suggesting or inviting the possibility of a posttermination sexual or romantic relationship with the client/patient. (See also Standard 3.05, Multiple Relationships.)

10.09 Interruption of Therapy

When entering into employment or contractual relationships, psychologists make reasonable efforts to provide for orderly and appropriate resolution of responsibility for client/patient care in the event that the employment or contractual relationship ends, with paramount consideration given to the welfare of the client/patient. (See also Standard 3.12, Interruption of Psychological Services.)

10.10 Terminating Therapy

(a) Psychologists terminate therapy when it becomes reasonably clear that the client/patient no longer needs the service, is not likely to benefit, or is being harmed by continued service.

(b) Psychologists may terminate therapy when threatened or otherwise endangered by the client/patient or another person with whom the client/patient has a relationship.

(c) Except where precluded by the actions of clients/patients or third-party payors, prior to termination psychologists provide pretermination counseling and suggest alternative service providers as appropriate.

History and Effective Date

This version of the APA Ethics Code was adopted by the American Psychological Association's Council of Representatives during its meeting, August 21, 2002, and is effective beginning June 1, 2003. Inquiries concerning the substance or interpretation of the APA Ethics Code should be addressed to the Director, Office of Ethics, American Psychological Association, 750 First Street, NE, Washington, DC 20002-4242. The Ethics Code and information regarding the Code can be found on the APA web site, http://www.apa.org/ethics. The standards in this Ethics Code will be used to adjudicate complaints brought concerning alleged conduct occurring on or after the effective date. Complaints regarding conduct occurring prior to the effective date will be adjudicated on the basis of the version of the Ethics Code that was in effect at the time the conduct occurred. The APA has previously published its Ethics Code as follows: American Psychological Association. (1953). *Ethical standards of psychologists*. Washington, DC: Author; American Psychological Association. (1959). Ethical standards of psychologists. *American Psychologist*, *14*, 279–282; American Psychological Association. (1963). Ethical standards of psychologists. *American Psychologist, 18*, 56–60; American Psychological Association. (1968). Ethical standards of psychologists. *American Psychologist, 23*, 357–361; American Psychological Association. (1977, March). Ethical standards of psychologists. *APA Monitor*, 22–23; American Psychological Association. (1979). *Ethical standards of psychologists*. Washington, DC: Author; American Psychological Association. (1981). Ethical principles of psychologists. *American Psychologist, 36*, 633–638; American Psychological Association. (1990). Ethical principles of psychologists (Amended June 2, 1989). *American Psychologist, 45*, 390–395; American Psychological Association. (1992). Ethical principles of psychologists and code of conduct. *American Psychologist*, *47*, 1597–1611.

Appendix C

CACREP Standards for Clinical Instruction

Clinical instruction includes supervised practica and internships that have been completed within a student's program of study. Practicum and internship requirements are considered to be the most critical experience elements in the program. All faculty, including clinical instruction faculty and supervisors, are clearly committed to preparing professional counselors and promoting the development of the student's professional counselor identity.

A. Each regular or adjunct program faculty member who provides individual or group practicum and/or internship supervision must have
   1. a doctoral degree and/or appropriate clinical preparation, preferably from an accredited counselor education program;
   2. relevant professional experience and demonstrated competence in counseling; and
   3. relevant training and supervision experience.

B. Students serving as individual or group practicum supervisors must
   1. have completed counseling practicum and internship experience equivalent to those within an entry-level program;
   2. have completed or are receiving preparation in counseling supervision; and
   3. be supervised by program faculty, with a faculty/student ratio that does not exceed 1:5.

C. A site supervisor must have
   1. a minimum of a master's degree in counseling or a related profession with equivalent qualifications, including appropriate certifications and/or licenses;

2001 CACREP Standards, Section III, Clinical Instruction. Permission granted by the Council for Accreditation of Counseling and Related Educational Programs.

2. a minimum of two (2) years of pertinent professional experience in the program area in which the student is completing clinical instruction; and
3. knowledge of the program's expectations, requirements, and evaluation procedures for students.

D. A clinical instruction environment, on- or off-campus, is conducive to modeling, demonstration, and training and is available and used by the program. Administrative control of the clinical instruction environment ensures adequate and appropriate access by the faculty and students. The clinical instruction environment includes all of the following:

1. settings for individual counseling with assured privacy and sufficient space for appropriate equipment (for example, TV monitoring and taping);
2. settings for small-group work with assured privacy and sufficient space for appropriate equipment;
3. necessary and appropriate technologies that assist learning, such as audio, video, and telecommunications equipment;
4. settings with observational and/or other interactive supervision capabilities; and
5. procedures that ensure that the client's confidentiality and legal rights are protected.

E. Technical assistance for the use and maintenance of audio and videotape and computer equipment is available as well as other forms of communication technology.

F. Orientation, assistance, consultation, and professional development opportunities are provided by counseling program faculty to site supervisors.

G. Students must complete supervised practicum experiences that total a minimum of 100 clock hours. The practicum provides for the development of counseling skills under supervision. The student's practicum includes all of the following:

1. 40 hours of direct service with clients, including experience in individual counseling and group work;
2. weekly interaction with an average of one (1) hour per week of individual and/or triadic supervision which occurs regularly over a minimum of one academic term by a program faculty member or a supervisor working under the supervision of a program faculty member;
3. an average of one and one half (1 1/2) hours per week of group supervision that is provided on a regular schedule over the course of the student's practicum by a program faculty member or a supervisor under the supervision of a program faculty member; and
4. evaluation of the student's performance throughout the practicum including a formal evaluation after the student completes the practicum.

H. The program requires students to complete a supervised internship of 600 clock hours that is begun after successful completion of the student's practicum (as defined in Standard III.G). The internship provides an opportunity for the student to perform, under supervision, a variety of counseling activities that a professional counselor is expected to perform. The student's internship includes all of the following:

   1. 240 hours of direct service with clients appropriate to the program of study;
   2. weekly interaction with an average of one (1) hour per week of individual and/or triadic supervision, throughout the internship, (usually performed by the on-site supervisor);
   3. an average of one and one half (1½) hours per week of group supervision provided on a regular schedule throughout the internship, usually performed by a program faculty member;
   4. the opportunity for the student to become familiar with a variety professional activities in addition to direct service (e.g., record keeping, supervision, information and referral, in service and staff meetings);
   5. the opportunity for the student to develop program-appropriate audio and/or videotapes of the student's interactions with clients for use in supervision;
   6. the opportunity for the student to gain supervised experience in the use of a variety of professional resources such as assessment instruments, technologies, print and nonprint media, professional literature, and research; and
   7. a formal evaluation of the student's performance during the internship by a program faculty member in consultation with the site supervisor.

I. The practicum and internship experiences are tutorial forms of instruction; therefore, when the individual supervision is provided by program faculty, the ratio of 5 students to 1 faculty member is considered equivalent to the teaching of one (1) three-semester hour course. Such a ratio is considered maximum per course.

J. Group supervision for practicum and internship should not exceed 10 students.

K. Clinical experiences (practicum and internship) should provide opportunities for students to counsel clients who represent the ethnic and demographic diversity of their community.

L. Students formally evaluate their supervisors and learning experience at the end of their practicum and internship experiences.

M. Programs require students to be covered by professional liability insurance while enrolled or participating in practicum, internship, or other field experiences.

Appendix D

NBCC Code of Ethics

Preamble

The National Board for Certified Counselors (NBCC) is a professional certification board which certifies counselors as having met standards for the general and specialty practice of professional counseling established by the Board. The counselors certified by NBCC may identify with different professional associations and are often licensed by jurisdictions which promulgate codes of ethics. The NBCC code of ethics provides a minimal ethical standard for the professional behavior of all NBCC certificants. This code provides an expectation of and assurance for the ethical practice for all who use the professional services of an NBCC certificant. In addition, it serves the purpose of having an enforceable standard for all NBCC certificants and assures those served of some resource in case of a perceived ethical violation. This code is applicable to National Certified Counselors and those who are seeking certification from NBCC.

The NBCC Ethical Code applies to all those certified by NBCC regardless of any other professional affiliation. Persons who receive professional services from certified counselors may elect to use other ethical codes which apply to their counselor. Although NBCC cooperates with professional associations and credentialing organizations, it can bring actions to discipline or sanction NBCC certificants only if the provisions of the NBCC Code are found to have been violated.

The National Board for Certified Counselors, Inc. (NBCC) promotes counseling through certification. In pursuit of this mission, the NBCC:

- Promotes quality assurance in counseling practice
- Promotes the value of counseling
- Promotes public awareness of quality counseling practice

- Promotes professionalism in counseling
- Promotes leadership in credentialing

SECTION A: GENERAL

1. Certified counselors engage in continuous efforts to improve professional practices, services, and research. Certified counselors are guided in their work by evidence of the best professional practices.
2. Certified counselors have a responsibility to the clients they serve and to the institutions within which the services are performed. Certified counselors also strive to assist the respective agency, organization, or institution in providing competent and ethical professional services. The acceptance of employment in an institution implies that the certified counselor is in agreement with the general policies and principles of the institution. Therefore, the professional activities of the certified counselor are in accord with the objectives of the institution. If the certified counselor and the employer do not agree and cannot reach agreement on policies that are consistent with appropriate counselor ethical practice that is conducive to client growth and development, the employment should be terminated. If the situation warrants further action, the certified counselor should work through professional organizations to have the unethical practice changed.
3. Ethical behavior among professional associates (i.e., both certified and non-certified counselors) must be expected at all times. When a certified counselor has doubts as to the ethical behavior of professional colleagues, the certified counselor must take action to attempt to rectify this condition. Such action uses the respective institution's channels first and then uses procedures established by the NBCC or the perceived violator's profession.
4. Certified counselors must refuse remuneration for consultation or counseling with persons who are entitled to these services through the certified counselor's employing institution or agency. Certified counselors must not divert to their private practices, without the mutual consent of the institution and the client, legitimate clients in their primary agencies or the institutions with which they are affiliated.
5. In establishing fees for professional counseling services, certified counselors must consider the financial status of clients. In the event that the established fee status is inappropriate for a client, assistance must be provided in finding comparable services at acceptable cost.
6. Certified counselors offer only professional services for which they are trained or have supervised experience. No diagnosis, assessment, or treatment should be performed without prior training or supervision. Certified counselors are responsible for correcting any misrepresentations of their qualifications by others.
7. Certified counselors recognize their limitations and provide services or use techniques for which they are qualified by training and/or supervision. Certified counselors recognize the need for and seek continuing education to assure competent services.

8. Certified counselors are aware of the intimacy in the counseling relationship and maintain respect for the client. Counselors must not engage in activities that seek to meet their personal or professional needs at the expense of the client.
9. Certified counselors must insure that they do not engage in personal, social, organizational, financial, or political activities which might lead to a misuse of their influence.
10. Sexual intimacy with clients is unethical. Certified counselors will not be sexually, physically, or romantically intimate with clients, and they will not engage in sexual, physical, or romantic intimacy with clients within a minimum of two years after terminating the counseling relationship.
11. Certified counselors do not condone or engage in sexual harassment, which is defined as unwelcome comments, gestures, or physical contact of a sexual nature.
12. Through an awareness of the impact of stereotyping and unwarranted discrimination (e.g., biases based on age, disability, ethnicity, gender, race, religion, or sexual orientation), certified counselors guard the individual rights and personal dignity of the client in the counseling relationship.
13. Certified counselors are accountable at all times for their behavior. They must be aware that all actions and behaviors of the counselor reflect on professional integrity and, when inappropriate, can damage the public trust in the counseling profession. To protect public confidence in the counseling profession, certified counselors avoid behavior that is clearly in violation of accepted moral and legal standards.
14. Products or services provided by certified counselors by means of classroom instruction, public lectures, demonstrations, written articles, radio or television programs or other types of media must meet the criteria cited in this code.
15. Certified counselors have an obligation to withdraw from the practice of counseling if they violate the Code of Ethics, or if the mental or physical condition of the certified counselor renders it unlikely that a professional relationship will be maintained.
16. Certified counselors must comply with all NBCC policies, procedures, and agreements, including all information disclosure requirements.

SECTION B: COUNSELING RELATIONSHIP

1. The primary obligation of certified counselors is to respect the integrity and promote the welfare of clients, whether they are assisted individually, in family units, or in group counseling. In a group setting, the certified counselor is also responsible for taking reasonable precautions to protect individuals from physical and/or psychological trauma resulting from interaction within the group.

2. Certified counselors know and take into account the traditions and practices of other professional disciplines with whom they work and cooperate fully with such. If a person is receiving similar services from another professional, certified counselors do not offer their own services directly to such a person. If a certified counselor is contacted by a person who is already receiving similar services from another professional, the certified counselor carefully considers that professional relationship as well as the client's welfare and proceeds with caution and sensitivity to the therapeutic issues. When certified counselors learn that their clients are in a professional relationship with another counselor or mental health professional, they request release from the clients to inform the other counselor or mental health professional of their relationship with the client and strive to establish positive and collaborative professional relationships that are in the best interest of the client. Certified counselors discuss these issues with clients and the counselor or professional so as to minimize the risk of confusion and conflict and encourage clients to inform other professionals of the new professional relationship.
3. Certified counselors may choose to consult with any other professionally competent person about a client and must notify clients of this right. Certified counselors avoid placing a consultant in a conflict-of-interest situation that would preclude the consultant serving as a proper party to the efforts of the certified counselor to help the client.
4. When a client's condition indicates that there is a clear and imminent danger to the client or others, the certified counselor must take reasonable action to inform potential victims and/or inform responsible authorities. Consultation with other professionals must be used when possible. The assumption of responsibility for the client's behavior must be taken only after careful deliberation, and the client must be involved in the resumption of responsibility as quickly as possible.
5. Records of the counseling relationship, including interview notes, test data, correspondence, audio or visual tape recordings, electronic data storage, and other documents are to be considered professional information for use in counseling. Records should contain accurate factual data. The physical records are property of the certified counselors or their employers. The information contained in the records belongs to the client and therefore may not be released to others without the consent of the client or when the counselor has exhausted challenges to a court order. The certified counselors are responsible to insure that their employees handle confidential information appropriately. Confidentiality must be maintained during the storage and disposition of records. Records should be maintained for a period of at least five (5) years after the last counselor/client contact, including cases in which the client is deceased. All records must be released to the client upon request.
6. Certified counselors must ensure that data maintained in electronic storage are secure. By using the best computer security methods available, the data must be limited to information that is appropriate and necessary for the services being provided and accessible only to

appropriate staff members involved in the provision of services. Certified counselors must also ensure that the electronically stored data are destroyed when the information is no longer of value in providing services or required as part of clients' records.

7. Any data derived from a client relationship and used in training or research shall be so disguised that the informed client's identity is fully protected. Any data which cannot be so disguised may be used only as expressly authorized by the client's informed and uncoerced consent.
8. When counseling is initiated, and throughout the counseling process as necessary, counselors inform clients of the purposes, goals, techniques, procedures, limitations, potential risks and benefits of services to be performed, and clearly indicate limitations that may affect the relationship as well as any other pertinent information. Counselors take reasonable steps to ensure that clients understand the implications of any diagnosis, the intended use of tests and reports, methods of treatment and safety precautions that must be taken in their use, fees, and billing arrangements.
9. Certified counselors who have an administrative, supervisory and/or evaluative relationship with individuals seeking counseling services must not serve as the counselor and should refer the individuals to other professionals. Exceptions are made only in instances where an individual's situation warrants counseling intervention and another alternative is unavailable. Dual relationships that might impair the certified counselor's objectivity and professional judgment must be avoided and/or the counseling relationship terminated through referral to a competent professional.
10. When certified counselors determine an inability to be of professional assistance to a potential or existing client, they must, respectively, not initiate the counseling relationship or immediately terminate the relationship. In either event, the certified counselor must suggest appropriate alternatives. Certified counselors must be knowledgeable about referral resources so that a satisfactory referral can be initiated. In the event that the client declines a suggested referral, the certified counselor is not obligated to continue the relationship.
11. When certified counselors are engaged in intensive, short-term counseling, they must ensure that professional assistance is available at normal costs to clients during and following the short-term counseling.
12. Counselors using electronic means in which counselor and client are not in immediate proximity must present clients with local sources of care before establishing a continued short or long-term relationship. Counselors who communicate with clients via Internet are governed by NBCC standards for Web Counseling.
13. Counselors must document permission to practice counseling by electronic means in all governmental jurisdictions where such counseling takes place.
14. When electronic data and systems are used as a component of counseling services, certified counselors must ensure that the computer appli-

cation, and any information it contains, is appropriate for the respective needs of clients and is non-discriminatory. Certified counselors must ensure that they themselves have acquired a facilitation level of knowledge with any system they use including hands-on application, and understanding of the uses of all aspects of the computer-based system. In selecting and/or maintaining computer-based systems that contain career information, counselors must ensure that the system provides current, accurate, and locally relevant information. Certified counselors must also ensure that clients are intellectually, emotionally, and physically compatible with computer applications and understand their purpose and operation. Client use of a computer application must be evaluated to correct possible problems and assess subsequent needs.

15. Certified counselors who develop self-help/stand-alone computer software for use by the general public, must first ensure that it is designed to function in a stand-alone manner that is appropriate and safe for all clients for which it is intended. A manual is required. The manual must provide the user with intended outcomes, suggestions for using the software, descriptions of inappropriately used applications, and descriptions of when and how other forms of counseling services might be beneficial. Finally, the manual must include the qualifications of the developer, the development process, validation date, and operating procedures.
16. The counseling relationship and information resulting from it remains confidential, consistent with the legal and ethical obligations of certified counselors. In group counseling, counselors clearly define confidentiality and the parameters for the specific group being entered, explain the importance of confidentiality, and discuss the difficulties related to confidentiality involved in group work. The fact that confidentiality cannot be guaranteed is clearly communicated to group members. However, counselors should give assurance about their professional responsibility to keep all group communications confidential.
17. Certified counselors must screen prospective group counseling participants to ensure compatibility with group objectives. This is especially important when the emphasis is on self-understanding and growth through self-disclosure. Certified counselors must maintain an awareness of the welfare of each participant throughout the group process.

Section C: Counselor Supervision

NCCs who offer and/or provide supervision must:

a. Ensure that they have the proper training and supervised experience through contemporary continuing education and/or graduate training
b. Ensure that supervisees are informed of the supervisor's credentials and professional status as well as all conditions of supervision as defined/outlined by the supervisor's practice, agency, group, or organization
c. Ensure that supervisees are aware of the current ethical standards related to their professional practice

d. Ensure that supervisees are informed about the process of supervision, including supervision goals, paradigms of supervision, and the supervisor's preferred research-based supervision paradigm(s)

e. Provide supervisees with agreed upon scheduled feedback as part of an established evaluation plan (e.g., one (1) hour per week)

f. Ensure that supervisees inform their clients of their professional status (i.e., trainee, intern, licensed, non-licensed, etc.)

g. Establish procedures with their supervisees for handling crisis situations

h. Render timely assistance to supervisees who are or may be unable to provide competent counseling services to clients and

i. Intervene in any situation where the supervisee is impaired and the client is at risk

In addition, because supervision may result in a dual relationship between the supervisor and the supervisee, the supervisor is responsible for ensuring that any dual relationship is properly managed.

SECTION D: MEASUREMENT AND EVALUATION

1. Because many types of assessment techniques exist, certified counselors must recognize the limits of their competence and perform only those assessment functions for which they have received appropriate training or supervision.
2. Certified counselors who utilize assessment instruments to assist them with diagnoses must have appropriate training and skills in educational and psychological measurement, validation criteria, test research, and guidelines for test development and use.
3. Certified counselors must provide instrument specific orientation or information to an examinee prior to and following the administration of assessment instruments or techniques so that the results may be placed in proper perspective with other relevant factors. The purpose of testing and the explicit use of the results must be made known to an examinee prior to testing.
4. In selecting assessment instruments or techniques for use in a given situation or with a particular client, certified counselors must carefully evaluate the specific theoretical bases and characteristics, validity, reliability and appropriateness of the instrument.
5. When making statements to the public about assessment instruments or techniques, certified counselors must provide accurate information and avoid false claims or misconceptions concerning the meaning of the instrument's reliability and validity terms.
6. Counselors must follow all directions and researched procedures for selection, administration and interpretation of all evaluation instruments and use them only within proper contexts.
7. Certified counselors must be cautious when interpreting the results of instruments that possess insufficient technical data, and must

explicitly state to examinees the specific limitations and purposes for the use of such instruments.

8. Certified counselors must proceed with caution when attempting to evaluate and interpret performances of any person who cannot be appropriately compared to the norms for the instrument.
9. Because prior coaching or dissemination of test materials can invalidate test results, certified counselors are professionally obligated to maintain test security.
10. Certified counselors must consider psychometric limitations when selecting and using an instrument, and must be cognizant of the limitations when interpreting the results. When tests are used to classify clients, certified counselors must ensure that periodic review and/or retesting are made to prevent client stereotyping.
11. An examinee's welfare, explicit prior understanding, and consent are the factors used when determining who receives the test results. Certified counselors must see that appropriate interpretation accompanies any release of individual or group test data (e.g., limitations of instrument and norms).
12. Certified counselors must ensure that computer-generated test administration and scoring programs function properly thereby providing clients with accurate test results.
13. Certified counselors who develop computer-based test interpretations to support the assessment process must ensure that the validity of the interpretations is established prior to the commercial distribution of the computer application.
14. Certified counselors recognize that test results may become obsolete, and avoid the misuse of obsolete data.
15. Certified counselors must not appropriate, reproduce, or modify published tests or parts thereof without acknowledgment and permission from the publisher, except as permitted by the fair educational use provisions of the U.S. copyright law.

SECTION E: RESEARCH AND PUBLICATION

1. Certified counselors will adhere to applicable legal and professional guidelines on research with human subjects.
2. In planning research activities involving human subjects, certified counselors must be aware of and responsive to all pertinent ethical principles and ensure that the research problem, design, and execution are in full compliance with any pertinent institutional or governmental regulations.
3. The ultimate responsibility for ethical research lies with the principal researcher, although others involved in the research activities are ethically obligated and responsible for their own actions.

4. Certified counselors who conduct research with human subjects are responsible for the welfare of the subjects throughout the experiment and must take all reasonable precautions to avoid causing injurious psychological, physical, or social effects on their subjects.
5. Certified counselors who conduct research must abide by the basic elements of informed consent:
   a. fair explanation of the procedures to be followed, including an identification of those which are experimental
   b. description of the attendant discomforts and risks
   c. description of the benefits to be expected
   d. disclosure of appropriate alternative procedures that would be advantageous for subjects with an offer to answer any inquiries concerning the procedures
   e. an instruction that subjects are free to withdraw their consent and to discontinue participation in the project or activity at any time.
6. When reporting research results, explicit mention must be made of all the variables and conditions known to the investigator that may have affected the outcome of the study or the interpretation of the data.
7. Certified counselors who conduct and report research investigations must do so in a manner that minimizes the possibility that the results will be misleading.
8. Certified counselors are obligated to make available sufficient original research data to qualified others who may wish to replicate the study.
9. Certified counselors who supply data, aid in the research of another person, report research results, or make original data available, must take due care to disguise the identity of respective subjects in the absence of specific authorization from the subjects to do otherwise.
10. When conducting and reporting research, certified counselors must be familiar with and give recognition to previous work on the topic, must observe all copyright laws, and must follow the principles of giving full credit to those to whom credit is due.
11. Certified counselors must give due credit through joint authorship, acknowledgment, footnote statements, or other appropriate means to those who have contributed to the research and/or publication, in accordance with such contributions.
12. Certified counselors should communicate to other counselors the results of any research judged to be of professional value. Results that reflect unfavorably on institutions, programs, services, or vested interests must not be withheld.
13. Certified counselors who agree to cooperate with another individual in research and/or publication incur an obligation to cooperate as promised in terms of punctuality of performance and with full regard to the completeness and accuracy of the information required.
14. Certified counselors must not submit the same manuscript, or one essentially similar in content, for simultaneous publication consider-

ation by two or more journals. In addition, manuscripts that have been published in whole or substantial part should not be submitted for additional publication without acknowledgment and permission from any previous publisher.

SECTION F: CONSULTING

Consultation refers to a voluntary relationship between a professional helper and a help-needing individual, group, or social unit in which the consultant is providing help to the client(s) in defining and solving a work-related problem or potential work-related problem with a client or client system.

1. Certified counselors, acting as consultants, must have a high degree of self-awareness of their own values, knowledge, skills, limitations, and needs in entering a helping relationship that involves human and/or organizational change. The focus of the consulting relationship must be on the issues to be resolved and not on the person(s) presenting the problem.
2. In the consulting relationship, the certified counselor and client must understand and agree upon the problem definition, subsequent goals, and predicted consequences of interventions selected.
3. Certified counselors acting as consultants must be reasonably certain that they, or the organization represented, have the necessary competencies and resources for giving the kind of help that is needed or that may develop later, and that appropriate referral resources are available.
4. Certified counselors in a consulting relationship must encourage and cultivate client adaptability and growth toward self-direction. Certified counselors must maintain this role consistently and not become a decision maker for clients or create a future dependency on the consultant.

SECTION G: PRIVATE PRACTICE

1. In advertising services as a private practitioner, certified counselors must advertise in a manner that accurately informs the public of the professional services, expertise, and techniques of counseling available.
2. Certified counselors who assume an executive leadership role in a private practice organization do not permit their names to be used in professional notices during periods of time when they are not actively engaged in the private practice of counseling unless their executive roles are clearly stated.
3. Certified counselors must make available their highest degree (described by discipline), type and level of certification and/or license, address, telephone number, office hours, type and/or description of services, and other relevant information. Listed information must not contain false, inaccurate, misleading, partial, out-of-context, or otherwise deceptive material or statements.
4. Certified counselors who are involved in a partnership/corporation with other certified counselors and/or other professionals, must clearly specify all relevant specialties of each member of the partnership or corporation.

Appendix: Certification Examination

Applicants for the NBCC Certification Examinations must have fulfilled all current eligibility requirements, and are responsible for the accuracy and validity of all information and/or materials provided by themselves or by others for fulfillment of eligibility criteria.

Approved on July 1, 1982. Amended on February 21, 1987; January 6, 1989; October 31, 1997; June 21, 2002; February 4, 2005; and October 8, 2005.

Acknowledgment

Reference documents, statements, and sources for the development of the NBCC Code of Ethics were as follows:

The Ethical Standards of the American Counseling Association (ACA), Responsible Uses for Standardized Testing (AAC), codes of ethics for the American Psychological Association and the National Career Development Association, Handbook of Standards for Computer-Based Career Information Systems (ACSCI), and Guidelines for the Use of Computer-Based Career Information and Guidance Systems (ACSCI).

REFERENCES

Abeles, N. (1980). Teaching ethical principles by means of value confrontations. *Psychotherapy: Theory, Research and Practice, 17,* 384–391.

American Counseling Association. (1995). *Code of ethics and standards of practice.* Retrieved February 10, 2003, from www.counseling.org

American Counseling Association. (2005). *Code of ethics and standards of practice.* Retrieved March 15, 2007, from www.counseling.org

American Counseling Association Office of Professional Affairs. (2007). *Licensure requirements for professional counselors: A state by state report.* Alexandria, VA: ACA.

American Psychiatric Association (2000). *Diagnostic and Statistical Manual of Mental Disorders* (4th ed., text revised). Arlington, VA: Author.

Auxier, C. R., Hughes, F. R., & Kline, W. B. (2003). Identity development in counselors-in-training. *Counselor Education and Supervision, 43,* 25–38.

Barnes, K. L. (2004). Applying self-efficacy theory to counselor training: A comparison of two approaches. *Counselor Education and Supervision, 44,* 56–69.

Barret-Lennard, G. T. (1981). The empathy cycle: Refinement of a nuclear concept. *Journal of Counseling Psychology, 28,* 91–100.

Beinart, H. (2003). Models of supervision and the supervisory relationship and their evidence base. In I. Fleming & L. Steen (Eds.), *Supervision and clinical psychology: Theory, practice and perspectives,* pp. 36–50. Hove, East Sussex, U.K.: Brunner-Routledge.

Beitman, B. D. (1987). *The structure of individual psychotherapy.* New York: Guilford.

Bernard, H. S. (1989). Guidelines to minimize premature terminations. *International Journal of Group Psychotherapy, 39,* 523–529.

Bernard, J. M., & Goodyear, R. K. (1992). *Fundamentals of clinical supervision.* Needham Heights, MA: Allyn & Bacon.

Bernard, J. M., & Goodyear, R. K. (1998). *Fundamentals of clinical supervision* (2nd ed.).Needham Heights, MA: Allyn & Bacon.

Bernstein, B. L., & Lacomte, C. (1979). Self-critique technique training in a competency-based practicum. *Counselor Education and Supervision, 19,* 69–76.

Bloom, B. S. (1984). *Taxonomy of educational objectives.* Boston: Allyn & Bacon.

Bloom, B. S., Engelhart, M. D., Furst, F. J., Hill, W. H., & Krathwohl, D. R. (1956). *Taxonomy of educational objectives: Cognitive domain.* New York: McKay.

Borders, L. D., & Benshoff, J. M. (1992). The mini-conference: Teaching professionalism through student involvement. *Journal of Counseling and Development, 7,* 39–40.

Borders, L. D., & Leddick, G. R. (1987). *Handbook of counseling supervision.* Alexandria, VA: Association for Counselor Education & Supervision.

Bordin, E. S. (1983). A working alliance model of supervision. *Counseling Psychologist, 11,* 35–42.

Boy, A. V., & Pine, G. J. (1980). Avoiding counselor burnout through role renewal. *Personnel and Guidance Journal, 59,* 161–163.

Bradley, C., & Fiorini, J. (1999). Evaluation of counseling practicum: National study of programs accredited by CACREP. *Counselor Education and Supervision, 39,* 110–119.

Bradley, L. J. (1989). *Counselor supervision: Principles, process, practice* (2nd ed.). Muncie, IN: Accelerated Development.

Cavanagh, M. E., & Levitov, J. E. (2002). *The counseling experience: A theoretical and practical approach* (2nd ed.). Long Grove, IL: Waveland.

Center for Credentialing and Education. (2005). *Approved clinical supervisor code of ethics.* Retrieved March 15, 2007, from www.cce-global.org

Connelly, A. R. (2005). What every graduate student needs to know. *Counseling Today, 22.*

Corey, G., Corey, M. S., & Callanan, P. (2003). *Issues and ethics in the helping professions* (6th ed.). Pacific Grove, CA: Brooks/Cole.

Cormier, S., & Hackney, H. (1999). *Counseling strategies and interventions* (5th ed.). Boston: Allyn & Bacon.

Deming, W. E. (1986). *Out of the crisis.* Cambridge: Massachusetts Institute of Technology.

Doehrman, M. J. (1976). Parallel processes in supervision and psychotherapy. *Bulletin of the Menninger Clinic, 40,* 1–104.

Edelwich, J., & Brodsky, A. (1980). *Burn-out: Stages of disillusionment in the helping professions.* New York: Human Services Press.

Eriksen, K., & McAuliffe, G. (Eds.). (2001). *Teaching counselors and therapists: Constructivist and developmental course design.* Westport, CT: Bergin & Garvey.

Fall, K. A., Holden, J. M., & Marquis, A. (2004). *Theoretical models of counseling and psychotherapy.* New York: Brunner-Routledge.

Fitch, T. J., & Marshall, J. L. (2002). Using cognitive interventions with counseling practicum students during group supervision. *Counselor Education and Supervision, 41,* 335–342.

Ford, G. G. (1995). *Teaching psychology students to reason ethically.* Poster session presented at the annual meeting of the American Psychological Society, New York, NY.

Forrester-Miller, H., & Davis, T. (1996). *A practitioner's guide to ethical decision making.* Alexandria, VA: American Counseling Association.

Garfield, S. L. (1994). Research on client variables in psychotherapy. In A. E. Bergin & S. L. Garfield (Eds.), *Handbook of psychotherapy and behavior change* (4th ed., pp. 190–228). New York: Wiley.

Gelso, C., & Woodhouse, S. (2002). The termination of psychotherapy: What research tells us about the process of ending treatment. In G. S. Tryon (Ed.), *Counseling based on process research: Applying what we know* (pp. 344–369). Boston: Allyn & Bacon.

Gibson, R. L., & Mitchell, M. M. (2003). *Introduction to guidance and counseling* (6th ed.). Columbus, OH: Pearson Merrill Prentice Hall.

Granello, D. H. (2000). Encouraging the cognitive development of supervisees: Using Bloom's taxonomy in supervision. *Counselor Education and Supervision, 40,* 31–46.

Henerson, M. E., Morris, L. L., & Fitz-Gibbon, C. T. (1987). *How to measure attitudes.* Newbury Park, CA: Sage.

Hiebert, B., Uhlemann, M. R., Marshall, A., & Lee, D. Y. (1998). The relationship between self-talk, anxiety, and counseling skill. *Canadian Journal of Counseling, 32,* 163–171.

Hill, C. E., Charles, D., & Reed, K. G. (1981). A longitudinal analysis of changes in counseling skills during doctoral training in counseling psychology. *Journal of Counseling Psychology, 28,* 428–436.

Hutchins, D. E., & Vaught, C. C. (1997). *Helping relationships and strategies* (3rd ed.). Pacific Grove, CA: Brooks/Cole.

Joint Committee on Standards for Educational Evaluation. (1981). *Standards for evaluation of educational programs, projects, and materials.* New York: McGraw-Hill.

Jourard, S. M., & Landsman, T. (1980). *Healthy personality* (4th ed.). New York: Macmillan.

Kesler, K. D. (1990). Burnout: A multimodal approach to assessment and resolution. *Elementary School Guidance and Counseling, 24,* 303–311.

Kiser, P. M. (2000). *Getting the most from your human service internship: Learning from experience.* Belmont, CA: Wadsworth.

Kitchener, K. S. (1984). Intuition, critical evaluation, and ethical principles: The foundation for ethical decisions in counseling psychology. *Counseling Psychologist, 12*(3), 43–55.

Kottler, J. A. (1986). *On being a therapist.* San Francisco: Jossey-Bass.

Kottler, J. A., & Brown, R. W. (2000). *Introduction to therapeutic counseling: Voices from the field* (4th ed.). Pacific Grove, CA: Brooks/Cole.

Larson, L. M., & Daniels, J. A. (1998). Review of the counseling self-efficacy literature. *Counseling Psychologist, 26,* 179–218.

Liddle, B. (1986). Resistance in supervision: A response to perceived threat. *Counselor Education and Supervision, 26,* 117–127.

Marx, J. A., & Gelso, C. J. (1987). Termination of individual counseling in a university counseling center. *Journal of Counseling Psychology, 34,* 3–9.

Megargee, E. J. (1992). *A guide to obtaining a psychology internship* (2nd ed.). Muncie, IN: Accelerated Development.

Morrison, J. (1995). *DSM-IV made easy.* New York: Guilford.

Murphy, J. F., & Cannon, D. J. (1986). Avoiding early dropouts: Patient selection and preparation techniques. *Journal of Psychosocial Nursing and Mental Health Service, 24,* 21–26.

Nelson, K. W., & Jackson, S. A. (2003). Professional counselor identity development: A qualitative study of Hispanic student interns. *Counselor Education and Supervision, 43,* 2–14.

Nichols, J. O. (1991). *A practitioner's handbook for institutional effectiveness and student outcomes assessment implementation.* New York: Agathon Press.

Ogrodniczuk, J. S., Joyce, A. S., & Piper, W. E. (2005). Strategies for reducing patient induced premature termination of psychotherapy. *Harvard Review of Psychiatry, 13,* 57–70.

Osborn, C. J. (2004). Seven salutary suggestions for counselor stamina. *Journal of Counseling and Development, 82,* 319–328.

Paniagua, C. (2002). A termination case. *International Journal of Psychoanalysis, 83,* 181–186.

Patton, M. Q. (1987). *How to use qualitative methods in evaluation.* Newbury Park, CA: Sage.

Penn, L. S. (1990). When the therapist must leave: Forced termination of psychodynamic therapy. *Professional Psychology: Research and Practice, 21,* 379–384.

Pope, K. S., Sonne, J. L., & Holroyd, J. (1993). *Sexual feelings in psychotherapy.* Washington, DC: American Psychological Association.

Pope, K. S., & Tabachnick, B. G. (1993). Therapists' anger, hate, fear, and sexual feelings: National survey of therapist responses, client characteristics, critical events, formal complaints, and training. *Professional Psychology: Research and Practice, 24,* 142–152.

Prochaska, J. O., DiClemente, C. C., & Norcross, J. C. (1992). In search of how people change. *American Psychologist, 47,* 1102–1114.

Prochaska, J. O., & Norcross, J. C. (2002). Stages of change. In J. C. Norcross (Ed.), *Psychotherapy relationships that work: Therapist contributions and responsiveness to patients* (pp. 303–313). New York: Oxford University Press.

Prochaska, J. O., Velicer, W. F., Rossi, J. S., Goldstein, M. G., Marcus, B. H., & Rakowski, W. (1994). Stages of change and decisional balance for 12 problem behaviors. *Health Psychology, 13,* 39–46.

Reis, B. F., & Brown, L. G. (1999). Reducing psychotherapy dropouts: Maximizing perspective convergence in the psychotherapy dyad. *Psychotherapy, 36,* 123–136.

Rodolfa, E. R., Haynes, A., & Kaplan, D. (1995). To apply or not to apply: That is the intern applicant's first question. *Professional Psychology: Research and Practice, 26,* 393–395.

Rodolfa, E. R., Vieille, R., Russell, P., Nijjer, S., Nguyen, D. Q., Mendoza, M., et al. (1999). Internship selection: Inclusion and exclusion criteria. *Professional Psychology: Research and Practice, 30*(4), 415–419.

Roe, D., Dekel, R., Harel, G., Fennig, S., & Fennig, S. (2006). Client's feelings during termination of psychodynamically oriented psychotherapy. *Bulletin of the Menninger Clinic, 81,* 68–81.

Rogers, C. R. (1961). *On becoming a person.* Boston: Houghton Mifflin.

Rogers, C. R., & Stevens, B. (1967). *Person to person: The problem of being human.* Lafayette, CA: Real People.

Ronnestad, M. H., & Skovholt, T. M. (1993). Supervision of beginning and advanced graduate students of counseling and psychotherapy. *Journal of Counseling and Development, 71,* 396–405.

Royse, D., Thyer, B. A., Padgett, D. K., & Logan, T. K. (2006). *Program evaluation: An introduction* (4th ed.). Belmont, CA: Thomson Higher Education.

Searles, H. F. (1955). The informational value of the supervisor's emotional experiences. *Psychiatry: Journal for the Study of Interpersonal Processes, 18*, 135–146.

Seligman, L. (1994). *Developmental career counseling and assessment.* Thousand Oaks, CA: Sage.

Seligman, L. (1998). *Selecting effective treatments* (2nd ed.). San Francisco: Jossey-Bass.

Skovholt, T. M., & Rivers, D. A. (2004). *Skills and strategies for the helping professions.* Denver, CO: Love Publishing.

Skovholt, T. M., & Ronnestad, M. H. (1992). Themes in therapist and counselor development. *Journal of Counseling and Development, 70,* 505–515.

Skovholt, T. M., & Ronnestad, M. H. (1995). *The evolving professional self: Stages and themes in therapist and counselor development.* New York: Wiley.

Spruill, D. A., & Benshoff, J. M. (1996). The future is now: Promoting professionalism among counselors-in-training. *Journal of Counseling and Development, 74,* 468–471.

Stedman, J. M., Neff, J. A., Donahoe, C. P., Kopel, K., & Hays, J. R. (1995). Applicant characterization of the most desirable internship training. *Professional Psychology: Research and Practice, 26*, 396–400.

Stewart, A. E., & Stewart, E. A. (1996a). A decision-making technique for choosing a psychology internship. *Professional Psychology: Research and Practice, 27*(5), 521–526.

Stewart, A. E., & Stewart, E. A. (1996b). Personal and practical considerations in selecting a psychology internship. *Professional Psychology: Research and Practice, 27*(3), 259–303.

Suarez, J. G. (1993). *Managing fear in the workplace* (TQLO Publication No. 93–01). Arlington, VA: Department of the Navy, Total Quality Leadership Office.

Summers, N. (2003). *Fundamentals for practice with high risk populations.* Pacific Grove, CA: Brooks/Cole.

Tedesco, J. F. (1979). Factors involved in the selection of doctoral internships in clinical psychology. *Professional Psychology, 10*, 852–858.

Thomas, S. R. (2005). The school counselor alumni peer consultation group. *Counselor Education and Supervision, 45*, 16–19.

Tryon, G. S., & Kane, A. S. (1993). Relationship of working alliance to mutual and unilateral termination. *Journal of Counseling Psychology, 40,* 33–36.

VanZandt, C. E. (1990). Professionalism: A matter of personal initiative. *Journal of Counseling and Development, 68,* 243–245.

Wachowiak, D., Bauer, G., & Simono, R. (1979). Passages: Career ladders for college counseling center psychologists. *Professional Psychology, 10*, 723–731.

Walitzer, K. S., Derman, K. H., & Connors, G. J. (1999). Strategies for preparing clients for treatment. *Behavioral Modification, 23,* 129–151.

Welfel, R. R. (1998). *Ethics in counseling and psychotherapy: Standards, research and emerging issues.* Pacific Grove, CA: Brooks/Cole.

Yager, G. G., & Beck, T. D. (1985). Beginning practicum: It only hurt until I laughed. *Counselor Education and Supervision, 25,* 149–157.

INDEX